ARIZONA
Historic Land

ARIZONA

Historic Land

Bert M. Fireman

With a Foreword by
Lawrence Clark Powell

ALFRED A. KNOPF · NEW YORK · 1982

THIS IS A BORZOI BOOK
PUBLISHED BY ALFRED A. KNOPF, INC.

Copyright © 1982 by Esther Fireman
Maps Copyright © 1982 by Don Bufkin
All rights reserved under International and Pan-American
Copyright Conventions.
Published in the United States by Alfred A. Knopf, Inc., New York,
and simultaneously in Canada by Random House of
Canada Limited, Toronto.
Distributed by Random House, Inc., New York.

All of the photographs in this book have been reproduced
with the kind permission of the Arizona Historical
Foundation, Hayden Library, Arizona State University.

LIBRARY OF CONGRESS CATALOGING IN PUBLICATION DATA

Fireman, Bert M.
Arizona, historic land.

Bibliography: p.
Includes index.
I. Arizona—History. I. Title.
F811.F57   1982   979.1   82-47807
ISBN 0-394-50797-5

Manufactured in the United States of America
First Edition

For Esther, Judy, and Janet,
who asked me to write this
informal history of Arizona

Contents

Foreword *by Lawrence Clark Powell*   ix

Introduction   3

1 Creation   17

2 Peoples of the Past   28

3 Enter the King's Captains   46

4 For the Glory of God and King   59

5 Time of the Apaches   69

6 Distant Trumpets   75

7 Ho for California!—and Back Again   84

8 Stopped at Stanwix Station   96

9 New Home in the West   108

10 Settling the Indian Question   120

11 The Wheel in the West   135

12 Hidden Wealth Revealed   147

13 Cowboys, Cattle, and the Law   162

14 South from Zion   173

15 Perils of Partisan Politics   184

16 Arizona Comes of Age   198

Contents

17 The Desert Blossoms   217

18 Ever Westward   229

    Bibliographical Essay   243

    Index   261

8 pages of photographs will be found following page 114

Maps will be found on pages 20, 50, 89, 155, and 232

Foreword

Bert Fireman and I became friends late in his life when an appointment to the University of Arizona lured me from longtime residence in California. Ours was an unusual friendship which accommodated wide differences of background, education, temperament, and philosophy. He was originally a disillusioned Democrat who in his passion for Arizona history joined forces with Barry Goldwater, while I was a Hoover Republican made a Democrat by the Great Depression. What united us was a devotion to historical truth and good writing. We both spoke out against the glorification of frontier violence and the clichés of the stereotype West. "The West was won by toil," Fireman insisted in a memorable address called *Mostly Sweat,* "by shovels, not by six-guns." When I told him that something I was writing on Arizona would not deign even to mention Tombstone and the O.K. Corral, Bert's rumble of approval reverberated throughout the library.

Envy and jealousy are common among writers in the same field. Fireman was free of those traits. When I was asked in 1972 to write the book on Arizona in the Bicentennial series called *The States and the Nation,* he was the first Arizona historian to offer his help. If he was, as he called himself, a self-taught historian, I wasn't any kind of historian—only a writer with a respect for history.

"You are the one to write it," I protested. "True, I am a better historian," he conceded, "but you are a better writer—and what they want is a history that will be read, not merely referred to." He was too modest. In this history which I am privileged to preface, Fireman

is revealed as both a good historian and a good writer. His book will
indeed be read as well as referred to.

Bert Fireman began as a newspaperman. His longtime daily column in the *Phoenix Gazette* called "Under the Sun" immersed him
in Arizona's history, current happenings, and local affairs. He wrote
about human concerns, causes, and civic progress; he succeeded in
preventing the city from uprooting its downtown palm trees and even
getting it to plant more; he called for more parks and malls and better
schools. This led to his own radio program, "Arizona Crossroads,"
which saw his interests and influence widen throughout the state.

The result was a cultural alliance with his fellow Phoenician
Barry Goldwater, and their creation of the Arizona Historical Foundation, devoted to research and publication of original material.
More than a dozen scholarly volumes on Arizona history ensued. In
1967 the foundation moved its offices and library to the Carl Hayden
Memorial Library of Arizona State University in Tempe, at which
time Fireman as curator began building the library's now outstanding
Arizona collection. He also commenced giving courses in Arizona
history as a lecturer in the university's Department of History. He
proved a dynamic and influential teacher.

Arizona history in all its aspects of research, teaching, and publication filled the remaining years of Fireman's life. He was a founding
member and on the Council of the Western History Association and
a longtime director of the Arizona Historical Society. He was especially proud to have founded and chaired the Arizona State Parks
Board, because without his efforts Arizona might still be the only
state without a park system. Another cause close to his heart was the
State Landmarks Committee. He was twice appointed to the President's Council on Historic Preservation, on which he worked assiduously in his last years.

No other Arizonan knew more or did more in these fields. As a
writer and lecturer he became known and respected statewide and
through the West. Historical museums at Tubac and Jerome and the
restoration of the state capitol in Phoenix were products of Fireman's
creative mind and skill as an organizer.

This untiring work and ever-willing participation as a writer and speaker for civic and scholarly groups made Bert Fireman nearly as well known in Arizona as his colleague Senator Goldwater. He knew everyone in historical studies and politics, and everyone knew him. His imposing stature made him visible in any gathering, campus conference or country barbecue. No wonder that he starred as a lineman in high-school and college football! An insistence on truth and accuracy and a blunt honesty made him sometimes a feared reviewer. But though he was tough, he was never a *mal hombre.* His earthy humor was only characteristic of the western frontier.

Yet he could also be a gentle charmer. Once when he spoke to my seminar, which included some determined feminists, Bert swiftly disarmed them with a tribute to pioneer Arizona women, some of whom he had sought out in their old age and interviewed. His wife, the former Esther Samuels of Douglas—whom he cherished as wise and stalwart, like her Biblical namesake—and and their gifted daughters, Judy and Janet, served to mellow his forthright masculinity.

Born in San Francisco in 1913, Bert Fireman was brought by his immigrant parents to Arizona as a child of three. He grew up in humble circumstances in Superior, Prescott, and Glendale. Except for war years in the San Francisco shipyards, he remained an Arizonan until his death in 1980. His Polish mother proved the family anchor and unfailing encourager of Bert's efforts to gain an education. They led eventually to an A.B. in Education from Arizona State College in Tempe.

Fireman had a rare gift for friendship on all levels of society. As president of the Phoenix Junior League, Sandra Day O'Connor sponsored Bert's popular winter lecture series at the Heard Museum. Upon his death, tributes came from governors, students, and lesser lights. No other Arizonan past or present was so deeply grounded in bedrock Arizoniana. The ethnic diversity, the history and lore, the economic, social, and political forces, as well as the land itself with its varied configurations and weathers, all went into the formation of Fireman's character and philosophy and colored and vivified his work.

Here now is the long-ripening history of his beloved state which he did not live to see published. It will take an honored place in

the long line of Arizona histories which began a century ago with
Bancroft. The learning and feeling, the humane values and human
judgments of this strong and good man are evident on every page.

Honesty, vigor, devotion, and love were hallmarks of Bert Fireman as man and historian. He was an essential part of my education
as I too came to claim Arizona as my adopted homeland, and I
proudly preface his book with these words of gratitude and affection.

                                           LAWRENCE CLARK POWELL

January 1982
Bajada of the Santa Catalinas
Tucson

ARIZONA
Historic Land

Introduction

That famous Civil War general who gave Americans a phrase to remember, the often-misquoted "war . . . is all hell," thought as little of Arizona as he did of the consequences of his profession. As commanding general of the United States Army, William Tecumseh Sherman accompanied President Rutherford B. Hayes on a railroad journey into southern Arizona in 1880. Obviously bored with the desert landscape, and recalling perhaps too vividly an earlier journey he had made in springless Army vehicles across the roadless, rocky, and sandy land, Sherman retorted explosively to a citizen's placation that Arizona "merely needed" less heat and more water, "Huh! That's all hell needs."

To compare Arizona to hell in 1880 was not overstating the case. The territory was raw, uncivilized, and thinly settled, except by Apaches, who were feared out of proportion to their numbers. In summer it *was* hot. And the desert was composed of prickly flora, hostile fauna, and a sea of dust churned by the iron-tipped hooves of mules drawing narrow wagon wheels that cut the landscape into clouds of grit and annoyance. Nonetheless, Sherman's remark has been neither forgiven nor forgotten by the twentieth-century discoverers of splendor and comfort in a prospering Arizona.

On his first trip into Arizona two years before, Sherman's dislike for the area had not been expressed so violently. His remarks had fallen upon ears more sensitive than those of the teamsters, railroad workers, tame Indians, and plain curious citizens at the rail siding of Maricopa who heard his oft-quoted comment. In 1878, at the conclu-

sion of an official inspection tour of Arizona's scattered military
posts, Sherman was traveling westward into California, leaving behind the discomforts of Arizona. A few miles west of Fort Yuma his
special train met another, bringing a new governor and old friend to
Arizona to take office as the territory's fifth chief executive.

The trains stopped so General Sherman could pay formal respects
to General John Charles Frémont. In the sunset of his life the Great
Pathfinder had been appointed governor of Arizona Territory. The
Frémonts were so impoverished they welcomed the scant $2,600
annual salary. President Hayes graciously acknowledged the Republican party's obligation to Frémont for withdrawing from the 1864
presidential campaign when Frémont's name on a third-party slate
threatened Abraham Lincoln's bid for re-election and thereby the
security of the Union. Frémont had waited fourteen years, until
necessity forced him to set aside his pride, to remind Republican
leaders of his past service to the political organization as well as his
need.

The appointment assured, the Frémonts interviewed old friends
who knew Arizona before leaving Washington in the summer of 1878.
Frémont himself had made only one journey through the territory,
in 1849, and it had been not a tour of exploration and glory but a sad,
hasty passage to meet his talented wife, Jessie Benton Frémont, in
California at the end of his tragic fourth expedition into the Rockies.
In Washington one hot evening before leaving for the West again, the
Frémonts were dinner guests of Edward Fitzgerald Beale, who
twenty years before had pioneered the use of camels across Arizona's
northern plateauland. Another distinguished dinner guest was General Sherman. Beale, even more than the Civil War hero, could
recount from personal experience the problems of travel in untracked
northern Arizona, but he also could and probably did recite for Jessie
and General Frémont the incomparable beauties of the San Francisco
Peaks, the Painted Desert, and that unique field of chalcedony that
is now called the Petrified Forest.

General Sherman at that very time was himself planning a trip
into the West for official inspections. He listened to Beale as eagerly
as did Jessie and General Frémont. If he and the Frémonts should
meet after he had made his tour of Arizona, and their schedules on

comparison indicated they might, General Sherman promised to fill them in with details more up to date than Beale's recollections of his travels in Arizona during the War with Mexico and again with the camels in 1857 and 1858. At this meeting General Sherman sat in Frémont's special car and told him what to expect once he had crossed the turgid Colorado River into Arizona Territory. Jessie was a careful listener. In her *Far West Sketches* she recalled Sherman's fiery description of the road she, the general, their son and daughter, their Chinese cook, and their dog Thor would take from the end of the railroad at Yuma. Sherman had just returned from Prescott, the territorial capital, which was their objective.

"I pity you. I pity you," he told Jessie, sounding strangely soft for the man who had allowed his undisciplined troops to ravage Georgia. "Going over that road, there are places where I shut my eyes and held my breath. You will cry and say your prayers."

Sherman misjudged Jessie Frémont and Arizona. Tears, which washed her handsome face often during the uncertainties of her husband's stormy career, were not to be part of the Frémonts' Arizona phase. Into her old age, a tear would come to Jessie's eye when she recalled the glories of the general's youth and the ecstasy of their love. But there was simply nothing about Arizona that made her cry. She adored it, enjoyed it, and brought to the rustic capital in the wilderness a gentling influence, with deft touches of culture that are not forgotten in the city where she made ladylike and agreeable adjustments to the exigencies of pioneer life.

General Sherman found Arizona akin to hell, but the gentle lady, without forsaking realism, had a different perspective. Later she recalled: "Even with government transportation which we had, climate and natural obstacles had to remain unchanged, while with the ordinary means, travel was a perfect nightmare of fatigue, discomforts, and some dangers." She did not despair, recalling rather that "it was a most interesting bit of travel."

The warrior and the gentle Jessie had traveled the same road. One found it unbearable, the other tolerable. The difference lay in the basic attitude of the viewer at a given time and place. The history of Arizona, its literature, and therefore its study have been influenced by this same individualistic perspective of the viewer. The purpose or reason for each traveler's visit to Arizona had much to do with what he observed, felt, and repeated for others. Which side of the looking glass had General Sherman stood on? In common with most fellow soldiers of all ranks, as well as touring journalists, railroad surveyors, and many professional writers, he had been brought to Arizona by his duty. That obligation often could not be fulfilled and passed by too soon. He and they avoided absorption or involvement in pioneer patterns of life, with strong feelings of bias and distaste for the duty imposed upon them.

Jessie Frémont, however, had come to Arizona with hope blooming brightly after years of business failure, military disgrace, and personal loss within her family. She had with her a son seeking the "cure" for consumption in the dryness of Arizona, and an old-maid daughter in need of a husband. One of her purposes sprang from the expectation that the Frémonts could restore their fortune on the mining frontier of the remote territory. She came, as did the majority of the pioneers, seeking opportunity. This was the sustaining force which, when multiplied by thousands of individuals and years of effort, brought a change to Arizona.

Pioneer builders and pioneer traditions emerged from attitudes and purposes such as those nurtured by Jessie Benton Frémont, while the ugly reactions and resentments of errant travelers and journalists of whom General Sherman was characteristic filled much of the literature of travel in Arizona for the first four centuries after it first was entered by Europeans. Unfortunately, few pioneers of the mine, canal bank, cattle ranch, or Indian reservation were as articulate as Jessie Frémont. Writers, generally a critical lot, left indelible impressions upon the news sheets and magazines and books about Arizona long after their shrill protests about the inconveniences of Arizona life had been forgotten by the hard-bitten, satisfied pioneers they encountered on travels into the territory.

General Sherman was far from being the first observer to translate the rugged and pristine beauties of Arizona into a fearful landscape. The most popular book about Arizona published before Sherman's two visits was *Adventures in the Apache Country: A Tour Through Arizona and Sonora,* written by an Irish wit, J. Ross Browne. The material in that book had been published previously to 1869 as a series of articles in *Harper's Magazine,* and even before that in the San Francisco *Bulletin.* Although Browne's impressions of Arizona were presented with undisguised strokes of humor (and, unfortunately, racism), in retrospect it was usually the dour and forbidding, rather than the odd or quaint, that readers remembered. His book had ended emphatically:

> No country that I have yet visited presents so many striking anomalies as Arizona. With millions of acres of the finest arable lands, there was not at the time of our visit a single farm under cultivation in the Territory; with the richest gold and silver mines, paper-money is the common currency; with forts innumerable, there is scarcely any protection to life and property; with extensive pastures, there is little or no stock; with the finest natural roads, travelling is beset with difficulties; with rivers through every valley, a stranger may die of thirst. Hay is cut with a hoe, and wood with a spade or mattock. In January one enjoys the luxury of a bath as under a tropical sun, and sleeps under double blankets at night. There are towns without inhabitants, and deserts extensively populated; vegetation where there is no soil, and soil where there is no vegetation. Snow is seen where it is never seen to fall, and ice forms where it never snows. There are Indians the most docile in North America, yet travellers are murdered daily by Indians the most barbarous on earth. The Mexicans have driven the Papagoes from their southern homes, and now seek protection from the Apaches in the Papago villages. Fifteen hundred Apache warriors, the most cowardly of the Indian tribes in Arizona, beaten in every fight by the Pimos, Maricopas, and Papagoes, keep these and all other Indians closed up as in a corral; and the same Apaches have desolated a country inhabited by 120,000 Mexicans. Mines without miners and forts without soldiers are common. Politicians without policy, traders without trade, storekeepers without stores, teamsters without teams, and all without means, form the mass of the white population. But here let me end, for I find myself verging on the proverbs.

Browne had come to Arizona in the midst of the Civil War, when the demands for military concentration in the main theaters of conflict had drained garrisons from scattered Arizona military posts and had permitted the Apache Indians to ravage the land. Actually, Browne's summary of desolation and despair was already several months out of date. Peace had settled again upon the land before his arrival in the territory on a pleasant and sunny Christmas Day in 1863. He came with a military escort, entering Arizona where the Frémonts and Sherman would, at the Yuma Crossing of the Colorado River. Browne confined his travels to the southern part of the territory, which until the war broke out had been the route of the Butterfield Overland Stage. This great pioneer mail line—less than twenty-six swaying days from Tipton, Missouri, to the Golden Gate —had quickened transcontinental travel, but had done even more for Arizona. The string of stage stations built from the Rio Grande to the Colorado River had changed the nomadic life of Apache tribes living between the Gila River and the Mexican border. Previously they had made their living by raiding, usually deep into the cattle and mining country and farming settlements of northern Mexico. Well-worn raiding trails led hundreds of miles into Mexico, where the great *haciendas* as well as isolated villages provided four-footed food that the Apaches drove and rode back to their brush-covered huts. Once the stage lines were pushed through, they had little need to seek the equine and bovine entrees of their diets at such great peril and discomfort. The "blue-eyed ones" had brought horses by the hundreds and cattle aplenty within easy range. These attractive nuisances were to appeal to Apache acquisitiveness and lead to open warfare between whites and reds in southern Arizona for a full quarter-century. Even the establishment of military posts did not abate the troubles, for, from the Apaches' opportunistic viewpoint, the Army was horse-mounted and cow-fed; thus opportunities for raiding mounted substantially, as General Sherman and other generals at his command increased the military force in Arizona in attempts to overwhelm the Indians. The Indians prospered and fattened on the whites' beasts of burden, mule meat being the first choice of the Apache palate.

But even before Browne with his tongue-in-cheek criticisms, General Sherman with his explosive revulsion against the entire territory, and Jessie with her solid pioneering spirit, Arizona had a romantic past more than three centuries old. Very little of this past was known to the average American, even to its historians, at mid-nineteenth century. American library shelves waited for the publication of *The Works of Hubert Howe Bancroft,* from his *Native Races* in 1880 to his *Literary Industries* ten years later, to obtain from these thirty-nine volumes the full scope and meaning of the Spanish penetration into the Southwest and along the Pacific Slope. It remained still for the inspiring Herbert Eugene Bolton, starting in Wisconsin, moving on to Texas and then to California, reaching his zenith amid the resources of the Bancroft Library at the University of California, to interpret the Spanish Borderlands as an earlier phase of colonial life in the Americas every bit as significant as the Puritan settlement of New England.

Almost a century before Plymouth Rock, Europeans had explored Arizona. There is some question whether credit for being the first non-American in Arizona should be given to Marcos de Niza, a Franciscan padre, or to his guide, a slave named Esteban. Historians recount variously that Esteban was a Moor and a Negro. He could have been both. All are agreed that he was black, massive, and spectacular. He was one of the four survivors who marched with Cabeza de Vaca from shipwreck on the Gulf of Mexico to haven at Culiacán near the Pacific shore in a seven-year ordeal of slavery, witchcraft, and survival that has no equal in American adventure. From Indians they encountered they acquired vague stories of golden cities to the north.

These tales excited Spanish ears that had been attuned by the success of Cortés and Pizarro to hope for other unlimited treasures in the Americas. Cabeza de Vaca's word-of-mouth account mentioned seven rich cities on as many heights. Willing Spanish listeners interpreted this to be tangible confirmation of the legend of Seven Cities of Cíbola which had been a standard fixture of Spanish folklore for some time. The viceroy of New Spain purchased Esteban so he could guide Fray Marcos on a tour of discovery into the far northwest, well beyond the sweep Cabeza de Vaca and his band had made westward across modern Texas, Chihuahua, Sonora, and Sinaloa. So they walked northward, Esteban wearing bells, amulets, and pend-

ants that jingled merrily as he strode magnificently among the adoring Indians, many of them women, who accompanied him. They were
his bearers, cooks, guides, and bed companions. Evidently he demanded and received many of each. A day or two behind was Fray
Marcos, bringing the blessings of the Roman Catholic Church to the
natives. After a triumphant march of feasting and many female favors, Esteban reached one of the pueblo villages near the modern
Arizona–New Mexico border, only to find entry denied him by a
people more advanced culturally than the brush Indians accompanying him. Unlike the sedentary and agricultural Indians of the Arizona
and Sonora lowlands, these mountaintop Indians did not believe that
hospitality extended to the bed—they killed Esteban for his forward-
ness. Warned by his fleeing companions, Fray Marcos crept under
cover to within sight of the village. In the sunset of the day, he said,
he saw a golden city much as the legends said Cíbola would be, rising
many stories high, covered with jewels, of great wealth and splendor.
Fray Marcos hastened back to the viceroy with an exaggerated tale.
He knew success was expected of his venture, so he did not disappoint
his listeners. There was a glorious land to the north—yes, seven cities
of gold on mountaintops. And so the following year, with Fray
Marcos as reluctant guide, Francisco Vásquez de Coronado led three
hundred soldiers and many more Indian helpers northward in an
army of strength and glory and color to envelop Cíbola into the
expanding Spanish Empire.

For his troubles, at the end of seventy-seven days of march across
a vast depopulated area of Sonora and Arizona, Coronado found only
misery and despair in the sky cities of western New Mexico. He took
them by conquest, getting little in return but a scant supply of stored
food, a few bits of turquoise, and two damaging clouts on the head.
Soon he was listening to a new tempting tale, that of a Gran Quivira
out on the plains of Kansas. His lieutenants followed that fool's trail
to further disappointment except for the proof they brought back of
the extent of the buffalo herds of the Great Plains. After two harsh
winters in New Mexico, Coronado turned back to Mexico to face
disgrace and prosecution. His eventual exoneration of blame for the
cruelties of conquest came too late to save his health or to give him

wealth such as Cortés and Pizarro had seized. But Coronado had pushed the limits of the Spanish Empire far northward and northeastward into the plains country; he had revealed—not so much himself as through the words of his chronicler, Castañeda—the great sweep of the southwestern country and the awesome beauty of the Grand Canyon, which his captains, Tovar and Cárdenas, had reached.

Thus, Arizona was opened for other explorers to follow. Permanent Spanish settlements first were made in the Rio Grande Valley of New Mexico, and from there exploring parties were to cross Arizona: Espejo in 1582–3, seeking and finding mineral ledges, but discoveries heavy in copper rather than rich in gold; Oñate in 1605, seeking anything spectacular to make his overlords in Mexico City forget his colonization reverses in New Mexico. Nothing tangible came of these explorations. Another century had almost passed before the sands of Arizona were crossed by the saintly Jesuit Father Eusebio Francisco Kino, putting down the foundations for missions at Tumacácori and San Xavier del Bac that would lead, decades after his death, to the establishment of military presidios at Tubac, Terrenate, and Tucson, and thereby to permanent Spanish settlement in Arizona.

So the story of settlement quickly unfolds. We find Spain attempting to contain the Apaches with a buffer of garrisoned forts, and approaching admission of failure therein when the revolution of 1810–21 rid Mexico of waning Spanish authority and left Arizona isolated and virtually abandoned on the northern frontier of a new republic born in poverty and political conflict. Then came the War with Mexico, making Arizona a pathway through which to extend American manifest destiny to the Pacific shore. Across Arizona marched Kearny's Army of the West, followed by Cooke's Mormon Battalion, clearing the only good wagon road south of South Pass—the only transcontinental east-west, all-weather wagon road anywhere between Canada and Mexico. Emory's *Reconnaissance* revealed to Americans for the first time the realities of the physiography of the Southwest. Earlier, Pattie's *Personal Narrative* had merely extended the dime-novel tech-

nique to a full-length book with some basis of truth. Soon it became
apparent that a railroad to the Pacific was not feasible within American territory either north of the Gila or within one marine league of
it, as the Treaty of Guadalupe Hidalgo allowed. The Gadsden Purchase in 1854 brought a practical railroad route into American hands,
but it would be twenty-three years before the iron rails would reach
Arizona. The Gadsden Purchase, however, brought Arizona the dramatic Jackass Mail, connecting San Antonio and San Diego in 1857,
and a year later the Butterfield Overland Mail, as well as a flock of
enterprising individuals who, having failed to find their El Dorado in
the California gold rush, sought fortunes in Arizona.

Crucial to this last population boom was a simple bit of American
ingenuity that has meant to the Southwest as much as McCormick's
invention of the reaper did to the economy and settlement of the
Great Plains. The modern invention was far less complicated than
McCormick's method of quick harvesting. The southern half of Arizona, that portion most richly endowed with sunshine, arable lands,
broad valleys, and vast grasslands, also harbors extreme summer
temperatures. Everybody who could do so in pioneer days left Arizona's summers behind, seeking either mountain or seashore relief
from the severe weather of June, July, August, and much of September. This problem drained Arizona of much of its human resources.
In a general way, as soon as a family made a stake, it pulled out for
a milder climate. Coastal cities are filled with former residents of
Arizona who brought with them their wealth, memories of the pleasant eight months of the year in southern Arizona, and usually a dread
of returning during the summers. The permanence of such detach-
ments often was strengthened when wives learned what their husbands' behavior had been while the good wife and children were away
at the seashore. Arizona summers for those left behind tended to be
lightened by the frivolities of summer bachelors at play with whatever
companions they could find tough enough to endure daytime temperatures and yet tender enough to be transformed after dark into gay
butterflies.

Early in pioneer life, farmers and ranchers had learned to preserve
butter and other perishables in so-called "desert coolers" placed in

the shade of tree or house. These were wooden frames covered with burlap, the upper edges immersed in pans of water. Capillary action and gravity caused the water to drip down the burlap. Since there usually is a breeze on the desert and humidity is very low except just prior to storms, the temperature in the "cooler" was reduced by evaporation of the water when kissed by the breeze. Ergo, butter could be kept firm even in hottest weather.

Suffering personally from high temperatures, residents often hung wet bedsheets over doorways and windows to take advantage of the same principle of evaporation. Or they wrapped themselves in wet sheets upon retiring. One large hotel, the Adams in Phoenix, operated a territorial-days cooling system by placing 300-pound cakes of ice in tubs around the lobby. Large fans blew over the ice, circulating a cooling breeze in the summer furnace.

About the time the Depression struck Arizona, the principle of the desert cooler was being adapted to cooling a room or two in houses in Arizona. Strips of burlap were hung over windows, with electric fans drawing air through them into the houses. This improvisation led to an even better means of distributing the moisture, with excelsior salvaged from packing cases becoming an immediate favorite. Soon the demand was so great, as neighbor copied neighbor in building each his own boxlike cooler attached to a window, that aspen forests in northern Arizona became the objective of firms which found profit in rendering wood into excelsior for this purpose. With a few pieces of board, several feet of chickenwire, a hose leading from a faucet to a distribution pan made of wood or tin, almost any handyman could build himself such a cooler. Temperatures could be reduced fifteen or twenty degrees in a room by use of a simple house-fan for power. Before long, enterprise flourished on the desert, and manufactured units were being sold and new fortunes were made by providing for this need peculiar to the sunny places of the earth.

It may be pointed out that Arizona-made evaporative coolers even now are exported to all continents. The basic concept is little changed from that of the original homemade "swamp coolers" (so called because they raised the humidity of a room), except that simple oscillating fans have been replaced with more efficient turbine-bladed blowers powered by stronger motors. It was a short next step to displacement of the evaporative coolers by refrigeration units in which freon and other rapidly expanding gases took the place of the simple but low-efficiency evaporative effect of water. The principle of the kitchen refrigerator was applied to home cooling in enlarged sizes.

A small home in Arizona requires perhaps a refrigeration unit of three-ton capacity, while a luxurious home may have a cooling capacity of fifteen or twenty tons distributed in two or three units cooling different parts of the house. Every commercial and office building built in central and southern Arizona for the past fifteen or twenty years, every warehouse and factory, every motel, hotel, and, in a few instances, bordello has been equipped with one kind or another of cooling unit. The rooftops of Arizona cities such as Tucson, Phoenix, and Yuma are cluttered with refrigeration units or evaporative coolers that make life bearable beneath ceilings where life once was a sweatbath all summer.

It is this factor more than any other that has allowed Arizona to take advantage of the accelerated westward movement of the American population. Without the cooler, Arizona still would be bypassed as it was during the great land boom in the early part of the twentieth century that brought a prosperity boom to California. It is possible to be more comfortable in Arizona throughout the summer than in the Midwest or East, where lower maximum temperatures are offset by the discomfort of high humidity. An Arizona home cooled to thirty degrees lower than outside temperatures by a modest-priced refrigeration system is a comfortable haven from summer's anger. Fully four-fifths of the passenger automobiles sold in Arizona today are equipped with refrigeration units, thus freeing their users from endurance of any more than a few minutes of heat a day. The passage from home-to-car-to-office-to-car-to-home for the clerk, businessman, or professional person is matched by the enterprise of shopping centers which are wholly refrigerated, even to malls where gardens grow and aviaries titillate the air with birdcalls. The housewife walks only a few yards from her cool car to the bliss of spending in air-cooled comfort. The pleasure this brings to residents also is profit to holders of stock in the three major public-utility firms which provide electricity to keep these hundreds of thousands of refrigeration units running twenty-four hours a day for months.

The effect of the cooling system on life in Arizona is drolly reflected in the experience of a traveler from a faraway state who drove into the desert town of Gila Bend in a state of collapse. He was barely able to stop his car at a service station. (Gila Bend is known as the Fanbelt Capital of the World, and the town's entire economy is based on the passing motorist. Taking advantage of the high summer heat, its service-station operators promote the desirability of carrying an extra fanbelt for emergencies.) The attendants rushed out and found the poor man suffering from heat prostration, but quickly had him comfortable in a room at a nearby motel. As fluids were replaced in his parched body and his fever and nausea receded, he gasped out a few questions: "How hot does it get in Arizona? . . . Don't try to kid me—you may say it is only 114 degrees, but the thermometer in my car passed 160 degrees before it burst. . . . Why did I have my windows closed? Simply because I learned long ago to do what the natives do. I saw all the Arizona drivers speeding along with their windows closed."

General Sherman said Arizona needed less heat and more water to make it less like hell. The first need has been modified by the use of coolers, as we have seen. The second requirement for improvement has been procured by storage dams along mountain streams, by deep-well pumping, and soon will be further augmented by the Central Arizona Project bringing Colorado River water into central Arizona. Tomorrow may bring conversion of seawater not far away in the Gulf of California. As for Browne's complaint on his visit of 1864 that Arizona had towns without population, now the reverse often is true. Subdivisions have pushed toward the mountaintops, and vast deserts are divided into estates.

In a century Arizona has developed prodigiously until in a composite of indices of growth for the past decade (1968–78), such as population (leading all states with 51.4 percent gain), personal income (growth of 246 percent), gain in retail sales (250 percent), increase in bank deposits (210.6 percent), manufacturing production (gain of 245 percent), and increase in nonfarm wages and salaries (up 86.6 percent), and other measures of material and financial gain, supporting cultural maturity and economic strength, Arizona astounds the nation and outstrips other states. How this has been achieved shall be told, briefly, historically, and informally, in the following chapters, with frequent expressions of opinion and analysis achieved through a quarter-century of serious and dedicated study and teaching of the state's history.

1

Creation

In the very beginning, with ardent labor during Six Days of Creation, God* formed the heavens and the earth. While resting on the seventh day, He felt very satisfied with that part of the land that would be known as Arizona. It was not entirely finished, but it was very good. Mostly, it was similar to another part of the earth He looked upon with special favor, called the Sinai. Essentially it was arid desert, rising away from a warm sea, a land of very little rain. Here many plants were thorny for protection; game animals were few and would develop special protective coloration and talents to endure the almost continuous aridity and rugged terrain. This, by God's will, was a land that would test man's faith and strength.

As compensation for these handicaps He provided the land with magnificent mountains flanking broad valleys and deserts. They were much loftier and more extensive than Mount Sinai itself, and stood out sharp and strong against the brilliant sky they seemed to support. At night this was strongly evident when a canopy of stars lighted the immense void between purple pillars circling the land. The flaming sun dropped behind such a range for its night's rest and would emerge from similar majestic mountains, renewed, in the morning.

*All references to God herein derive from Judeo-Christian concepts of the earth's creation, and are provided for readers with fundamentalist or orthodox beliefs. The author, neither an agnostic nor an atheist, associates himself with deists such as Thomas Jefferson and with naturalists such as Darwin, who believed the processes of evolution have been operating for millions if not billions of years.

He provided an incomparable color spectrum for this landscape in a stupendous chasm that Adam's descendants were to call by many names in many tongues before settling conclusively upon a descriptive term that has become known the world over: the Grand Canyon.

Arizona's limits were not narrowly circumscribed—although God provided the silt-laden Colorado River, roaring through and out of the Grand Canyon, to mark immutably the territory's western limits. Left to mere men was the chore of drawing straight lines upon and across deserts and mountains to mark Arizona's other boundaries. It would be many centuries before that was accomplished.

God thoughtfully surveyed this favored land of Arizona.

When finished, it would be only eight short of 400 miles from north to south, and 338 miles wide at the broadest point, encompassing 113,909 square miles of territory.

It was and is a land of many contrasts in climate and geography, reaching from about 90 feet above the level of the sea—actually, the Gulf of California or, as our Mexican neighbors prefer to call it, the Sea of Cortés—to nearly 13,000 feet into the sky at the San Francisco Peaks, standing as sentinels guarding the Grand Canyon.

Native Americans of the Hopi and Navajo tribes insist that their gods dwell among those crags and snowy peaks, from which they can look down upon man in his mortal, often feeble struggles and striving.

If man would commune with those native gods, he must climb the tortuous sides of the triple peaks, a severe test of lungs, legs, and heart, upward through forests of pine, maple, aspen, spruce, and fir that surround the peaks, guarding the eminence from vast surrounding grasslands of the Colorado Plateau, on which the peaks are the tallest but not the only sentinels.

As He rested on the seventh day, it was with warm and satisfied accomplishment that He surveyed the sun-bathed land His creation had wrought. Starting at the sea to the southwest, Arizona was spread out in three great steps or planes progressing northeastward to enclose those snowy peaks and the Grand Canyon.

THREE BIOLOGICAL ZONES

First is the Lower Desert province, often called the Sonoran Desert. Together with an eastern extension composed of slightly higher Lower Basin country reaching to the New Mexico border, the Lower Desert stretches as a giant, imperfect crescent northwest to southeast, straddling Arizona's border with Mexico and reaching more than halfway along the Colorado River border with California and Nevada. It is like a saucer with edges tipped north, east, and south, draining westerly. This is the heartland of Arizona's richness, the sun belt that is home to three-fourths of its wealth and population, its two largest metropolitan areas centered on Phoenix and Tucson, and most of its major mines, industries, and agriculture.

Fitting into the concave portion of that crescent, likewise oriented northwest to southeast, is a tumbled, mountainous segment of Upland Desert, ranging in altitude from 3,000 to 5,500 feet, forested by ponderosa pine, shaped prophetically similar to a Clovis point with the broad base toward the southeast, where such earliest absolute proof of man's presence in Arizona was uncovered at the Lehner ranch in Cochise County early in the twentieth century. This mountain zone is transitional geologically as well as in flora and fauna, marking the crumbling-off of the higher Colorado Plateau, which rises from about 5,500 feet altitude to 9,000 feet and which stretches northward to near the Continental Divide at the Four Corners where Utah, Colorado, and New Mexico join Arizona, and then westward to the edge of the Great Basin in southern Utah.

By the measure of rainfall, a universal yardstick that determines climate and the density and distribution of growing things upon the earth, Arizona is a desert, falling as it does totally within the arid designation since it receives less than twenty inches of rainfall a year, except for a few isolated patches and peaks. Twenty inches of rain is the accepted borderline between desert and temperate lands. With that much or more, crops will grow to maturity with regularity. Beneath that standard, man must employ ingenuity and engineering skill to grow his food, fodder, and fiber by irrigation.

Although an arid land, Arizona has a well-defined river system, allowing that less than a dozen of its rivers flow the year around.

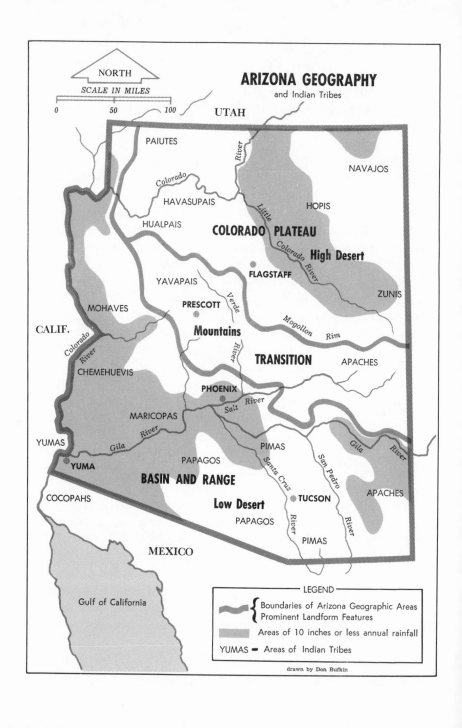

ARIZONA GEOGRAPHY
and Indian Tribes

NORTH

SCALE IN MILES

0   50   100

UTAH

PAIUTES

Colorado River

NAVAJOS

HAVASUPAIS

HOPIS

HUALPAIS

COLORADO PLATEAU

Little Colorado River

High Desert

FLAGSTAFF

YAVAPAIS

ZUNIS

MOHAVES

PRESCOTT

Verde River

Mountains

Mogollon Rim

CALIF.

Colorado River

TRANSITION

APACHES

CHEMEHUEVIS

PHOENIX

Salt River

MARICOPAS

Gila River

PIMAS

Gila River

YUMAS

YUMA

PAPAGOS

Santa Cruz River

San Pedro River

BASIN AND RANGE

APACHES

COCOPAHS

Low Desert

TUCSON

PAPAGOS

River

River

PIMAS

MEXICO

Gulf of California

─── LEGEND ───

{ Boundaries of Arizona Geographic Areas
  Prominent Landform Features

Areas of 10 inches or less annual rainfall

YUMAS ━ Areas of Indian Tribes

drawn by Don Bufkin

Most are moist only after torrential thunderstorms of summer or gentle winter rains, but nevertheless they are rivers which define avenues of travel, cultivated crops, habitable places, and evidence of the endless erosion that has formed this wrinkled, lovely land.

RIVER SYSTEMS

The major internal river system in Arizona—the Gila—bisects the Lower Desert and its Lower Basin appendage, running almost directly from east to west to confluence with the Colorado River at Yuma, and thence flows southward to the Sea of Cortés. The Gila River forms in the mountains of western New Mexico. On its left or southern bank, as it meanders slowly toward the setting sun, it collects seasonal floods (if any) from the San Simon and the Santa Cruz, and a small, constant flow from the San Pedro—all three rivers coming into Arizona under the barbed-wire fence that divides the state from Mexico, flowing first northward down the saucer's slope to the immense alluvial trough through which the Gila moves westward.

From northern and higher mountains the Gila accumulates the bulk of its flow, in turn taking in the San Francisco River near the New Mexico border; then the San Carlos, coming quickly out of mountains in eastern Arizona; Mineral Creek, which when first mapped by the United States Topographical Engineers was described as the Ink River, since it was blue-colored from running over copper deposits in the Pinal Mountains; and finally, west of Phoenix, the Gila joins up with the Salt River, which is a more muscular stream than its parent. The Salt is formed of the White and Black rivers in the snow-covered White Mountains, picks up additions from Carrizo, Cherry, and Tonto creeks (above Theodore Roosevelt Dam), and then adds the healthy Verde River thirty miles east of Phoenix. Together this system drains about a third of Arizona, providing domestic, industrial, and irrigation demands of the great Salt River Valley, population center of the state. After its confluence with the Salt, and before man-made dams sucked up its flow, the Gila once was a respectable river, filled with fish and beaver, a dependable highway and route of exploration and conquest in the great westward flow of population to the Pacific shores. Were not the water impounded in reservoirs and used to irrigate crops and serve domestic and industrial demands in the state's population center, it could contribute handily to the flow of the Colorado. But the waters of these streams have been put to man's everyday use in this century, with very little surplus floodwater reaching the sea.

The combined flow of the intermittent Big Sandy and Santa Maria rivers in the northwest corner of the Lower Desert province midway up the western boundary—neither ever more than a mere trickle except in the rainy season—forms the Bill Williams Fork (*not* a river), which formerly emptied into the Colorado. With most of its historic flow impounded behind Alamo Dam, the Bill Williams eases a scant few drops into blue Lake Havasu, a reservoir formed by Parker Dam on the Colorado, backing water several miles up the fork as well as far up the main stream.

One other river of some consequence in the Arizona system drains that portion of the Colorado Plateau south of the Grand Canyon which slopes northward away from the Mogollon Rim and the heights of the White Mountains. The Little Colorado River trickles off the north and east slopes of that range, opposite the Black and the White, gathered from tiny creeks to flow northwestward to join the mighty Colorado in the middle of the Grand Canyon. There it dumps a muddy patch into the clear, cold main stream, from which the mud and silt that gave the Colorado its name have been settled out in the vast, quiet reaches of Lake Powell.

LAND OF SCANT RAINFALL

The bulk of the Lower (or Sonoran) Desert is prickly and usually parched, receiving as little as two inches of rainfall upon the lowest, southwesterly portion where the Colorado runs into the sea. East from the coast—the direction of winds blowing in from the Pacific Ocean and the Sea of Cortés—rainfall is more abundant, especially as the edges of the desert crescent curl upward. The southern fringe laps into the highlands of Mexico's border state of Sonora. Rain also is heavier on the concave northern edge nestled against the mountain-rim country. Mountain ranges obtruding above the desert floor, in a general north-south configuration, intercept warm, damp clouds scudding in from the sea, forcing them upward into cooler drafts where moisture is released to give most of the Lower Desert up to ten or twelve inches of rain, with higher points receiving as much as twice that amount.

The almost equal distribution of rainfall between summer and winter rainy seasons nurtures superior grasslands, particularly in the eastern half of the desert crescent, creating Arizona's finest cattle rangeland. Dual rainy seasons also make for a great variety of natural growth on the slopes and mountainsides between the Lower Desert and a scattering of skyscraping peaks which are never out of sight in southern Arizona. Within a scant few miles the nature of plant life and, consequently, the variety of animals that feed upon it (and in turn upon each other) will vary from sterile flats to alpine glens. In a single day's hiking, one can cherish both environments in southern Arizona. If a resolute hiker makes a morning start among the salt-bush of alkali flats and creosote *bajadas* along the Cañada del Oro near Tucson, sunset can find him plucking columbine and fairy ferns at a spring trickling from granite ledges high in the Santa Catalinas.

Because of mountain intrusions, rainfall is almost invariably lighter on eastern slopes, away from prevailing winds. Hence there are dry patches of severe desert everywhere. Several varieties of cactus are found even on the slopes of the San Francisco Peaks and Mount Baldy above 8,000 feet altitude.

DESERT GROWTH ABUNDANT

But desert in Arizona does not conjure up marching sand dunes as in the Saharan stereotype. The Lower Desert is an arboreal desert, characterized by a great variety of trees and sturdy plants rooted deeply to gulp passionately the torrential summer rains and the more gentle winter rainfall. Flying over Arizona, one sees veins of darker green foliage, highlighted by the bright sunshine, lining the wrinkled terrain and drainage slopes; the darker the vegetation, the richer the water supply. These indicate that rain flowing into a vast network of sandy watercourses provides an improved environment and thus heavier growth than is possible on rocky slopes.

Principal trees of the Lower Desert are several varieties of mesquite; the palo verde, which breaks into golden globs of blossoms in the spring; lavender-hued ironwood along watercourses; and on southwestern slopes the cylindrical, branched saguaro cactus, whose early summer crown of blossoms is the state's official flower. The large, flat, cream-colored petals of the saguaro, which blossom rapidly, grow into fruity pods of carmine seeds later ravished by whitewing doves, which migrate northward each summer for their harvest, and which themselves are greeted by hordes of hunters with shotguns.

Covering the desert floor and mountain slopes are countless varieties of cactus and thorny brush, defying the common belief that the desert is drab and barren. Indians who inhabited the Sonoran Desert counted around a hundred trees, plants, and grasses that yielded them food in some form. The most dependable desert manna in Arizona is the sugary seedpod of the mesquite, which gave the Papago (bean-eater) Indians their name. The saguaro is the most stately of the cacti, followed by related organ-pipe and pitahaya varieties. The bisnaga or barrel cactus (whose pulp is glutinous and bitter, therefore *not* drinkable) makes splendid cactus candy. The needlelike cholla, staghorn, pin cushion, prickly pear (similar to Israel's sabra), hedgehog, and beavertail are among varieties that in springtime (especially after plentiful winter rains) make Arizona deserts a contradiction in terms. Where there are not cacti, there are the equally thorny ocotillo, with blazing wands of red flowers particularly attractive to hummingbirds, tall creamy sprays of yucca or Spanish bayonet and Joshua, irascible catclaw, and a variety of wildflowers that defy description.

Where nothing else thrives, there is the omnipresent creosote bush—despised as stinkbush or larrea by the 49ers—durable, medicinal, and delightfully pungent after a desert rainstorm. In the poorest of soils and minimal moisture the scraggly burro bush thrives.

There is little commonality among desert plants, except in their thorniness and the defensive devices that nature has provided as additional protection in their severe environment. Few have flat leaves common to domestic plants, because evaporation is too rapid with such normal apparatus. Desert growth tends to have waxy or varnished coverings that conserve water and also, by odor, taste, and cathartic or emetic qualities, discourage animals from feasting upon the plants when grass is scarce.

Some naturalists have described desert plants as growing upside down, with little exposure aboveground but extensive root systems larger than the visible foliage. Root systems reach far down for water, storing a reserve supply within underground stems or above the ground under waxy covers, safe from searing evaporation. Some cactus varieties—the saguaro and organ-pipe types especially—have accordion-style trunks which are in effect expandable tanks of pulp filled with water to tide them over dry spells.

Where water is more abundant, the desert growth multiplies, and with it the number of animals who make their living in austere surroundings.

THE BUSY DESERT

The desert has often been called a silent land. Don't believe it. In May or June, when the palo verde is showering golden petals with tiny reddish inserts, sit for a few moments in the shade, watching and listening. Ladybugs may be dangling from the soft, needlelike leaves; bees will be gathering nectar, contesting with hummingbirds for access to the flowering glory; Sonora doves may be nesting in the tree's branches, and fluttering sparrows come visiting; the sandy ground will be marked with the footsteps of a mother Gambel quail and her children, who are calling and skipping under surrounding creosote growth; mockingbirds scold and finches chatter; an owl softly protests the sunshine; buzzards wheel on thermals rising from sunning slopes, hunting for fallen prey; hawks swoop in to scoop up some snake or burrowing owl *(tecolote)* emerging recklessly from a cool subterranean dwelling. Quiet? The desert is alive with the sounds and visible signs of its many inhabitants: coyote, kit fox, jackrabbit, bobcat, badger, raccoon, ground squirrel, kangaroo rat, gopher, tortoise,

Gila monster, mule deer, desert sheep, roadrunner, and snakes. Their tracks are everywhere, as are gnats and flying varmints of many kinds, including the ubiquitous housefly.

Many crawling and flying things add to the abundance of life forms in the Arizona desert. Summers can be dreadfully hot, especially to the west and close to the Sea of Cortés, but everywhere in the desert country—which is most of Arizona—winters are relatively mild.

The Lower Basin adjunct to the Lower Desert is one of the prized regions in the nation for bird-watching. Flanking the Mexican border, especially in the Huachuca and Chiricahua mountains, and along ever-flowing Sonoita Creek and the San Pedro River, is an area described by ornithologists as the richest bird-exploring area in the United States. Of roughly 650 known American nesting birds, nearly 200 have been identified and observed in southeastern Arizona on the fringe of the Sonoran Desert, where a combination of ideal weather and an ample water supply, which provides adequate food and excellent cover, makes the area a favorite stopping place on a major North American flyway.

Every corner of the nation inevitably has its horror stories, of diseases, foods, beasts, swamps, or haunted houses to avoid. Of Arizona it often has been said the poisonous animals of the desert are a hazard. The litany of things to avoid begins with the rattlesnake, includes the Gila monster, the tarantula, the scorpion, and, for good measure, even degrades the horned toad. All exist in Arizona, but not to worry. The risk of any of these creatures actually harming someone is less than that involved in crossing Fifth Avenue, State Street, or Market Street at noon on Sunday *with* the green light.

The rattler is largely nocturnal, because the desert's summer heat is too severe for him. He cannot survive in the noonday sun. There is little danger from his kind, except when climbing a rocky slope hand-over-hand. Normally, the rattler will flee if he hears any strange noise, especially one made by alien humans. The Gila monster, beautiful in a repulsive way, is extremely sluggish and would never mouth anything but an egg unless provoked to do so. Even then, while his mouth is filthy and his poison sacs will do some little harm, deaths from Gila monster bites are unknown. The scorpion is more to be feared than other desert denizens, and the smaller the beast, the greater the potential impact of his sting. He carries a sharp wallop in a spike and venom in a tail that strikes with fury. But antiscorpion treatment is readily available, and packing infected areas with ice minimizes spread of the venom. Few adults suffer seriously from scorpion stings, though they can be fatal to small children. But since scorpions usually hide in damp places, under rocks or trash, the danger from them is minimal—why mess with desert debris when everything else is so beautiful? The tarantula is a huge, ferocious-looking, hairy spider who can take a good nip with his pincers, but he is not poisonous and not hostile. Quaint characters sometimes keep tarantulas for pets, which speaks little for human normalcy.

As for the horned toad, he is a totally harmless lizard, protected by Arizona law, who when cornered or frightened squirts a liquid that looks like blood from his eyes. He's about as dangerous as Grandma Moses, and equally shy.

2

Peoples of the Past

Even the most chauvinistic of American anthropologists do not assert that mankind originated in this hemisphere. Man in America is recognized as an immigrant, although lively arguments rage about when and how he arrived on these shores. Recent attempts to interpret ancient art inscriptions and figures cut into rocks have stimulated anew the diffusion theory: that Phoenicians or Iberians or Babylonians or Celts somehow crossed the Atlantic Ocean into the Gulf of Mexico, made their way up the Mississippi and followed its drainage to the Continental Divide, walked the few miles to the western slope, and then traced the Gila River into New Mexico and Arizona. As an exercise in important or simply divergent speculation in a world fraught with nuclear fears, there is no apparent harm in that theory, or similar ones of trans-Pacific migrations by Polynesians.

More acceptable is the broader consensus that ancestors of today's Native Americans were Asiatics who entered the Americas via the Bering Sea land bridge, to wit:

THE HUNGRY:
HUNTERS AND HOME SEEKERS

Hunger brought them, gnawing at their innards, neutralizing the icy winds and subordinating the dangers. They traveled slowly, tagging behind herds of imperial mammoths and other beasts of the Pleistocene Age, skirting great glaciers which formed a mountainous barrier to fog-shrouded Arctic wastes, a cap of ice on a shivering world. Rivulets and streams of chilling water crept from beneath the ice pack, cutting furrows between greening banks, and then were lost in the great gray sea, spotted with broken floes of ice, that stretched south of the marshy land they were crossing.

Thus man came to America, braving danger from animals which had the capacity to kill a dozen men in one assault. Man was afraid, but fear is rarely an emotion as motivating as hunger. Sooner or later one of the great beasts would get mired in a swampy place, or a calf would wander from its mother or the protective ring of bulls. Then hungry men would swarm in for the kill, wielding stone clubs and spears, driving stone points toward vital organs, thrusting and club-bing and hammering until the beast would fall. Jubilant, with shar-pened flat rocks used as knives, their women and children would join the hunters in butchering the animal before it was cold.

They satisfied their hunger on the almost-living flesh, tepid blood pouring over and warming bodies protected from biting wind only by animal skins. Gorged, they left most of the animal undevoured. Wolves would feast on what they left. Only a few tender parts, such as the liver, would be carried along as these people of the past faced the rising sun the following morning and plodded again into the marshes. They were following the path of animals which instinctively were migrating gradually eastward from the frozen inner wastes of Asia, skirting the receding ice cap, feeding on grasses thrusting out of the soaked earth as the ice withdrew and exposed to a strengthen-ing sun earth that had been covered with ice for centuries.

The best of modern man's technology of time measurement—radiocarbon dating added to chemical analysis, geologic stratigraphy, and dendrochronology—correlated with archeological studies of northeastern Asia and the Bering Strait area, have produced a con-sensus that these hunters (clearly not an intermediate step in evolu-tion, but *Homo sapiens* himself) came to the Americas something short of 30,000 years ago. Advancing dating techniques periodically tend to roll the entry date back in multiples of a few thousand years. A half-century ago, many scientists believed man had been in the Americas only 10,000 years; some now say it has been longer than 30,000 years. Geologists believe that glaciers grow and shrink with changing climatic cycles. The Bering land bridge could have been free of ice blockage 28,000 years ago but closed in a following cold spell that might have lasted 5,000 years or more, thus opening a door to admit man to the Americas in two separated eras—allowing respectability to variant calculations of an entry date. (Recently, a new technique of measuring traces of amino acid in the bones of ancient man and animals has thrust back to 48,000 or 50,000 years ago the threshold of that first human migration, although this finding has not as yet won general acceptance.)

The best of scientists cannot agree when ancient man first came to Arizona any more than they can define or pinpoint when he ceased being an Asiatic and became a Native American. Nor can the best minds calculate how much earlier ancient forms of animal life had preceded man to Arizona. What does it matter? Coal and iron deposits along the nearly 400-mile north-south axis of the state, buttressed by scattered fossil and faunal remains, clearly indicate Arizona was alive with animal forms long before ancient man's presence was recorded by the artifacts and garbage he left behind.

Some indication of the span of animal life in Arizona is given by the fossilized head of an animal with crocodile features that was collected near the Little Colorado River and has been on display at the American Museum of Natural History in New York City. This form of animal life which once lived in Arizona has been gauged to be millions of years old, possibly the best-preserved artifact of early animal life in Arizona.

THIS BEAST WAS MAN-KILLED!

In 1951 two alert, thoughtful ranchers of southern Arizona, father and son, contacted the Arizona State Museum in Tucson. For some years they had been observing water erosion along Greenbush Creek near the town of Naco on the Mexican border. They had noticed a few remnants of strange bone washed free of sand and gravel. Recently a summer storm had exposed something larger, so tantalizing in scope they asked experts to examine two man-made points they had found near exposed bones and teeth of an animal enormously larger than horses and cattle on their small ranch. Archeologists hurried to the site and were stunned by the discovery. Excavation revealed considerable remains of a Pleistocene beast, unquestionably a mammoth *(Mannuthus columbi),* and in and near the skeletal structure, mostly between the head and chest, were eight (not just two) beautiful points of the Clovis fluted type, a style fashioned and used in the Southwest about 10,000 to 9,000 B.C.

A cluster of charcoal, remains of a fire on which some parts of the animal may have been roasted, told that these hunters were not primitive eaters of raw flesh, such as their ancestors welcomed to America on the Bering Sea land bridge, but were advancing gourmets whose skills enabled them to build fires and manufacture killing tools. The Naco site gave scientists stronger evidence of early occupation of Arizona by man than had any previous scattered signs of his presence.

Only two years later a rancher about twenty miles away reported another find to the Arizona State Museum. This time, bones of nine animals had been exposed—mammoths again, but also an extinct bison or long-horned buffalo, the giant tapir, and a tiny horse. Clovis-type points were augmented in this, the Lehner ranch discovery, by tools of butchering as well as of the kill. The application of dating techniques reached deeper into the past. Borrowing a term previously applied to hunters on the plains east of Arizona, archeologists provisionally designated these people Llano Man.

Both these sites yielded man-made tools, but no skeletal evidence of man himself. Geologic stratigraphy has established the era when such animals as the mammoth and tapir became extinct as from 10,000 to 9,000 years ago. Subsequent carbon-dating of charcoal (a useful, peaceful fallout of nuclear science) rolls the date of the mammoths' death and this first known outdoor barbecue feast in Arizona to 11,300 years ago.

Early man and the party who fed on mammoth tenderloin or tongue along the San Pedro River at the Lehner ranch could have been part of a slow-moving migration of man southward. Eventually mankind was to populate South and Central America, in the latter developing a culture so progressive and prolific that it produced the Toltecs, Mayas, and Aztecs; these peoples became so numerous and warlike as to produce a reverse migration northward 10,000 years ago.

While the first weapons with points found in Arizona were of the Clovis type, later finds of tools and archeological remains would be categorized as Folsom type. For more precise identification and localization, the earliest residents of Arizona have been designated Cochise Man, named for the county in which major remains of their existence have been uncovered.

Man the hunter, whether identified initially by the use of Clovis or Folsom projectiles or eventually localized as Cochise Man, was caught in a changing climatic cycle as the world warmed. Abundant rain and luxuriant near-tropical growth that had supported camels, mammoths, sloths, tapirs, bison, and horses diminished, being replaced by more arid conditions and smaller animals. As big game became extinct, early man came to rely more on his intelligence than on his brawn as a hunter, adapting to a changing environment, learning to gather fruits, berries, seeds, roots, and nuts. Instead of gorging on meat, he adjusted and balanced his appetite to smaller animals that provided less protein. This dependence upon a greater variety of growing things, floral more than animal, led into a new life-cycle and a new designation for it—the Desert Culture. Thousands of years passed as man in the Southwest moved through this process of earning his living by adapting his tastes and tools to the diminishing availability of meat on the hoof.

MAN AT VENTANA CAVE

In the Sonoran Desert eighty-five miles west-northwest of Tucson and seventy-five miles directly south of Phoenix, an overhanging cliff of the Castle Mountains created a cave in which a small spring perpetually yielded the single most important necessity of life— water. This is called Ventana ("window") Cave. As glaciers receded and the warming earth reduced their food supply, big game animals of the Pleistocene period discovered this trickle of water in their relentless search for sustenance. They found the shelter of the cliff accommodating even though its location at 2,500-foot altitude never was extremely cold. They quenched their thirst after feeding in a luxuriant valley several miles to the east. They lingered near the spring, and there some died. Whether their death came naturally, the result of the reduced food supply, or was inflicted by hunters who followed these animals to the site, their demise in Ventana Cave coincided with the presence there of Cochise Man.

Digging through nearly fifteen feet of midden, or human litter and garbage that had been preserved and kept dry by the overhanging cliff, archeologists uncovered a record that indicates man lived there, intermittently if not continuously, for 10,000 years. Skeletal remains of thirty-nine persons buried beneath the cliff, thousands of stone and bone tools, weapons of the hunt and domestic life, woven and fur coats, pottery in which food was cooked and served, bits of cotton cloth and clothing, personal adornments, storage jars and baskets, unconsumed morsels of food, some art forms painted on walls, well-picked bones and discarded corncobs—these reveal the history of man at Ventana Cave. It was literally a window to people of the past, a material encyclopedia of Native American lore encompassed in a garbage heap only fifteen feet deep, yet plunging 10,000 years into antiquity. The stratigraphy at Ventana Cave was the ideal sought by geologists and archeologists. Protected from moisture and erosion by the cliff, overlapping and interwoven layers of history were stacked one atop the other, the oldest at the bottom, the most recent on top.

Papago Indians still made seasonal use of the spring when excavation began in 1941. Because the first burials discovered near the surface obviously were not of modern origin, apparently not of their own tribal group, the Papago workmen had no religious objection to further excavation. Carefully they peeled away the debris of centuries and epochs, a half-meter in depth at a time, in squares two meters to the side. Each wheelbarrow of refuse was screened. Material artifacts were bagged and marked. The workmen quickly passed through midden deposited by their own people, who in the past few centuries have gathered saguaro cactus fruit near there in the summer, camping in the cave with its dependable spring. Deeper layers revealed the burials that experts dated before the Spanish *entrada* of the sixteenth century A.D. Beneath these were thousands upon thousands of pottery shards representing many cultures and tribes which met there. Ventana Cave was a crossroads and watering place in the desert, but, because of the scarcity of streams and arable land nearby, was never a population center. The pottery represented the product of cultural intrusions from many directions—a conclusion based on the differences in texture, color, composition, style, and decoration of the pottery shards.

The vast accumulation of pottery and other fragments told of trading and traveling, of intercourse with neighbors, of borrowing and lending skills. About 2,000 years into the trash, the shards bottomed out. Beneath that level, diggers had entered into a pre-ceramic age when shells or basketry served as water receptacles and for other household purposes. Simultaneously, or nearly so, it was learned, corn and pottery came to Ventana Cave, perhaps a few centuries before the time of Christ, brought there by northward-moving Hohokam people yielding to the pressure of warlike foes, such as the Teotihuacanos, who dominated central Mexico. Later inhabitants of Ventana Cave are identified as Desert Hohokam, cousins of the better-known and more progressive River Hohokam of the Gila and Salt River valleys.

In the age before pottery there was a greater accumulation of bones than later, and more basketry and woven plants. This told archeologists that the introduction of corn (or maize) had marked a major change in the diet of the Desert Culture. Since the time of Cochise Man, the economy had been shifting from hunting to gathering, and now men advanced toward irrigated agriculture. Meat which once had been the principal element in the diet was now flavoring for a stew of corn, beans, squash, nuts, seeds, and pods, gathered painstakingly from the natural growth.

Encyclopedic as was the dig at Ventana Cave, it failed to reveal any evidence that architecture was among the arts or skills of the residents. The cave home was comfortable and safe; the climate was mild; apparently they felt no pressure or need to build ticky-tacky houses.

FIRST MAN-BUILT HABITATIONS

We turn back to Cochise Man to reconstruct as logically as we can an orderly progression of Desert Culture into the style that evolved into the southwestern tradition in which some Indian bands still live in modern Arizona. When man the hunter faced a food dilemma with the extinction of big game and became a desert dweller, some of his numbers apparently followed animal prey to the shelter and water provided by Ventana Cave, thus becoming part of the astonishing monolithic calendar of man preserved at that site. Material remains indicate that Ventana Cave was visited and intruded upon by many regional cultural bands, although it was not a favorable living site, merely a crossroads. Information derived from Ventana Cave indicates that the main cultural flow was northward, perhaps following the coast of the Sea of Cortés away from the hostility of warlike Mesoamerica, and finding in the Sonoran or Lower Desert province a likely habitat in which to root, gain strength, and then move on again. The first of the three great geographic planes into which Arizona is divided was to become a homeland for the Hohokam. This was the Lower Desert. Entrenched on this first step in a lovely land, man would again look northward.

Adapting their way of life initially to gathering and eventually to intensive agricultural endeavors as corn and other new food crops were introduced from cultures to the south, these desert dwellers began also to restrict their nomadic ways. In a loose sense they became the first builders and urban developers in Arizona, establishing small groups of simple daub-and-wattle pithouses on high ground along streams that could easily be diverted to irrigate fields planted on the lower terraces beside streambeds. Sedentary life was dictated by the length of the growing season. From the time corn seeds were planted in the early spring or late summer (the desert supported a two-crop maize economy) until harvest, maturing took three to four months, during which weeding was necessary, irrigation had to be repeated, and animals attracted by growing plants—rabbits, rats, gophers, deer, and others—had to be frightened away or slaughtered to add flavor and some protein to the mass of vegetables and carbohydrates eaten.

From these first sedentary sites in the Lower Desert, seasonal entry is indicated into a higher mountainous corridor located between the Sonoran Desert to the south and the elevated Colorado Plateau and the Great Basin to the north. During the waiting or growing season for crops, even the farming people hunted a little and gathered cactus fruits, mesquite beans in great quantities, seeds, berries, roots, and nuts such as jojoba, acorns, and piñons from the mountains jutting out of their desert province and bordering it to the north. In the early summer, before the corn was ripe, most of the able-bodied Hohokams trekked to the mountains rimming the desert for the harvest of the maguey, the plant that produces mescal and tequila in Mexico, and whose sugar-laden flowering heart was harvested and roasted to preservelike consistency, providing a staple of life for colder months of the year and for times of low-yield irrigated crops.

During such gathering and hunting expeditions the more adventuresome of Cochise Man found pleasing little valleys and river terraces at higher altitudes, where summer temperatures were less severe and where a broader range and variety of food products could be found because of increased rainfall at higher elevations. Some of these people parted from their Hohokam friends who clustered along the river valleys of the desert, moving up into mountain valleys, taking with them skills they had learned on the desert floor as well as seeds of cultivated crops.

Hinged on the east at the Rio Grande Valley and on the northwest in west-central Arizona where origins of the Verde River mark western limits of the Mogollon Rim, this mountain-midland province shaped similar to an elongated Clovis point came to support a modified life-style called the Mogollon Culture. It was developed by migrated desert dwellers who readily borrowed cultural elements from other peoples they contacted to the east, west, and north. This culture roughly occupied the 10,000 years of evolution and human expansion between the Paleo origins of Cochise Man and the classic period of the River Hohokams who dominated the Lower Desert after the introduction of maize, beans, squash, and pottery several centuries before the dawn of Christianity. Thus the second step on the three planes of Arizona cultural development was occupied. The Desert Culture was followed in time by the Mogollon Culture, with migratory bands from both of these life-styles gradually moving up onto the Colorado Plateau to develop there the Anasazi Culture.

THE MOGOLLON CULTURE

The mountainous Mogollon homeland, the drainage basin of the Salt and Gila rivers, was the closest thing to a temperate climatic zone in Arizona. Its variety in terrain and temperature, plus an abundant water supply, stimulated development. The Mogollons were to outstrip their southern neighbors in the pace of change, aided by a central location that enabled them to become a marketplace for surrounding areas. Their trinkets and jewelry of seashell speak eloquently of trade with bands or individuals who trekked from the Sea of Cortés and the Pacific shore with trade goods. Salt from Mogollon deposits was traded for macaw feathers and bells from deep in Chihuahua, for cotton from Hohokam lands, and for Hopi pottery.

Although not its inventors, the Mogollons improved pottery substantially in both utility and artistic quality. As had the Hohokams, they first learned of ceramics from Mexican migrants. From the same source they acquired their first bows and arrows as weapons superior to the older atlatl or throwing stick. In forested, game-abundant country their hunting skills improved with superior weaponry. High ground along narrow valleys provided them strategic defensive sites on which to build their homes and protect themselves from enemies.

The Mogollons made their greatest contribution to man's progress in the desert with architecture. Improving vastly upon the very simple and temporary circular pithouses of Cochise Man and the Desert Hohokams, the Mogollons began building clusters of dwellings of a more permanent nature. They began scooping out pits several feet deep, piling dirt around walls reinforced with heavy poles instead of flimsy brush. A strong center pole supported a conical roof. Permanent firepits and then storage bins and pits were added, where surplus supplies of food could be stored in jars and baskets to relieve the Mogollons of seeking food during the harsh days of winter. That time could be devoted to improving their skills in tanning hides, basketry, and pottery arts. And it gave them more time for religious ceremonials. By deepening and enlarging pithouses for ceremonial purposes, the Mogollons created the first kivas, or underground religious centers, in the Southwest. Man had now learned to survive by storing the surplus of bountiful crops, and had proper facilities for expression of his religious faith and aspirations. It was a great step forward for mankind in the Southwest, while to the north a new culture was developing in the rock country of the Colorado Plateau.

PEOPLE OF THE ROCK

Easily the most spectacular although not a particularly fecund section of Arizona, the Colorado Plateau for the first dozen centuries of the Christian Era supported the dynamic Anasazi Culture. The Navajos provided that name, meaning "ancient ones," for the early basket-maker and pueblo people who inhabited the enormous rocky province that stretches across northern Arizona with its cultural epicenter near the Four Corners, the only place in the U.S. where four states' borders come together: Utah, Colorado, New Mexico, and Arizona.

The heartland of Anasazi achievement was in the drainage of the San Juan River, slightly east of Four Corners. Dual concentrations of amazing size and sophistication existed at Pueblo Bonito in the Chaco Canyon area of northwestern New Mexico, and contiguously around the gorgeous Mesa Verde cliff dwellings in southwestern Colorado. Arizona had slightly less imposing structures and population concentrations in Canyon de Chelly and in the Tsegi Canyon–Kayenta area with the dramatic Inscription House, Keet Seel, and Betatakin sites.

The earliest phase of Anasazi tradition is described by anthropologists as Basket Maker, in tribute to the excellence and variety of woven and plaited items created by these people as a counterpoise to their lack of the pottery which neighboring cultures were utilizing at the same time.

By the fifth century of the Christian Era the Anasazi were moving out of the caves in which they first found shelter, and were building crude pithouses, often circular and fairly shallow, frequently roofed with a combination of logs and mud mortar, easily recognizable as an introductory phase of the mud-and-log hogans of the Navajos, who eventually succeeded the Anasazis as principal residents of the Colorado Plateau.

These early Basket Makers began building dwellings closer to
fields of flint corn and later beans and squash and perhaps cotton,
planted in deep alluvial valleys that had been created by the timeless
erosion of soft sandstone of the plateau. In time, some of these buildings were deepened and lined with masonry, becoming centers for
communal affairs and progressively religious ceremonial chambers
such as the Mogollons also were developing. These were the first
kivas of the pueblos, the urban communities created as the Anasazis
conjoined homes into extensive apartment structures covering in
some cases several acres and including housing facilities for thousands of persons. With this remarkable and creative life-style the
Anasazis entered the second aspect of their rich tradition. Their
culture, dating from about the seventh century A.D., has been designated the Pueblo tradition, the Spanish name for town.

Developing great skill as masons, they added contiguous rooms
to dwellings and kivas until their multistoried apartment and plaza
compounds had grown into small cities. One archeologist has said
that the Pueblo Bonito complex was the largest apartment or housing
structure in the world until surpassed by a modern building in New
York City in the 1880s. Apace with architectural achievements, they
became pottery makers of inordinate decorative and utilitarian skill.
These handicrafts, buttressed with ardent moral attitudes that
emerged from their kivas and close family life developed in clan
structures, enhanced their influence. Anasazi Culture encompassed a
vast area east of the Colorado Plateau, occupying much of the middle
and upper Rio Grande Valley, and in Arizona spread southward over
the ebbing Mogollon world. Branches of the Anasazis who lived
along the Little Colorado River and south of San Francisco Peaks,
identified as the Sinagua and Salado cultures, were to reach into the
Lower Desert to be absorbed or interwoven with or even to dominate
the late River Hohokam Culture.

The exact causes of Anasazi decline are uncertain. Drought, internal epidemics, and loss of vitality due to cultural superiority leading
to complacency and then nonproduction have been advanced as possible contributory causes. The truth is locked up in the mysteries and
secrets of the beautiful, rocky land. The dynamic and vibrant Anasazi
Culture flourished for several centuries, leaving elaborate ruins as

monuments beyond the mortal span of human life. Even before severe drought swept over the Southwest in the last quarter of the thirteenth century, some Anasazi sites had been vacated. The lack of rain is given as a major cause of decline of all three cultures in Arizona during that era. Another major factor contributing to the dislocation and diffusion of the Mogollon and Anasazi cultural patterns was the gradual impact of a vast in-migration of hunting newcomers from the north and east, threatening rather than destroying the sedentary villagers and their fields. Some anthropologists believe the first intruders were Shoshoneans, from farther north in the Rockies. As the newcomers advanced, many Anasazis and Mogollons moved away, entire villages trekking eastward to resettle in the Rio Grande Valley. Others found mountains and mesalands easily defendable, and became entrenched as enduring pueblo communities of Acoma, Laguna, Zuñi, and Hopi, isolated enclaves of Anasazi people becoming in time the modern Pueblo culture of great virtue and surpassing artistic skills, often said to be the epitome of all Native American achievement.

Whether or not Shoshoneans began the devastating invasion, the occupation of Arizona north of the Gila and east of its union with the Salt was to be fulfilled in the sixteenth century by Athapascan bands of hunters who had arrived in North America many thousands of years after the primary immigration of man the hunter across the Bering land bridge in the waning Ice Age. Archeological discoveries along the Aleutian Islands suggest that this final great migration from Asia may have been accomplished by island-hoppers who, upon reaching the North American mainland, moved down into the Athapascan Valley of the Canadian Rockies before flooding onto the Upper Great Plains. Eventually they migrated southward in the buffalo country east of the Rockies until overwhelming resistance from other migrants, possibly the Comanches of the upper plains of modern Texas, turned them westward across the backbone of the continent.

These newcomers, who swept over the remaining Anasazis and Mogollons and their Sinagua and Salado subcultures, were eventually to become the Apaches and the Navajos. The Athapascan language used by peoples far to the north, in British Columbia, is close to that spoken by these two interrelated groups of the Southwest with only slight dialectic differences, reflecting a common root of language and culture.

LAND OF THE STONE HOE

Mogollon culture lost its separate identity, yielding to intrusions and finally disappearing entirely two centuries before the arrival of the Spaniards. To the north the Anasazi Basket Maker culture had gradually grown into the monumental Pueblo period, whose enduring qualities and architectural style survive in many places despite the Athapascan blitzkrieg. Meanwhile, to the south and west the River Hohokams were achieving the highest level of prehistoric progress in Arizona.

The center of Arizona population today is in the Salt River Valley, the identical center of habitation in prehistoric days before the arrival of the twin scourges, Athapascans and Europeans, and it is such a center for the identical reasons that it was a thousand years ago. Here, near the confluence of the Salt, Gila, and Verde rivers, fertile soil and a dependable water supply are brought together under the life-giving sun.

Working only with stone hoes and tools of wood and bone, the River Hohokams developed a sophisticated system of water diversion and delivery, thereby advancing on material and social levels not achieved by other native cultures in the Southwest. Their bountiful crops provided more leisure time for creative endeavors than was possible among gathering and hunting people endlessly searching for edible plants and animals to fill their cooking pots. The Desert Hohokams created decorated pottery and fine basketry, etched shells with fruit acid, built semipermanent homes of wattle-and-daub, made attractive mosaic and turquoise ornaments, beads and other personal decorations, mirrors, and cosmetic palettes, constructed ball courts similar to those in Mesoamerica, and evolved a social system with separate warrior groups trained for and capable of repelling the thrusts of the aggressive Athapascan raiders.

When Salado bands moved southward from the Anasazi region, bringing more sophisticated pottery designs and architectural skills that resulted in great buildings such as Casa Grande and Pueblo Grande, the Hohokams absorbed these newcomers without disastrous conflict. The Hohokams evidently continued their custom of cremating their dead, while the newcomers practiced inhumation, to the confusion at times of present-day archeologists who find Salado and Hohokam material intermingled.

The valleys of the Salt and Gila rivers spawned the Hohokams' greatest achievement. Their largest urban center was Los Muertos, stretching several miles south and southeast of the modern city of Tempe, now totally eradicated by suburban dwellings but fortunately mapped and parts of it crudely excavated—thus exposing it to widespread vandalism—by the pioneer Hemenway-Cushing Archeological Expedition of 1887-8. They dug a dozen canals running southward from the Salt River to hundreds of earthen homes that sheltered several thousand residents. Freeway and subdivision construction has given scientists a second chance to study portions of Los Muertos, although much of this scientific data as well as the ancient residents are, as the name of the site suggests, *muerto*—dead.

Much of the early farming and older residential section of Phoenix was built on the ruins of similar canal systems and colonies of Hohokam residents who tilled fields by day and at night gathered in adobe apartment compounds where a thousand years later high-rise apartments and skyscrapers have been erected.

Twenty miles south of Los Muertos, on the north bank of the Gila River, is Snaketown, a complex second in size but of even greater scientific importance because it escaped early white settlement and destruction. Snaketown is destined to be developed as a national monument of major significance to illustrate the complex irrigation culture of the Hohokams.

The Casa Grande, most impressive of Hohokam-Salado structures, stands on the south bank of the Gila, about twenty-five miles east of Snaketown. West of Los Muertos and on the north side of the Salt, on the fringe of the busy Phoenix airport, is Pueblo Grande, a house structure eclipsed in size and grandeur only by Casa Grande. It stands guard over a Hohokam complex that includes Park of the Four Waters, one of several remaining sections of canals constructed by the Hohokams with their stone hoes and carrying baskets.

This great farming center thrived for a thousand years, but was abandoned in the late thirteenth century, possibly the result of a devastating drought that swept the Southwest. The ancient Hohokams departed. Eminent archeologists believe they merely moved out of the Salt River drainage into the Gila River Valley, and that their strain and skills have been preserved by the friendly Pima Indians who were living there when the first Europeans arrived and marveled at the progress they had made.

THIS LAND WAS THEIR LAND

While archeologists cannot agree on the arrival date of the Athapascan hordes—estimates range from the tenth to the sixteenth century—the catastrophic impact of their takeover is unquestionable. The Athapascans, divided into numerous small Navajo and Apache family bands reaching from Four Corners to Mexico, dominated the eastern half of Arizona. Their only unity was in language and the commonality of a nomadic, raiding culture with little in the way of fine arts but advanced skills in martial pursuits. They had by the sixteenth century forced older groups into settlement patterns that have been modified but little through succeeding centuries.

People generally believed to be descendants of the Hohokams, largely the peaceful Papagos and Pimas, occupied the Lower Desert and river valleys. The Desert Hohokams are thought to have become the Papagos, while the River Hohokams we now know as the Pimas.

Along the Colorado River were pressed tribes of possibly earlier origin—at least, they spoke dialects of Uto-Aztecan derivation, believed to have come out of Mesoamerica prior to the Hohokams. There were the Cocopahs, living near the mouth of the Colorado River, the Quechans or Yumans near the confluence of the Gila with the Colorado, and the Chemehuevis and Mohaves, sharing the middle portion of the western river boundary. Farther north, around the big bend where the Colorado emerges from the Grand Canyon and turns south, were scattered bands of impoverished Paiutes, closely related to inhabitants of the Great Basin. The life-styles of these people living along the Colorado had not changed greatly from the meager economy of Cochise Man and the earliest patterns of desert dwellers from which the more progressive Mogollon and Hohokam cultures also developed.

Life was very simple for these people, depending basically upon gathering, with a rudimental agriculture in the river floodplains. In the center of Arizona's vast desert and stretching toward the Colorado River were the Yavapai and Hualpai peoples, also living by a combination of hunting and gathering patterns virtually unchanged by the centuries.

Before the European invasion Arizona belonged completely to Native Americans who, by the most definitive of cultural yardsticks, were still living in the primitive Stone Age. They had not learned to make tools of metal, although some relatively advanced bands in Mexico manufactured and traded small copper bells into Arizona, whose presence in ruins gave rise to a belief that Arizona copper deposits were mined in pre-Columbian times. They did dig some turquoise and sulfites, but only for ornamental and cosmetic uses, not for smelting and use as tools.

The only domestic animals raised by Native Americans in Arizona were dogs and turkeys, both food items. The wheel was unknown. The bow-and-arrow was the most advanced weaponry. No metal existed to ease the struggle for existence.

Agriculture, supplemented by gathering and the little hunting possible in an arid land, was the mainstay of human survival. Along the southern river valleys farming progressed with meritorious engineering skill. Brush dams, canals, and well-tended irrigation patterns produced bountiful crops of corn, squash, beans, and cotton. Along the Colorado River and on scattered patches of ground in many areas the inhabitants simply poked seeds into wet soil after spring rains or floods, depending upon water absorbed by the earth to bring their plantings to maturity. Variations in the river's flow, however, made such cropping patterns unpredictable, and the frequent result was deprivation and starvation, and equally negative raids upon neighbors.

The Athapascans and western desert people lived very much as desert dwellers had when they emerged from the original life-style of Cochise Man. They erected temporary brush hovels, moving in small bands in a repetitious seasonal pattern, usually in a prescribed and restricted area, gathering roots, seeds, fruit, and nuts, and trapping or shooting animals that lived in the varied environments of different altitudes. Once corn was established as the basic food staple, even wandering bands would plant tiny fields at some fertile spot, returning after a few months of gathering wild plants to harvest the corn, if it had not already been consumed by deer, antelope, or rabbits and other rodents. These little patches of corn in hidden places and the early summer migration of both mountain and river-valley residents to the flowering maguey forests on the slopes of the midland mountains brought the bands into competition for food and often conflict over women and children sought as slaves and mates. Seasonal raiding excursions by mountain people to the river valleys at harvest time also shattered peace in the land. The farming people defended their crops and habitations so vigorously that Apache tradition came to characterize the Hohokams and their Pima and Papago descendants as fierce warriors, although these people when encountered by entering Europeans were described as gentle and peaceable.

It was not an abundant life that most Native Americans had achieved in Arizona, nor an idyllic one. Because of varying seasonal rainfall, gathering and hunting did not produce uniform results. Hard times in the high mountain country could intensify raiding by hungry hill residents on their own neighbors or the river people. The inhabitants lived in a constant state of physical danger as well as on the fringes of starvation. Isolated in scattered bands, each preoccupied with the vital, basic problems of survival, these peoples of the past achieved little in the way of political unity or organization.

As compensation for the daily stringencies of an austere life, they were completely free of limiting restraints until cycles of white conquest first engulfed them midway in the sixteenth century.

3

Enter the King's Captains

Fantastic legends, beautiful dreams, and great expectations first lured Europeans to Arizona early in the sixteenth century, disturbing the tranquility that had settled upon the land after the severe drought of the late thirteenth century and the following Athapascan assault. Within a half-century of Columbus's landing on San Salvador while seeking the East Indies, Native Americans of the Southwest were drawn into the first of a series of conquests that continues to this day.

Returning to Spain after his second voyage, Columbus brought a few vials of fine placer gold that he had purchased from natives on Hispaniola for a few trinkets. Spanish reaction was doubly adverse: initially that Columbus had failed to reach the Indies with their spices or find China with its riches in silk, but also there were bitter complaints about the token amount of gold that he brought home as a substitute for the wealth expected.

When Columbus landed after his fourth and final journey in 1502, his morale fractured and his health destroyed by hardships, disgrace, and his own mismanagement, his crew unloaded a small fortune in gold and copper garnered in Central America. His death followed soon after, in 1506, before this source of new wealth could be exploited.

Little appreciation was forthcoming for his discoveries and the opportunities now available to Spanish adventurers, but there was a murmur of excitement in revival of the unbelievable legend of the seven banished bishops of Mérida (sometimes they are described as Portuguese) who had built the same number of lovely cities on blessed islands in the faraway land of Antilia. Henceforth two small chains of islands in the Caribbean have been called the Greater and the Lesser Antilles.

Perhaps Antilia was not the Lost Atlantis after all, not hidden, as some imagined, in the treacherous Sargasso Sea. Criticism continued: clumsy Columbus and his feckless brother Diego could not even find Antilia when it was right under their noses! Part of the myth told of fantastic crystal-clear rivers flowing over sands of pure gold!

Within a few years the audacious Cortés had conquered Mexico (1519–21) and dispatched to the Spanish homeland staggering shiploads of gold and silver, the spectacular treasure of Montezuma accumulated by the Aztecs from conquered satellite tribes on the mainland. This golden trove so enriched a privileged few in Spain that rampant inflation resulted, putting ordinary bread beyond the reach of the average peasant. It also stimulated the emigration of a horde of disenfranchised minor nobility, unemployed soldiers, and officeholders to the New World, especially from the dry plains of Estremadura which had produced the hardbitten Cortés himself, as well as the Pizarro brothers, who in 1536 were loading their ships with Inca gold after putting to the sword the advanced welfare society of Peru.

The nationalization of Spain that followed the marriage of Ferdinand and Isabella and their successful conquest in 1492 of the last Moorish stronghold, the Alhambra at Granada, had fallen hard upon functionaries and satraps of the many small feudal states and dukedoms they brought under the unified flag of Spain. Grateful to Catholicism for its role in the expulsion of the Moors, Spain's rulers invoked the Holy Inquisition to eliminate all opposition, secular and religious, that might threaten the realm. Many independent and ambitious persons saw its harsh injustices as another reason to seek adventure, freedom, and fortune in the New World.

The Americas did not receive all their explorers and settlers munificently. Cortés and the Pizarros were the luckiest of dozens of leaders of expeditions that radiated from the permanent settlements of Hispaniola and Cuba to all shores of the Caribbean and Gulf of Mexico. Only the conquerors of Mexico and Peru found wealth equal to that mythical El Dorado of Spanish folklore which at the end of each day was covered with glittering gold dust.

FLORIDA TO SONORA

Pánfilo de Narváez, who had served with Cortés in Cuba before the conquest of Mexico and against him on the mainland, and who complained of receiving bad treatment from Cortés and is said to have lost an eye in an encounter with him, sought his own fame and fortune in Florida. (He was perhaps the first one-eyed celebrity to contribute substantially to Arizona's history: In the twentieth century Arizona would have a popular one-eyed governor, Jack Williams, and a witty, ambitious congressman, Morris Udall, who played professional basketball and made a remarkable record in government despite such a handicap.*)

Narváez brought 600 colonists and five ships from Spain to colonize Florida, which had withheld its fabled fountain of youth from Ponce de León, but which might still contain gold deposits and other riches. A hurricane robbed the expedition of two ships carrying families of colonists and reserve supplies. Fighting his way up the peninsula as far as modern Tallahassee, Narváez encountered alligators and vipers in endless swamps instead of golden amulets and pearls of great price. On the Gulf coast in 1527 he slaughtered his horses, used their hides to cover hulls made of wooden poles, and constructed five awkward boats on which he hoped to sail along the coast, ever westward, knowing that eventually that course should raise the Río Pánuco near Tampico on the east coast of Mexico. The five ungainly tubs bearing more than 200 men sailed and rowed past the delta and mouth of the Mississippi, only to be storm-wrecked on the coast of Texas near Galveston Island. Narváez disappeared into the grasping sea. Some eighty men were thrown up on the island, to be enslaved by hostile Indians. In six years all were dead except three Spaniards, including the expedition's treasurer, Cabeza de Vaca, and an African named Esteban, the slave of a Spaniard named Dorantes.

Miraculous good fortune brought the three Spaniards and the

*The author lost vision in one eye when he was a boy.

stalwart slave together. Cabeza de Vaca cleverly capitalized upon the native belief that the Spaniards' Catholic prayers and sign of the cross could effect cures. He traded upon this notion with adroit showmanship and some elementary knowledge of folk medicine to obtain food and Indian guides. Passed from one tribe to another as miracle workers, the party traversed Texas on a northwestward tangent to the high buffalo plains, possibly fording the Rio Grande north of El Paso and coming into or near the southeastern corner of Arizona. Curious, cooperative Indians told them that bearded men like themselves had been seen beyond the high, piney mountains stretching across the sunset horizon. With Indian help they managed to cross the Sierra Madre and enter a river valley flowing down into the Sea of Cortés.

In March of 1536, eight years after they had been shipwrecked, they encountered slave-hunting Spaniards in the mountains of Sinaloa, and soon were taken to the most remote frontier outpost of northwest New Spain, Culiacán. From there they were taken before the erstwhile president of the *audiencia* or high court of New Spain, Nuño de Guzmán, who, to offset slanders against his name, had been exploring northward from Mexico City, hoping to discover another cache of gold the size of Montezuma's to clear his reputation and make his fortune. In an earlier expedition along the coast of the Gulf of Mexico, Guzmán had encountered an Indian who described seven great cities on golden mountains far to the north. Was it Providence rather than coincidence that Indians in the Rio Grande country had told these four rescued travelers an almost identical tale of great cities to the north? Guzmán hurried the four to Mexico City to repeat that portion of their adventures to Viceroy Antonio de Mendoza, who had been sent to Mexico to curtail and limit the unauthorized explorations of the ambitious Cortés. The conqueror of Mexico had built ships on the Pacific shore that explored as far north as Baja California, where pearl-bearing oysters existed, and in which vicinity dreamers expected to find the fabled Island of the Amazons. It was not until the twentieth century that the amoral, topless, swinging starlets of Hollywood would come close to approximating the fantasies then associated with the Amazon legend.

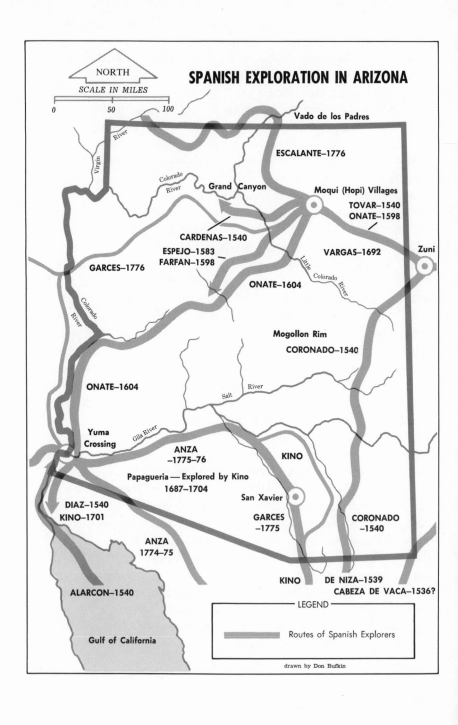

SPANISH EXPLORATION IN ARIZONA

NORTH

SCALE IN MILES

0   50   100

Virgin River

Colorado River

Vado de los Padres

ESCALANTE–1776

Grand Canyon

Moqui (Hopi) Villages

TOVAR–1540
ONATE–1598

CARDENAS–1540

ESPEJO–1583
FARFAN–1598

VARGAS–1692

Zuni

GARCES–1776

ONATE–1604

Little Colorado River

Colorado River

Mogollon Rim

CORONADO–1540

ONATE–1604

Salt River

Yuma Crossing

Gila River

ANZA
–1775–76

KINO

Papagueria — Explored by Kino
1687–1704

San Xavier

DIAZ–1540
KINO–1701

GARCES
–1775

CORONADO
–1540

ANZA
1774–75

KINO   DE NIZA–1539
CABEZA DE VACA–1536?

ALARCON–1540

Gulf of California

LEGEND

Routes of Spanish Explorers

drawn by Don Bufkin

FOR GOLD AND GLORY

That he was the king's representative in New Spain, charged with curtailing the far-ranging plunders of Cortés, did not foreclose Viceroy Mendoza's personal pursuit of gold and glory. With cold logic Mendoza concluded that since Cortés had found a bonanza in central Mexico and the Pizarros were raking in riches in Peru, certainly there must be great treasure awaiting the valiant and the bold to the north. He made plans to explore that far country. As a start, he would send a fleet of his own up the coast to nudge aside Cortés's sailors and bring home the pearls and a few Amazons. He already had connived with Pedro de Alvarado, who had sailed to Peru as a supply associate of the Pizarro expedition, to be his admiral in the northern venture. When Alvarado became bogged down in other matters, the viceroy recruited Hernando de Alarcón for that role.

As head of his land forces, the viceroy had focused on wealthy, young Francisco Vásquez de Coronado, governor of the vast northwestern province known as New Galicia, as Galicia was the northwest corner of Mother Spain. Coronado was married to a granddaughter of King Ferdinand, whose fortune helped outfit the Coronado expedition in grand style.

The arrival of Cabeza de Vaca and his three companions in Mexico City inflamed the viceroy's ambitions. Although the survivors of the Narváez catastrophe did not say that the seven cities Indians had mentioned were festooned with jewels and riches, it was in the proximity of Cíbola, the name given to the buffalo country, and the account generally corroborated that heard by Guzmán near Tampico, which was more detailed and left little doubt about great riches. To souls begging to be salved with gold, it was simple enough to superimpose these hopes upon the earlier fable of the seven bishops, which also dealt with unlimited riches. How could such circumstances lead but to glory?

In planning his northern foray, Viceroy Mendoza could speculate hopefully upon matching the golden reward achieved by Cortés in Mexico and Pizarro in Peru, but he consciously wished to avoid the mortal sins of the two brazen explorers, the murder of the Aztec Montezuma in Mexico and the Inca Atahualpa in Peru. To send an army into unknown lands as they had was to court damnation.

To the viceroy's court had come a pliant Franciscan friar, one Marcos de Niza, whose name indicated origin on the French Riviera. The priest had recently returned from introducing Catholic piety to natives in Peru and Guatemala. Why not send this pious friar, experienced in entering new lands, to feel out the hospitality of the north country and pave a peaceful path for Coronado and the band of conquistadors he was gathering?

Marcos de Niza was willing, and royal and Franciscan authorities approved the venture, so the viceroy acquired the slave Esteban from his owner, Dorantes, to serve as a guide for Fray Marcos. Although slavery officially was banned in New Spain, that peculiar institution was effectively maintained in Mexico into the twentieth century under the guise of peonage. Esteban was eager for the assignment. Along with other vestiges of Grecian and Roman culture, Spain had retained the tradition that slaves could win their freedom by deeds of valor or remarkable public service.

THE ADVANCE BEGINS

The friar, his guide, and a second priest, Fray Honorato, whose illness or distaste for frontier hardships soon led to his withdrawal from the party, were accompanied as far as Culiacán by Coronado, who went there to put down a minor Indian uprising and to recruit native porters to accompany Fray Marcos. These included some Indians who had followed the Cabeza de Vaca party across the Sierra Madre to the Pacific coast.

The viceroy sent elaborate instructions for the peaceful *entrada*. Copies of his directive preserved in the great Archive of the Indies at Seville spell out in detail what the friar was to achieve as he penetrated the interior for the honor and glory of the Holy Trinity and the exaltation of the Holy Catholic Faith. The priest was to make careful observations of the people, where and how they lived, of the land in all its features and resources, its plants and animals, and especially its minerals. He was to locate rivers, mountains, and any all-water passage leading to the South Sea, or Pacific. Spaniards devoutly believed in the Strait of Anían, their term for the imaginary

Northwest Passage. He was to bring back samples of everything, to send secret reports of his discoveries, and to take possession of the whole land for his majesty the emperor in the name of the viceroy. (Similar instructions, lacking the religious overtones, were given to the Lewis and Clark expedition dispatched by President Thomas Jefferson to explore the Missouri drainage two and a half centuries later.)

The viceroy's directive contained this final instruction: "You must explain to the natives of the land that there is only one God in heaven, and the emperor on earth to rule and govern it, whose subjects they must all become and whom they must serve."

This last admonition was part of the universal *Requerimiento* by which Spanish explorers in the New World, led by Columbus, unfurled the banner of Spain, erected a cross, and had a priest proclaim such an edict as a safeguard and warning to negate native hostility. Unfortunately, the message usually was read in Latin, an archaic tongue unknown to anybody within hearing except the priest.

Fray Marcos's advance party departed Culiacán in March of 1539, Esteban joyously in the lead and retracing portions of the route he had followed nearly three years before. Burdened with porters carrying supplies, and busily collecting information and Christian converts, the main party moved too slowly for Esteban. Anxious to perform feats that could lead to his freedom, the slave received Fray Marcos's permission to scout ahead. He sent back reports in the form of improvised crosses, sized to reflect the importance of resources on the trail ahead. The crosses soon began to grow dramatically larger. Creating a sensation, Esteban was dressed with jingling bells and ornaments and accompanied by two large greyhounds. He remembered the hospitality with which the Cabeza de Vaca party had been received when Indians believed the Spaniards could perform miraculous cures. He played the part also.

A retinue of admiring Indians fell in behind him. As Esteban moved from village to village, collecting gifts of turquoise and female companions, the crosses he sent back to the friar grew ever larger. Esteban and Marcos de Niza were greeted warmly by curious Indians who had never seen such unusual individuals. At the same time they cherished the trinkets the friar distributed as he gathered the Indians for prayer and blessings. Gratefully the Indians produced their best foods and softest beds for the visitors. No wonder the friar would report the route northward was such a smooth road, bountifully supplied with food and comforts. For a small, unique party, it was; for the locust swarm of Coronado that followed, it was something else!

Esteban rapidly outstripped Fray Marcos, who used his time in conveying the Holy Gospel to the Indians, and in diversions to the west to find a road to the Sea of Cortés so the fleet that was to parallel Coronado could easily load expected treasures. By the time Fray Marcos reached present-day Arizona, penetrating possibly only as far north as the Gila River, frightened Indians who had gone ahead with the black man came running back with sad news: Esteban had crossed an unpopulated desert area and reached a group of six or seven mud pueblos (was this Cíbola?), where his journey ended. There he was confronted by suspicion rather than hospitality, by challenge instead of generosity. He explained to the alien reception party his role, told of Fray Marcos following him, and sought the cozy comforts of the fairest of Hawikuh's maidens. Instead, he was stoned to death by indignant elders, who a year later told Coronado's men of Esteban's obvious lies and arrogance. How could he, a black man of insatiable lust, be the representative of a nation of holy white people who knew the whole truth about the Ruler in the sky?

ON TO CIBOLA!

Although Fray Marcos later wrote that he advanced to within sight of Hawikuh, observing it was a city as large as Mexico City itself, most scholars doubt that he actually came to this first Zuni outpost of the Land of Cíbola. He hurried back to Culiacán and then to Mexico to report to the viceroy, wildly exaggerating his discoveries, but turning back to join Coronado's army gathered at Compostela, near modern Tepic. Permission came from Spain for the expedition to proceed, so the viceroy traveled to Compostela as Coronado paraded more than 200 mounted conquistadors, a smaller foot contingent, and 800 native packers, servants, and herdsmen driving a commissary of cattle, sheep, goats, even turkeys, and a *remuda* of spare horses. Meanwhile, the fleet under command of Hernando de Alarcón sailed from Acapulco to meet the land party at the head of the Sea of Cortés.

Even a small advance party of soldiers led by Captain Melchior Díaz encountered resentment and difficulty on the road that Fray Marcos had reported as smooth and hospitable. A dozen mounted men with servants and pack outfits called for far more food, forage, and water than the small native villages could spare. The novelty of the flamboyant Esteban and the humble friar had given way to the insistent demands of conquistadors of the advance party and the overwhelming mass of Coronado's main force, which swept over the land like a swarm of locusts devouring everything in sight.

With a third of his force, Coronado reached Hawikuh on July 7, and had to fight his way into the little adobe-and-stone village. It lacked gold, silver, and the glitter reported by Fray Marcos, who hid his embarrassment in prayers and then returned to Mexico as soon as he could. A few storage bins filled with corn were the only treasure found. Indians told of richer lands *"más allá"*—a little farther along the road. Coronado sent out parties to see. Don Pedro de Tovar discovered the Hopi villages to the northwest, never to know his name would be perpetuated by the handsome El Tovar Hotel on the brink of the Grand Canyon, which itself was first seen by Captain Cárdenas, whose accomplishment has been stingily noted by a miserable little creek flowing into the Colorado River.

Disappointed and hungry after searching through the five or six other small Zuni villages in the Cíbola grouping, Coronado sent parties eastward where the Indians spoke, truthfully this time, of richer places *"más allá."* By the time the main party had advanced from Sonora to Hawikuh, the richer Rio Grande Valley and the neighboring Pecos River country had been entered. The conquistadors moved into the province of Tiguex, the area around present-day Albuquerque. Although pueblos along the Rio Grande were numerous and more prosperous than those of the first-plundered Cíbola and Acoma, they possessed little to feed and enrich the Spaniards during a forlorn winter in which Indian distaste for the visitors brought an increasing pattern of raids and disturbances.

TROUBLE—NOT TREASURE

In the spring of 1541 Coronado was lured eastward into the plains of modern Kansas, among the buffalo which gave Cíbola its name, in search of a golden land called Quivira. He had a willing guide called El Turco, who recited splendors that proved another myth. The deceptive guide was garroted after he finally confessed that he had been bribed to deliberately lead the Spaniards away from the Rio Grande and Pecos valleys. Coronado's party went as far east as modern Wichita in a fruitless search for riches, but were the first Europeans to learn the magnitude of the land and the extent of the endless herds of bison that occupied the plains. Quivira was just another delusion.

Back on the Rio Grande for a second winter, fortunately not as severe as the first, the disappointed and frustrated Spaniards wished only to go home to Mexico. When Coronado suffered a riding accident, he agreed to the return. Three Franciscan priests remained behind to teach the Indians, but became the church's first martyrs in the American Southwest. The other Spaniards and many of their Indian servants took the trail south. By July of 1542 Coronado was humbling himself before the viceroy, explaining that the arid land and its unfriendly inhabitants were not as they had been represented. The Golden Cities were made of rock with mud for mortar. The only gold there was the everlasting sunshine that bathed and burned the land. The only wealth he had brought back was his own life and soul, after two personal injuries and many narrow escapes.

After his confession of failure, and of the financial loss which he shared with many participants and the viceroy, Coronado had to face the legal probing of the *residencia* which sat in judgment on every high Spanish official at the conclusion of his appointment. Some of his followers had accused Coronado of cruelty and other crimes against the native people. He was lucky to be exonerated of such offenses, while unlucky in all else. His reputation and fortune were gone, and his future was bleak.

CURTAIN OF SILENCE

For the following forty years the inhospitable frontier of the future Arizona and New Mexico was closed off by a curtain of silence. When again Spaniards ventured northward, they followed the Conchos River and then the Rio Grande on a route avoiding the Sonora highlands and the Arizona deserts, learning that the three Spanish priests had been killed by natives to whom they had attempted to teach the lessons of Christian love. Again priests ventured into the unknown to save these poor souls, and again the pantheon of martyrs was enlarged. Nevertheless, in 1582 a pious adventurer, Antonio de Espejo, obtained official permission to penetrate the pueblo country, to rescue the lost missionaries if they had survived, and to explore carefully the land where Coronado and the priests had failed to find riches that should be there. Already wealthy, Espejo was willing to risk his neck and invest his money for another chance at fame, greater fortune, and eternal glory. East of the Rio Grande the expedition, led jointly by Espejo and a Franciscan, Bernaldino Beltrán, found nothing. Turning westward, at the Hopi villages in Arizona they were told of mines to the southwest. They entered the Verde Valley and skirted gaunt Mingus Mountain in central Arizona, which four centuries later yielded millions in copper and a king's ransom in residual gold and silver. Espejo and Beltrán found copper-stained ore with a show of silver in a land far from mining equipment, workmen, military protection, and food supplies. The mantle of darkness fell over Arizona again.

The Franciscan hope of converting heathens to Christianity, coupled to the magnetism of the gold that *must* be there, even if still unfound, was to resurrect Spanish dreams of permanent colonies along the upper Rio Grande. After three years of preparation Juan de Oñate, already rich by virtue of his father's one-fourth share of the spectacular silver vaults of Zacatecas, led a large expedition northward in 1598. He spent nearly half-a-million pesos of his own funds to outfit the colony and supply it with livestock, equipment, and seed, while the crown provided priests, artillery, and auxiliary supplies to establish a new outpost in New Mexico. Oñate was its governor and captain-general, determined and brave but not always wise. His best efforts were blocked by severe and clumsy treatment of Indians by priests and military personnel. Besides, the land simply would not feed and supply all the needs of the colonists and their protective troops.

His reputation suffering and the colony weakened, Oñate undertook a desperate journey to restore his leadership. With only thirty soldiers and one priest, he followed the Espejo-Beltrán route to the Hopi villages, then down the Verde River valley, passing near the site of modern Prescott, where they missed placer gold underfoot, but picked up some traces of silver to the west while finding their way to the Colorado River. They followed the Colorado all the way to the Sea of Cortés, believing it was the Pacific. Oñate returned safely to New Mexico and more internal troubles. Later the viceroy cynically summarized what Oñate had found: "Nothing but naked people, false bits of coral, and four pebbles." By 1605 the explorations into Arizona by the conquistadors had all ended in failure.

Nearly a century later, messengers of God's grace would enter Arizona again, as had Marcos de Niza and Coronado's friars, from the south. This time they would not be Franciscans, who continued to labor with scant success among the Hopis until 1680. The new *entrada* was led by priest-soldiers of the militant Society of Jesus, which had inherited the responsibility for leading Indians living west of the Sierra Madre to an understanding of God and the glory of the king.

4

For the Glory of
God and King

Failure of the Espejo and Oñate explorations to find mineral deposits that could be immediately exploited halted European ventures into Arizona. Only the persistent Franciscan priests from northern New Mexico endeavored to establish the Holy Trinity in place of native beliefs in the Hopi villages. The effort cost six Franciscan martyrs, and in the end the peaceful kachinas still reigned.

The colonization of New Mexico financed by Oñate had devolved into a struggle for power between inept civil and military authorities and zealous Franciscans who devoutly believed that conversion of the Indians was highest priority. Unaccompanied missionaries moved westward along the trail Cárdenas and Tovar had marked to the Hopi villages.

By 1629 many residents of the village of Awatovi on Jeddito Mesa, several miles southwest of the modern settlement of Keams Canyon, had joined the padres in erecting the Mission of San Bernardino and professed belief in Christianity. Still, fierce opposition existed which by 1633 brought death by poisoning to Father Porras. Franciscan fervor continued, creating mission churches at Oraibi and Shungopovi. Native hostility increased in all of New Mexico under pressure of harsh Franciscan demands that idolatry be suppressed, combined with unreasonable levies upon the Indians to support the civil population with supplies and labor. Meanwhile, incessant squabbling between state and church functionaries undermined Spanish unity on this frontier. In 1680 the Hopis joined other natives in the bloody Pueblo Revolt, during which hundreds of Spanish soldiers and settlers and several priests were killed. Most of New Mexico was abandoned. The Hopis killed the four missionaries living with them.

In the following decade of reconquest many Indian village groups from the Rio Grande sought refuge in the Hopi country and established new pueblos. Priests gradually drifted back to Hopiland, and Awatovi once more became a Christian center. In 1700 it was assaulted by anti-Catholic Hopis and burned, with male converts and the priest perishing together as torches and dried chili peppers were tossed into a flaming underground kiva whose one exit was closed.

Priests and pagan belief continued to coexist in conflict in Hopiland for the next century. The isolation of the pueblos and the poverty of the region protected them from total military subjugation. Meanwhile a new religious force, the most militant in Spanish history, moved toward Arizona from the south.

Only a few years after Coronado's failure, treasure *was* found north of Mexico City, but, unlike the golden storehouses of the Aztecs and the Incas, this wealth was in silver and was *in situ* in the wrinkled Sierra Madre waiting for miners to extract and refine it. Great silver mines at Guanajuato and Zacatecas and eventually much farther north at Alamos and Parral brought Spanish miners and colonists northward. Inevitably a cattle frontier to feed the new settlements and a missionary frontier to pave paths to heaven moved ahead of the miners.

JESUIT ARMY ADVANCES

To fill the need for education and conversion to the Holy Faith, members of the vigorous new Society of Jesus arrived in Mexico in the 1570s and soon were carving out a vast missionary field west of the Sierra Madre (since Franciscans were firmly established on its eastern flanks), along the Gulf of Mexico, and northward along the Rio Grande.

From Compostela, where Coronado had rallied his conquistadors, and from Culiacán, where Cabeza de Vaca's small band had been reunited with their countrymen, the Jesuits moved slowly up the west coast, carrying their *reducción* or conversions from one river valley to another, building pueblos and missions as they progressed from one tribe to another. Under their guidance the mission as a colonizing institution of Spanish government achieved major importance.

The Jesuits were pious, organized, and firm. Each pair of missionaries generally was accompanied by a like number of soldiers. The sword and cross advanced together for the glory of God and king, bringing the Indians with love into the church, and with force if needed to the responsibilities of Spanish citizenship, which included service in the militia, growing crops for the support of priests and soldiers, learning the Castilian tongue, paying taxes, and obedience to all the laws of God and king, generally as interpreted by black-robed priests.

As an institution of the dual realm of God and king, the mission was to achieve three broad purposes on the frontier: to convert Indians to the Catholic faith; to protect them from their enemies, such as hostile tribes, colonists, or maldoers who might exploit them; and to civilize them in skills and arts of Spanish custom, including obedience, as preparation for citizenship. The missionaries, supported by the crown, were to reach these goals in a decade, hand over the civilized Indians to diocesan priests and civil authorities, and then move on to a newer, more distant frontier to repeat the process.

Originally all missionaries were native-born Spaniards. When a manpower shortage developed at home, *criollos*—Spaniards born in the Americas—became acceptable seminarians, and eventually even Indians and *mestizos* or mixed-bloods were taken into the priesthood. Nations affiliated with Spain in the Holy Roman Empire were, in time, allowed to provide Jesuits to staff missions on the frontiers of New Spain.

ENTER FATHER KINO

Thus Arizona was to acquire its first outstanding European-born personality, the Indians of northwest New Spain a defender and apostle, and the capable Jesuits another candidate for sainthood. He was an Italian, born in the Tyrolean Alps, trained as a Jesuit in Bavaria. He hispanicized his family name of Chini to Kino, and when he came to the Sonoran frontier in 1687 was called Eusebio Francisco

Kino. His statue stands in Statuary Hall in the United States Capitol in honor of his contributions to the settlement of Arizona.

Although he had hoped to be a missionary in the Far East, as his distant cousin had been, Kino was destined by a roll of the dice to be assigned to the desert rim of Christendom when a luckier priest won the last open assignment to the Orient. Kino's first post was the failing Jesuit effort to colonize the tip of Baja California, where insufficient rainfall doomed the colony. After it failed, Kino was sent northward to a remote mission on the obscure San Miguel River in Pimería Alta, the name given then to modern southern Arizona and northern Sonora.

Father Kino was to make the Mission of Nuestra Señora de Dolores (Our Lady of Sorrows) the hub of his uniquely energetic accomplishments. During twenty-four years on the desert frontier he established an equal number of new missions. He made forty extensive tours of his realm. By tracing the origin of blue abalone shells to the Pacific shore he proved that Baja California was not an island. By effective training of Indian cowboys he raised prolific cattle herds whose surplus provided seed stock for the cattle industries of California and Arizona. He produced the best map of the Southwest available for two centuries. By his friendship with the captain-general of the Jesuit order he was able to obtain additional missionaries to extend conversions in Pimería Alta, but never enough to satisfy his devotion to his native flock and their needs. He was such a valiant protector of Indians that even now on borderland backroads he is credited reverently as founder of all old churches and missions. When his friend Father Saeta was martyred by discontented Indians at Caborca, Kino bound the church's wounds by showing continued confidence in the perpetrators as innocent children of God. His virtues and deeds are at present undergoing review, looking toward his possible canonization by the Roman Catholic Church.

With Kino's death in 1711 following his dedication of a new chapel at Magdalena in Sonora, Spanish influence on the frontier weakened. The lessons taught by Kino were forgotten and his inspiring presence was missed. Forty years later, as other Jesuits struggled to hold the advances he had achieved, Pima Indians became discontented and rebelled on a broad front, killing many settlers. Spanish arms were called in to subdue and punish them. This incident in 1751 proved to be a turning point in Spanish policy in the region: The next year a presidio, or military garrison, was established at Tubac on the Santa Cruz River in southern Arizona. Love having failed to hold the Indians, now the sword would rule the northwest frontier. The Jesuits were pained at this sad turn of events, but only fifteen years later, in 1767—through no fault of mission management or immorality—they were banned from all Spanish domains. The secular church had grown jealous of dominant Jesuit influence in the courts of Portugal, France, and Spain in turn, and with papal consent had persuaded King Charles III to punish the order by banishment.

FRANCISCAN REALM

Expulsion of the Jesuits in 1767 thrust upon the Franciscans extra responsibility to take over mission duties in New Spain. Although friars already were spread thinly from the Sabine River to the Pacific, their seminaries and colleges were scoured for priests ready to take up the Jesuits' unfinished tasks. God smiled upon Arizona when young Francisco Tomás Garcés left the seminary at Querétaro to come to San Xavier del Bac near Tucson. Strikingly similar to Kino, with a restless passion to carry the gospel to the far corners of Pimería Alta, and equally devoted to conversions and betterment of native life-style, Garcés found himself stationed at San Xavier del Bac, which had been Kino's favorite outlying mission. A small adobe church had been built in 1700 at Kino's direction. Now a domed edifice of grand proportions made of fired brick was erected. Ornately decorated by native artists trained by artisans imported by the Franciscans, San Xavier became an impressive showplace of frontier achievement. Garcés did not live to see completion of this brilliant White Dove of the Desert, but the spirit of his devotion surrounded its completion.

Even before the Jesuit expulsion, Spanish strategists had planned to occupy and settle upper California. This task fell to the Franciscans, led by Friar Junípero Serra. In 1769 they moved by land and by sea to the task, establishing, at great hazard and cost in souls and pesos, the presidio and mission of San Diego. The mission's role of converting, protecting, and civilizing the Indians had by this time superimposed upon it the extra burden of supplying and populating California for internal development and settling it as protection against alien invasion. The threat consisted mainly of an exaggerated fear of English explorers and freebooters in the Pacific and Russian fur hunters who had begun to move southward from Alaska toward the California coast. These foreigners might threaten the Manila galleons which sailed from Acapulco to the Philippines, returning laden with Oriental silks and spices. On the perilous return to Acapulco the inbound galleons followed the Japanese current flowing northward along the Asiatic coast, skirting the Aleutian Islands and arcing southward along the northwest coast of America. The presence of European powers anywhere in the Pacific, considered a "Spanish lake," was cause for alarm.

As Kino wrote that someday it would, Arizona thus gained increased importance as the logical supply road to California. The road through Pimería Alta could supply necessities for California more cheaply and safely than a water route. Pacific Ocean winds were adverse to northbound coastal shipping between Mexico and Alta California.

PROTECTING THE FRONTIER

A new viceroy of New Spain, Italian-born Frey Antonio María de Bucareli y Ursúa, urged his representatives on the borderlands to expedite this strategy, while simultaneously he supported the king's edict to create a cordon of presidios or garrisons stretching all the way from California to the Texas coast. This line of forts was designed to repel bloody incursions by Apache and Comanche raiders mounted on horses acquired from Spanish settlements, which made them a mobile enemy of mission Indians and colonists of the cattle and mining frontiers. The presidio of Tubac in Arizona and others at nearby Altar, Terrenate, and Fronteras were part of the new military structure called the Provincias Internas with headquarters at Arizpe in Sonora.

Fray Garcés's eager curiosity about natives in every corner of Pimería Alta was to reveal this needed road to California. As Kino had done before him, Garcés followed the Gila River to its union with the Colorado, preaching to the Indians as he passed from one *ranchería* to another. At the present site of Yuma he met a runaway Indian who had come across the western sand dunes and desert from the sea coast, where he had seen men dressed as Garcés was, in robe and sandals.

The excited friar hurried to Tubac to report the land route to the sea to Captain Juan Bautista de Anza, born at Fronteras of a father with the same name who had achieved a fine reputation for military leadership. Captain Anza relayed the news to Viceroy Bucareli, in return receiving orders to explore the road. The year 1774 was a week old when Captain Anza with thirty-four soldiers, Indian guides, the irrepressible Fray Garcés, and his companion, Fray Juan Díaz, headed straight west from Tubac, crossing the parched Papago country by a route later known as El Camino del Diablo. Winter rains had left sufficient water in holes known to the Indians.

At Yuma they persuaded the California Indian who had told Garcés of the trail to guide them to the coast. He led them around the creeping sand dunes west of the river, through the sunken area now called Imperial Valley, and over coastal mountains, all the way to Mission San Gabriel a few miles from today's famous Pasadena Rose Bowl. Franciscans there were delighted to see Garcés and directed the party northward along El Camino Real, the highway connecting the chain of missions the friars were building all the way to Monterey, capital of Alta California. Praise and promotion were bestowed on the military captain. The humble friars had followed God's will. The road to California was open. Spain's fears about the safety of the northwest frontier were, in part, allayed.

The following year a party of 240 colonists, recruited in Mexico City and in Sinaloa and Sonora, collected at Tubac to march to Monterey. The party followed the Santa Cruz River through Tucson to the Gila and then turned westward along the trail Kino and Garcés knew so well. Captain Anza proudly rode as their leader. Garcés went only as far as Yuma, then turned off on a special mission. Fray Pedro Font accompanied the main party as chaplain and chronicler. Finding the best farmlands near Monterey already taken, the colonists moved inland and northward. Where the peninsula sheltered the site from the open sea the Spaniards built a mission, near which the hamlet of Yerba Buena (renamed San Francisco) later developed as an important rewatering and provisioning site for whaling and trading ships.

LINKING OUTPOSTS OF EMPIRE

Accompanied only by friendly Indians, with whom he shared dog stew with equal relish, and whom he loved as dearly as he did his fellow friars, Garcés went north along the Colorado River to the modern site of Needles, there turning west to follow a dry desert watercourse and scattered waterholes into the Mohave Desert sink, over the Tehachapi Mountains, and into the great central valley of California. His assignment was to find a second road from Monterey on the coast to Santa Fe, New Mexico. The Spanish engineer Costansó had reported to the viceroy that these capitals of the two northern fingers of Spanish colonization were on approximately the same latitude. They should be joined by a road, thus strengthening the northern frontier against either Russian or British intrusion. Garcés went to see. He followed the San Joaquin River northward to near present-day Fresno, where again Indians told of men dressed in robes and sandals beside the sea, across the swampy valley and over the Coast Range. Knowing that he was now directly east of Monterey, Garcés retraced his trail to the Colorado River. Next he would find the way to Santa Fe. Hualpai Indian guides who had been there before on trading expeditions led him to the Hopi Indian village of Oraibi, where he was coolly received because of the natives' remembrance of Franciscans who nearly a century before had been killed during the Pueblo Revolt. Recently a Franciscan from Zuñi pueblo farther to the east, Fray Silvestre Vélez de Escalante, had come to the Hopi villages seeking help to locate a ford across the Colorado River, but had been turned away without such guidance. Escalante, like Garcés, had set out in response to the viceroy's request that the northern road be charted.

The natives of Oraibi were disdainful of Garcés's friendly mien. Spaniards were not welcome at Oraibi or neighboring villages. On

July 4, 1776, the day that liberty was proclaimed for a new nation across the continent in Philadelphia, Garcés sadly turned back toward San Xavier del Bac, his love for the Indians undiminished. He accepted their inhospitality as a message from God that he must serve the heathen more intently to achieve grace sufficient to win their favor.

A NOBLE EXPERIMENT

To bolster the Sonora road, Spanish authorities decided to establish a new type of colony at Yuma Crossing. Missions had not been universally successful under the ethereal management of some priests. Military presidios often were characterized by harshness and force little appreciated by the victimized Indians. Colonists frequently made excessive supply and labor demands on the native people. Perhaps a settlement combining the best features of these three types would succeed. So twenty civilian families were sent to Yuma Crossing as the core of an agricultural settlement. They were accompanied by soldiers, but only by married soldiers with families, who also would be encouraged to establish farms. Four priests went along, their function restricted to ecclesiastical duties. Father Garcés was among them. Two missions were formed on the California side of the river, overlooked by a military post and a central church on the hill that later became the site of Fort Yuma.

This noble experiment, however, issued in discord. The missionaries were less able than ever to deliver the material gifts their Indian neophytes expected. Colonists seized the finest farming land for themselves, dislocating Indians. The soldiers were brazenly severe, joining colonists in brutal flogging of flagging native workmen. The military and religious forces were in disagreement. The Indians were confused, oppressed, and angry.

A climax came when Captain Fernando de Rivera y Moncada, one of the pioneer founders of California, arrived from Sonora driving a herd of horses to the coast. His men turned the horses into Indian fields to feed, precipitating on July 18, 1781, a violent native uprising that brought death to Rivera and all Spanish men except three soldiers and four lucky settlers. Women and children were spared, but the Indians clubbed to death Father Garcés and his three fellow priests.

The Yuma Massacre closed the overland road to California, effectively ending Arizona's participation in affairs of the Spanish Empire in North America; precisely four decades later, in 1821, the flag of Spain would be lowered from the presidio and walled town of Tucson, to which the garrison had moved in 1776 from Tubac.

The mission frontier in Arizona had reached the Gila River but did not cross because of the unconquered Apache menace. San Xavier del Bac was completed in magnificence before the end of the century, and soon a less imposing mission was built farther south at Tumacácori as the Franciscans clung to their responsibility to teach the gospel to the Papago Indians.

While decline and decay settled over Pimería Alta, far across the Atlantic, with the opening of the nineteenth century, Napoleon conquered Spain. This became the signal for widespread native and *criollo* revolt against the festering incompetence and failure of Spanish rule in the New World. As the Spanish flag was assaulted at presidios and missions on the frontier and a new red-white-and-green flag of Mexico appeared in a few populated centers, Apache raiders gloated at the weakness and civil strife of the white intruders, who cowered in fear in undermanned presidios and pueblos. The intensity of the Apache raids increased until a reign of bloodshed and terror plagued the Southwest.

5

Time of the Apaches

Harshness has often been cited as a significant and debilitating quality of Spanish colonial administration. Vastly outnumbered by a resistant native population and themselves only recently released from Moorish bondage, Spanish civil and military personnel strangely were deaf to the avid preaching of Christian charity and love by priests who accompanied them on their task of stabilizing far frontiers.

The missionaries had a more receptive audience in Indians who hardly understood the gospel but who responded with open curiosity to friendly strangers, with innocent glee to their songs and pictures of heaven, with appreciation for gifts, and, as their sophistication increased, with that gratitude understandably changing to greed for material things. Their life-style long had tottered on the brink of starvation. Father Kino proved centuries before marriage counseling became popular that domestic happiness is enhanced by a full stomach. He and other wise missionaries made substantial contributions to a better diet and improved standard of living for Indians, knowing that conversions would be stimulated more by the material blessings of Christianity than by spiritual glories promised by the priests. Natives who accepted subordinate local offices assisting Spanish officials were rewarded with wonderful new foods, tools, and clothing in payment. To the Indian, living within earshot of the bell of the local church meant a more fruitful life, if not necessarily a holier one.

IMPROVED LIFE-STYLE

In such an arid land, hunting did not return rich rewards for the chase. Gathering roots, seeds, cactus fruit, acorns, and pine nuts, and growing small plots of corn, beans, and squash left the natives generally lean and lank before the Spaniards came. Once the missionaries introduced their supermarket of new products—wheat, garbanzos or chick-peas, grapes, peaches, citrus, quinces, pomegranates, figs, olives, and, above all, domesticated animals: sheep, goats, cattle, hogs, chickens, donkeys, mules, and horses—a bountiful new life was available to mission Indians in Pimería Alta.

While an aura of contentment often surrounded such missionized inhabitants, their peaceful appreciation of the new life was interrupted by occasional revolts and uprisings by dissidents who sensed that their loss of freedom was not sufficiently compensated by material returns. Such brushfires could be stamped out by greater Spanish generosity, by removal of haughty and cruel officials, by armed suppression, and—the most obvious of solutions—by kind treatment.

A greater danger lurked at the rim of Christendom, outside the missions and pueblos. The Spanish introduction of the horse probably had a more important effect upon native life in North America than any other action of the invaders. As Cortés's mounted soldiers had terrorized Indians on the east coast of Mexico, thereby hastening his conquest of Mexico, three centuries later the Spaniards were under attack in Mexico, cringing from the terror created on the northern frontier by Indians who had become fearful horsemen.

Hunter-raider tribesmen of the Great Plains and the Southwest had become ferocious with the mobility provided them by the horse. Animals that escaped settlements or were stolen provided mobility that converted foot-weary Indians into expert horsemen, capable of striking fierce blows against pueblos and missions and then withdrawing heavily laden with booty to the safety of their favorite haunts. The problem of a winter food supply often was met by killing the horses and mules they stole on raids, with the comfortable awareness that the Spaniards would have a new herd in time for next summer's raids.

Buffalo hunting on the Plains had been tedious and dangerous when the Indians were afoot. The horse enabled them to harvest the hump-backed beasts either with bow-and-arrow or by driving them over high riverbanks and cliffs to their deaths. The horse permitted Indians from north of the Gila and from the parched lands beyond the Rio Grande to raid deep into cattle and mining areas of the northwest borderlands. Settlements hundreds of miles south of the Gila were subjected to sweeping raids by whooping bands of Apaches, Navajos, and Utes coming south along the river valleys from Arizona, and by Comanches, Kickapoos, and Lipán or Kiowa Apaches from beyond the Rio Grande. This raiding into Mexico added a devastating new dimension to the uncertainties of the Spanish effort to colonize and hold Pimería Alta.

MOBILITY OF THE HORSE

Raids by Apaches and other mounted bands were not punitive or retaliatory—that is, not the result of injustices against Indians by the Spaniards. Raiding for booty had for countless centuries been the way of life of these peoples. Since their arrival from Asia they had preyed upon each other. With horses secured from the Spaniards, they could strike and steal what they desired with greater speed and impunity. They swept into the Spanish outposts to satisfy their tastes for the needs and luxuries of their new life-style: women and children to be captive slaves but eventually to enliven and rejuvenate their extended families; food of all kinds, including horses and mules which would be eaten after serving their first purpose of transportation; clothing better than their own buckskin or plaited pants; distilled *aguardiente* or brandy and mescal made of native maguey, for which the Indians easily developed a craving; iron tools and modern weapons. Almost as soon as iron and forges were brought to the frontier, the Indians learned to make points of metal for their spears and arrows, finding metal more efficient and less laborious than chipped stone or bone points. They were equally alert to the power of firearms, and returned home with muskets taken from their fallen victims. Later they would return for a supply of gunpowder and shot.

When increasing incursions of this sort threatened the safety of the frontier in depth, the Spaniards called out militia formed of mission Indians and colonists in attempts to punish the raiders. Such

efforts were ineffective in stopping the raids, especially after unscrupulous traders—the Spaniards generally blamed such crimes on
the French and English—bartered superior guns and ammunition to
the Indians for furs and later sold them outright when the raiders
learned to plunder mines, mints, and treasuries on the frontier.

CRUMBLING DEFENSES

The cordon of presidios built across the borderlands during the last
quarter of the eighteenth century and the organization of the administrative jurisdiction known as the Provincias Internas were a
direct reaction to the inability of the militia, soldiers from the missions, and Indian auxiliaries to cope with raiding Indians. Even with
such garrisons, presidial soldiers often were poorly trained, badly
armed, underpaid, constricted by crown regulations, and haphaz-
ardly led. When the chain of forts failed to halt the raiding, outland-
ish efforts were made to create havoc among the Indian enemy by
stirring up hatred and differences between tribes, by debauching them
with liquor, by selling them obsolete and inferior guns with a view
to creating a trade dependence for ammunition and repairs, and by
adopting an extermination policy, with cash bounties for scalps. This
last vile tactic backfired when unprincipled scalp hunters delivered to
officials in Chihuahua the hairlocks of murdered Mexicans who had
carelessly wandered outside settlements and whose dried scalps could
not be distinguished from those of Indians. All of these devices failed,
while only one other approach, of lesser inhumanity, was partially
effective. As late as the nineteenth century, Apache Indians were
living at Tucson supported by crown grants or doles, paid to remain
peaceful; but these docile Apaches were very few in number con-
trasted to hordes who warred on the settlements.

When Spain collapsed to Napoleon's invading army and revolution broke out throughout Mexico beginning with Father Hidalgo's
grito or cry of revolt in 1810, the last five viceroys at Mexico City felt
compelled to call in Spanish troops from frontier posts to hold the
capital against the growing armies of independence. Frontier Indian
raiders immediately found the resulting weaknesses in the defensive

structure and increased their raids to loot the presidios of weapons of war as well as consumable booty.

TIME OF THE RAIDERS

As freedom from Spanish rule came to the unprepared young Republic of Mexico in 1821, the Apache raiders became lords of Arizona. Cattle ranches and the few mining enterprises on the frontier were abandoned. Priests stayed close to the frightened presidial troops at Tucson, who prudently took down the Spanish flag and raised the new Mexican banner in its place, meanwhile intensifying prayers for deliverance from the encouraged enemy.

Cut off from financial support from Mexico City, where chaos and disorder, punctuated by the frequent shots of firing squads, hampered efforts to establish a stable government after freedom came in 1821, governors of the frontier provinces of California and New Mexico had to use ingenuity to support themselves and the troops abandoned with them in the danger zone. Spain traditionally had prohibited trade with foreigners, since under its rule mercantile rights and virtually all other civil ventures were authorized, licensed, and even sold by the crown to favored petitioners. Under the weak Mexican governments, foreign trade was unofficially condoned and even encouraged as means of bringing needed supplies to the bazaars of Monterey and Santa Fe, and to produce sales and import taxes to pay officials and troops. Yankee trading ships began calling openly at California ports. Entrepreneurs, headquartered in the great fur-trading center of St. Louis or the Missouri River outpost of Westport (now Kansas City), started visiting and trading with merchants in Santa Fe. The famous Santa Fe Trail was now a lifeline to bring supplies from the United States, often in trade for Mexican mules. Fur buyers openly traded with Taos and Santa Fe in an expansion of business previously conducted surreptitiously at various fur fairs or rendezvous at Taos and in hidden valleys in the Rocky Mountains.

THE AMERICANS ARRIVE

After the northern beaver plews had been depleted, the fur trade had moved down into the lower Rockies. This southward relocation of the centers of the fur trade, coupled with the development of the Santa Fe Trail, greatly increased the number of independent traders, hunters, and mountain men who drifted across Arizona, following the easy grades of the Gila River valley to reopen the road to California. This time it was to be not a feeble, misdirected Spanish effort to supply a distant colony but the vigorous vitality of the amoral new nation flexing its muscles.

The hardy men trapping Sonoran beaver and other fur-bearing animals in the heart of the Apache country, along creeks and rivers draining Arizona mountains into the Gila and the Colorado, were not passive, lovable, but often unworldly priests in Jesuit or Franciscan robes, nor were they civil vassals of Spanish royal monarchy. These were a new breed of frontiersmen. Imbued with a restless, self-serving, nationalistic fervor soon to be categorized as manifest destiny, they were striking out on their own, without governmental license or support for the most part, to conquer new worlds of their own. Whereas exploration on the frontiers of Spain universally was licensed, sanctioned, and financed by the home government, in this awakening of western America the individual pioneers were the leaders. Their number probably included more renegades than patriots, not so many explorers as exploiters, not adjusters but conquerors, more adventurers than settlers—but this was a new, victorious wave of the future. From the land of sunrise they were bringing new American ideas and the American flag to a land not yet known as Arizona.

6

Distant Trumpets

As unchecked Apache marauders forced abandonment of cattle and sheep ranches and the few mining ventures on the Arizona frontier in the first third of the nineteenth century, distant trumpets sounded in Texas that heralded a coming decade in which Hispanic influence in the Southwest would wane as the Anglo-American presence escalated.

Repeating a Spanish folly in colonial administration although it had recently won its independence from Spain, in 1821 Mexico invited land-hungry American colonists into its troubled province of Texas, hoping the hardy newcomers would build a bulwark against hostile Indians whom Mexican troops could not control. Although this *empresario* system had been attempted by the Spaniards in Florida and failed, liberal land allotments were offered to American settlers. In exchange, they were to join the Roman Catholic Church and become citizens of Mexico, thus standing as brothers with Mexican settlers to subdue heathen and hostile Comanches and plains Apaches.

These new Texas colonists, pouring across the Mississippi from the dark and bloody lands west of the Appalachians where they had proved their pioneering mettle, were more successful than Mexicans believed possible. Generally of Scotch-Irish stock, they were mostly Protestant and fiercely independent. Many took dual oaths of Catholic and Mexican allegiance with grave reservations. Others simply did not bother. Many brought slaves from the cottonfields of Tennessee, Mississippi, and Alabama. Texas had an ideal climate for cotton, tobacco, and rice—crops with heavy labor demands. The official ban on slavery in Mexican territory was ignored by the newcomers.

The stunning success and growth of the Texas-American colony became a convenient political issue for the quixotic Mexican general and often dictator Antonio López de Santa Anna. On becoming president in 1833, Santa Anna postulated to his disorganized country that opportunistic Texans were a major cause of Mexico's many troubles. Harsh regulations and restrictive constitutional provisions were invoked to withdraw the self-rule by states that was specifically allowed in the colonists' contracts. Not surprisingly, the Texans reacted vigorously, in part because they were receiving covert support from expansionists back home in the United States. President Andrew Jackson was openly sympathetic. His close friend Davy Crockett had resigned from Congress to join Texas adventurers. The swashbuckling Sam Houston, former governor of Tennessee, had Jackson's support in aggressive efforts to ascend to political control in Texas.

TEXAS'S FREEDOM FIGHTERS

As resistance to Santa Anna's harsh edicts grew in Texas, colonists whose fathers and grandfathers had participated in the American War of Independence armed themselves to oppose the army Santa Anna led into the province to suppress the rebellious settlers. A makeshift Texas force, bolstered by volunteers recruited in New Orleans on the promise of generous land grants for military service, routed the Mexican garrison and captured an old fortified church called the Alamo in the city of San Antonio de Béxar, the modern San Antonio. Two men later to be prominent pioneers in Arizona's settlement participated in that First Battle of the Alamo, a forgotten Texas victory. They were William S. Oury, twenty years later a mail and express agent for Butterfield's stage line and Wells Fargo in Tucson and one of the first Anglo cattlemen in southern Arizona, and Herman Ehrenberg, a German youth who as a mining engineer would help find and publicize Arizona's mineral wealth at midcentury. Both had been sent to other fighting fronts by the time Santa Anna's army overran and killed the sacrificial defenders of the Alamo. A few weeks later Texas bugles trumpeted in triumph when General Sam Houston surprised the Mexican main force at its siesta hour near boggy San Jacinto and brought a quick and victorious close to the Texas revolution.

Thereupon Texas was for several years an independent republic, which obligated itself for financial support to Britain and France, but eventually, as destiny dictated from the outset, sought and accepted annexation to the United States. Worsening relationships between Mexico and the United States now became official, hinged emotionally but not exclusively on the southern border of Texas. The United States contended that the border should be the Rio Grande, while Mexico insisted that the Nueces River had been the historic boundary between the provinces of Texas and Coahuila. The Mexican Congress and officials had repudiated Santa Anna's surrender document following his defeat at San Jacinto, which Texas said gave it the Rio Grande boundary. Fearing for his life, Santa Anna had conceded territory to the Texans as far as the Rio Grande. Maps, however, showed clearly that the 1816 Spanish frontier of Texas had been marked more than a hundred miles farther northeast on the Nueces River. Lands between the two streams were lightly populated, and never had been considered part of Texas. Greed was in the eyes of American expansionists. The dispute over the Rio Grande, which the Mexicans called Río Bravo del Norte, merely blanketed other American aspirations.

An even greater prize—California—was attracting American interest. Yankee traders and whalers and overland explorers, notably the eager John Charles Frémont, had reported on the fertility and potential wealth of the great valleys of California. With manifest destiny calling for a nation fronting on two oceans and the Orient trade beckoning as railroad construction encouraged commercial interests, both Britain and France were fearfully viewed as potential possessors of California in satisfaction of Mexican debts to those countries.

MANIFEST DESTINY DOMINANT

California gained more favor as a goal of American political expansion at the urging of land speculators and commercial interests. Frémont's father-in-law, United States Senator Thomas Hart Benton of Missouri, vigorously trumpeted the glories of the Far West, encouraging Americans to push out to Texas and California and Oregon after purchasing outfits and supplies in the great markets of St. Louis.

In 1842 rumors of war with Mexico plus American anxiety to seize California sent a naval flotilla commanded by Thomas ap Catesby Jones into the port of Monterey, capital of upper California. Jones captured the presidio and ran up the American flag despite Mexican protests that the two nations were not at war. This bloodless assault, for which Commodore Jones apologized and withdrew within thirty-six hours, was based upon a rumor circulated in South America that Mexico and the United States were at war. Such tension and action were indicative of the American passion for California, where several hundred Americans were established as merchants, ranchers, professional men, and speculators. Some had married native California women and had connived to acquire land grants which could be obtained easily from Mexican officials or purchased at very small cost.

Among the Americans were men keenly aware of the process by which Texas had become independent of Mexico and had then been annexed to the United States. Secretary of State James Buchanan was willing to buy California, but encouraged the American consul at Monterey to pass the word that Washington would look favorably upon annexation if California through its own efforts should set itself free, on the example of Texas. Many Californios were unhappy with the province's budgetary and military abandonment by Mexico City and had begun acquiring large land grants in anticipation of a change.

When Frémont arrived in northern California with a party of sixty mountain men and mercenary Indians posing as trappers in early 1846, his presence in strength exceeded that of Mexican troops in the area and precipitated the creation of the abortive Bear Flag Republic, which saw Californios joining American squatters to hasten the separation from Mexico then believed inevitable. Established American businessmen were embarrassed by the revolt and decried it as predatory and unnecessary. They had been waiting for a ripening of the separation movement or open war. Three weeks later news of war arrived with American warships. Down came the flag of the California Republic, to be replaced by the Stars and Stripes.

THE U.S. HURTLES INTO WAR

Humorless President Polk had relieved all anguish and doubt from those who questioned American policy about Texas and manifest destiny. Soon after Texas was annexed officially in 1845, the president sent General Zachary Taylor to occupy coastal lands between Corpus Christi, at the mouth of the Nueces, and Matamoros, the most easterly remaining Mexican garrison, on the south bank of the Rio Grande. Taylor's troops planted artillery on the north bank of the Rio Grande, threatening Matamoros. This of itself was barely short of war. Back in Washington, Polk was fidgeting, anxious to begin his war of expansion but impatiently waiting for an incident or excuse to shift blame to the Mexicans. In a few days, accommodating Mexican troopers crossed the Rio Grande several miles above Matamoros and fired upon some of Taylor's troops, killing a few. The president's message to Congress announcing the outbreak of war had been written—with a pious apology that the Sabbath had been violated in its preparation—even before news of that invasion of American territory and slaughter of United States troops reached the White House.

Arizona as an entity of the United States was to emerge from the War with Mexico, since the desert lowlands along the Gila River were to provide the transportation corridor for one of three campaigns that soon were launched against Mexico. Arizona was the road to California, richest prize of the war.

Although political jealousies denied him adequate troops and supplies, General Taylor drove quickly toward Monterrey, industrial center of Mexico, defeating Mexican defenders in successive battles. General Winfield Scott, with effective naval support, landed an army near Veracruz and followed Cortés's route of conquest in a drive for Mexico City. His campaign was beset by political blundering and intrigue in which the United States helped restore Santa Anna to leadership in Mexico in what proved to be a vain hope that he would hasten Mexican capitulation. But, despite Santa Anna's treacherous anti-American program, by September of 1847 United States marines had stormed the heights of Chapultepec and all Mexico had submitted to the American conquerors.

While the principal theater of war was directed toward conquest of central Mexico and its government, drums of war swept across Arizona as United States dragoons hastened to seize California.

ARMY OF THE WEST

Upon mounted forces that had been operating on the western plains against Indian hostiles fell the responsibility for seizing all territory west of the Rio Grande. Brigadier General Stephen Watts Kearny rode out of Fort Leavenworth along the Santa Fe Trail as commander of the Army of the West to take the frontier provinces one after the other. Already alienated from Mexico City by isolation and fiscal neglect, New Mexico did not resist as Kearny advanced into Santa Fe without firing a shot. After organizing a civil government under questionable military authority, he led 300 dragoons southward on the first leg of a dash to California. Kearny was near Socorro, ready to leave the Rio Grande behind, when he met Kit Carson, diminutive but dynamic mountain man, riding east from California with official dispatches reporting that Frémont and Commodore Robert F. Stockton had conquered the northern part of California. Carson and twelve Delaware Indians had been guides in Frémont's party which had supported the Bear Flag Republic and then openly warred on Mexican authorities. Kearny ordered Carson to return with him to California as guide for his occupying force, calling upon another famous scout, Thomas "Broken-Hand" Fitzpatrick, to carry the dispatches on to Washington.

Carson convinced General Kearny that a force of 300 men with wagons could not travel rapidly on the Gila River route which lay before them, so Kearny sent the wagons and 200 men back to Santa Fe. Led by Carson and his loyal mercenaries, the tiny Army of the West hurried toward the setting sun. Near the Continental Divide they encountered cordial Apaches led by a regional chief, Mangas Coloradas, who welcomed news of the war with Mexico, volunteering to join the Americans against Mexico, raiding victim and constant foe of the Apaches. Mangas was stunned by Kearny's refusal, but caused the Americans no serious trouble.

BATTLE OF SAN PASCUAL

Familiar with the route he had traveled often as trapper and horse trader, Carson led the force rapidly along the Gila River. In a few weeks they had crossed the Colorado River and the Salton Sink beyond, and were approaching their goal of San Diego, where American warships were in control. As they came near the hamlet of San Pascual, two days' march northeast of San Diego, they were attacked by a band of Californio lancers, expert horsemen led by General Andrés Pico, brother of the last provincial governor of California. In a fog-shrouded battle that stretched into two days, the Californios soundly defeated the invaders, killing fifteen officers and men. Carson and a Navy lieutenant with the party, Edward F. Beale, managed to slip through the lines of the celebrating victors to reach San Diego and direct sailors to the rescue of Kearny's crippled army.

As Kearny hurried westward from Santa Fe, his second in command, Colonel Philip St. George Cooke, was organizing a force of volunteers to build a military road to San Diego. For this purpose the United States Army had recruited more than 500 members of the Church of Jesus Christ of Latter-day Saints, then migrating from Nauvoo, Illinois, to an as yet undetermined new refuge or Zion in the Far West. In responding to the Army's needs, Brigham Young, president of the church, negotiated for the men's pay to be delivered to their families, thus obtaining support for the exodus; at the same time he confirmed the loyalty of the Mormons to the nation, an allegiance which had been questioned during their persecution and troubles.

SAINTS MARCHING WEST

Cooke's Mormon Battalion marched farther south on the Rio Grande than had Kearny, seeking the lowest point on the Continental Divide before turning southwest. He led a working party rather than a traditional army, most of the men being equipped with shovels and pickaxes to construct a wagon road through mountain passes and across streams to supply San Diego from the plains arsenal at Fort Leavenworth. Among guides for 400 Mormon men (and five wives who refused to be parted from their husbands) was the most famous baby in Far West history, now grown to manhood and serving Cooke as a scout. This was Baptiste Charbonneau, son of the Indian Sacajawea, famed guide of the Lewis and Clark Expedition.

As the battalion approached Tucson, officers of the Mexican garrison attempted to bluff Cooke into bypassing the presidio, threatening a stiff defense. The next morning his force marched into Tucson uncontested. The garrison had sought sanctuary at San Xavier del Bac Mission to the south. Townspeople were happy to sell their meager supplies to the American enemy. Marching on, the Mormons celebrated Christmas Day visiting Pima Indians on the Gila River near present-day Sacaton, feasting on a surprising delicacy, watermelon, and trading with friendly natives. They marched on to California without incident and were later mustered out of Army service at San Diego by Colonel Cooke, with ardent praise for loyal service in extending the military road from Santa Fe to San Diego.

Maps and descriptions of routes followed by Kearny and Cooke were published about a year later in a government volume prepared by Lieutenant William H. Emory of the Army topographical corps, who had accompanied Kearny. It was widely distributed in time to serve the great wave of Forty-niners who rushed westward after gold was discovered near Sacramento while American and Mexican officials were drawing up the Treaty of Guadalupe Hidalgo ending the war with Mexico.

MEXICO HUMBLED

Mexico lost one-third of its territory as a result of its defiance of American manifest destiny, yet Americans who argued for "All Mexico" considered the treaty soft or generous. All of California, Nevada, New Mexico (then including Arizona), Utah, and parts of Colorado and Wyoming were ceded to the United States, for which Mexico received $15 million, while claims of United States citizens against Mexico were assumed by the United States government. The United

States had offered Mexico $20 million for the same territory before the war began.

In the new treaty the Rio Grande was clearly designated the boundary of Texas, rather than the Nueces, as Mexico had claimed. The Gila River became the principal boundary between Mexico and the United States from the Rio Grande to the Colorado, from which a straight line was drawn to San Diego to separate Baja California, which Mexico retained, from richer Upper California. The United States guaranteed the new boundaries with Mexico against Indian incursions, and extended full rights of citizenship to Mexicans who chose to remain in the ceded territory, along with a guarantee of land grants perfected before the war. A joint Mexican-American commission was to survey and mark the new boundaries.

For three centuries since the time of Coronado the Spanish mode had enveloped the Southwest. Crown authority was pervasive in settlement patterns, exploration, social and business organization, and religious life. Licenses were required for exploration, travel, mining, most businesses, ranching, and all but the simplest of daily occupations. Religious thought and action which deviated from official Catholic patterns brought repression and punishment. Yet control of all processes of civilization had failed to maintain Spain's grip on its colonies. Neither had it prepared the Indian population and Spanish settlers for self-rule.

Until the War with Mexico the direction of travel and control in Arizona had been the north-south axis: the Spaniards pushing north from Mexico for treasure and souls to convert, building a defense in depth along an extensive frontier, while Indian bands made their living by raiding southward to the frontiers of settlement. As the Treaty of Guadalupe Hidalgo in February of 1848 marked the triumph of American manifest destiny, a new east-west road was being marked across Arizona as a major route to the Pacific shore. Soon the drum of thundering hooves was heard in the province in place of the trumpets of war. Travel to California accelerated due to the lure of gold discovered in and wrested from the Mother Lode. These two highways of destiny in the Southwest crossed at the only town in Arizona, the walled presidio of Tucson. Arizona was at the dawning of a new era and importance under Anglo-American leadership.

7

Ho for California!—
and Back Again

As the magnetism of gold had lured the conquistadors into a vast
unknown land where they met failure instead of fortune, the discovery of gold in California was the most magnetic event in the life of
the young American republic. The multiple hazards of desert travel
—thirst, hunger, heat, rough country, sand, rocks, fatigue, unending
search for grass and water, and often lurking human enemies—did
not deter thousands of adventurers from rushing to California to
either mine the golden treasure or exploit its existence as artisans,
farmers, ranchers, or entrepreneurs of a thousand crafts and callings.

Cooke's wagon road built by the Mormon Battalion became an
important route to California, funneling immigrants from the southern part of the nation to the Pacific Coast. It had two natural advan-
tages over the better-publicized Oregon Trail, which crossed the
Rockies at South Pass in Wyoming and divided at Fort Bridger,
Utah, the lower fork becoming the Emigrant Trail to California.

Travelers leaving trading centers on the Mississippi and Missouri
rivers to follow the Oregon Trail could not venture onto the western
prairies until late May or even June, when grass first began its spring
greening. Oxen, mules, horses, and accompanying herds of cattle and
sheep found fresh feed on the southern route—Cooke's road—many
weeks earlier. Too, once the Rio Grande was passed, the desert was
not as forbidding as it first appeared, despite Kit Carson's blasphe-
mous comment that a wolf couldn't make a living in that country.
Southeastern Arizona is blessed by two rainy seasons, in midwinter
and midsummer; hence the good earth provided year-round proven-

der for stock, and the streambeds, although rarely filled, would yield water to those willing to dig a few feet into sand.

The Mexican Cession having added goldfields to the United States without their existence being known to the signators, soon after their discovery the federal government turned quickly to binding the Pacific Coast to older parts of the nation. Army topographical engineers were dispatched to explore the vast territory from the Great Plains to the ocean with dual purpose: to find and map the best railroad route to the Pacific and to identify and evaluate the resources acquired by the war.

Arizona provided two adequate railroad routes, along the 35th and 32nd parallels, the latter and more southerly being clearly the most economical of all to construct and maintain because the Rockies flattened in New Mexico and the desert was relatively inexpensive to cross. Ultimately the railroad route priority was a political decision made by Congress rather than a practical one based on need, ease, or economy. As a result, the first transcontinental railroad was built farther north, although the second and third did in fact cross Arizona.

BOUNDARY TROUBLES

Meanwhile, an incompetent American boundary commissioner added to Mexican frustrations as a faulty map used in writing an ambiguous boundary description in the Treaty of Guadalupe Hidalgo provided for an artificial border to be marked from the Rio Grande to the Gila River. John Russell Bartlett, a noted bibliophile with proper political connections but with little administrative ability, was unequal to his Mexican counterpart, General Pedro García Conde, in the negotiation for the new boundary. Surveys disclosed that the Gila River railroad route as allowed in the treaty was too beset with deep canyons for railroad construction. A route slightly more southerly would be ideal for American purposes. Factors in the dispute between Bartlett and Conde soon were overwhelmed by re-emergence of the "all of Mexico" argument among American expansionists. Despite the dismemberment of Mexico in 1848, railroad promoters wanted more land from its northern frontier, and some were willing to see blood spilled to achieve that end. A second war with Mexico was briefly imminent until President Pierce sent a southern senator and railroad promoter to Mexico City to mesmerize Santa Anna with his perpetual need, gold.

James Gadsden at first offered to buy all of Mexico north of the mouth of the Rio Grande. Santa Anna envisioned a pile of gold pieces and demurred: *"Un poquito, sí, pues todo—no!"* Patiently Gadsden negotiated for a railroad route passing near Tucson, but is damned to this day in southwest Arizona for alleged failure to obtain Baja California and the head of the Gulf of California, which would have given the United States a seaport there. It matters not that the upper end of the Gulf is filled with islands, shallows, shoals, and a bad tidal bore, making it unsuitable for large seagoing vessels; the issue frequently is reborn at election time. Mexico steadfastly retained a land bridge between Sonora and Baja California, and has linked those prospering frontier states with a railroad and a major highway.

The new international boundary as finally approved on June 30, 1854, stretched from twenty miles below Yuma to a point a few miles north of El Paso, separating Arizona and New Mexico from Sonora and Chihuahua. The Gadsden Purchase included the area disputed by the original boundary commissioners, and added 29,670 square miles to the United States. Gadsden achieved his primary goal, an ideal, economical railroad route from the Rio Grande to the Pacific. Mexico was paid $10 million as compensation, of which Santa Anna skimmed off a fourth for personal needs. Gadsden also won abandonment of a careless article in the Treaty of Guadalupe Hidalgo which had obligated the United States to keep Indians out of Mexico and to compensate that nation if they did damage there. The United States obtained transportation rights across the Isthmus of Tehuantepec in southern Mexico, a concession never used, and waived in 1937. By the Gadsden Treaty the United States again offered full citizenship to Mexicans who remained in the ceded territory.

FRENCH IN SONORA

Before the United States settled on its Arizona boundary with Mexico, filibusters had attempted to occupy the same lands. The boldest of these invasions was generated by faraway circumstances. Discovery of gold in California virtually coincided with 1848 social upheavals in France and the Germanic states. With the failure of the French revolution, companies were organized to sail for California, there to get rich and perhaps help build the new social order that France would not accept. Many of these urbane Frenchmen were unsuited for the hardships in the goldfields, although French Gulch and similar names testify to Gallic presence in the Sierra Nevadas. Drifting back into San Francisco from the goldfields, disgruntled Frenchmen were readily recruited for colonizing adventures in northern Mexico. That struggling country, despite its experience in Texas and California, authorized and encouraged a French colony at the border to protect itself from white Yankees and red raiders. The border region was largely undeveloped, but had enough vestiges of mineral wealth to excite reckless endeavors. After lingering awhile at Saric, one of Kino's remote missions some twenty-five miles southwest of Nogales, a French party led by the spirited Count Gaston de Raousset-Boulbon actually captured and held Hermosillo, the capital of Sonora, for two weeks in late 1852. After returning to California, the determined Raousset was called back to Mexico by Santa Anna, ostensibly to colonize 6,000 Frenchmen along the American border. Once he was there, the proposed French Legion shrank to 500 men who were to fight Apaches. Santa Anna's usual treachery in reversing promises, bolstered by Mexican patriotism, brought the young count before a firing squad at Guaymas on August 12, 1854. Even in their futile effort the French filibusters advertised Sonora's resources and charms.

The constitutional duty of the United States Senate to evaluate and approve the Gadsden Treaty, and inferentially to modify terms negotiated earlier, had not been completed when the first significant, legal American party prepared to enter the Gadsden Purchase. Filibusters had been encouraged by Mexican officials to develop and settle unoccupied lands, a policy designed to insulate the border while foreign firms in partnership with well-placed Mexicans undertook exploitation of undeveloped resources. Concurrently a lively market in Sonora and Baja California land grants developed in San Francisco, with a few genuine parcels and much spurious paper being offered for sale. A purveyor of such tantalizing tracts won the attention of two bold adventurers who were willing to buy, but not until they had personally inspected the farming and mining lands offered for sale.

POSTON LEADS EXPLORATION

Thereupon Charles D. Poston and Herman Ehrenberg began an enterprise that opened Arizona to serious mineral exploration and settlement, simultaneously beginning a strong backwash of goldseekers from California to Arizona. Only a small fraction of the Argonauts to California found financial success in the goldfields or in business pursuits. Many returned to their homes in despair and poverty. But the desire for a pot of gold was irrepressible in many men, Ehrenberg and Poston distinctly among these. As gold excitement diminished after the first wild years of discovery, the backwash began. California's superb attractions did not universally favor those who went there. Arizona became a convenient and favored residence for many who failed in California.

Although Poston and Ehrenberg were neither the only nor the first Americans to venture into the Gadsden Purchase, their undertaking was the most spectacular and best publicized. Both men had a flair for advertising their adventures.

After escaping with his life from the massacre at Goliad in the Texas War of Independence, Ehrenberg returned to Germany and wrote a book of his experiences. That work paid for his education as an engineer. In 1844 he came back to America, made an overland trek to Oregon, sailed to Hawaii and the South Seas, served with Americans in Baja California during the War with Mexico, discovered gold-bearing sands on the scenic Oregon shore, sold land and sought public office with no luck, and finally, needing work, returned to San Francisco, where he found employment as a mapmaker and engraver.

Ehrenberg and Poston had a common love for adventure and journalism. Born in Elizabethtown, Kentucky, near the birthplace of Abraham Lincoln, Poston had been an apprentice printer and deputy county recorder, had read law, but left home, wife, and daughter to seek his fortune in California in 1850 when he was twenty-five years old. As his political job in the custom house in San Francisco was

ARIZONA BOUNDARIES

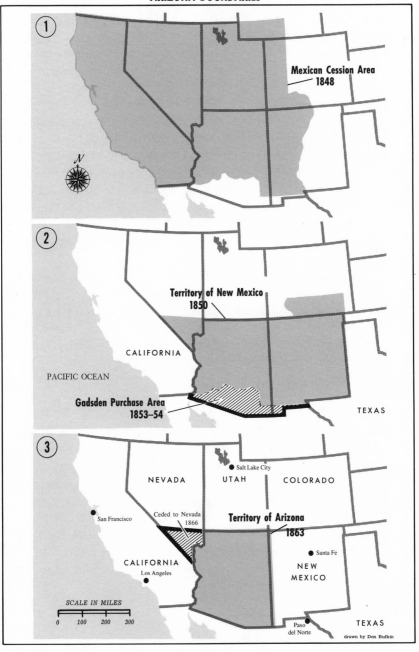

1

Mexican Cession Area
1848

2

Territory of New Mexico
1850

CALIFORNIA

PACIFIC OCEAN

Gadsden Purchase Area
1853–54

TEXAS

3

Salt Lake City

NEVADA   UTAH   COLORADO

San Francisco

Ceded to Nevada
1866

Territory of Arizona
1863

CALIFORNIA

Los Angeles

Santa Fe

NEW
MEXICO

SCALE IN MILES

0   100   200   300

Paso
del Norte

TEXAS

drawn by Don Bufkin

nearing an end late in 1853, Poston's mercurial dreams perceived golden opportunity in Mexico.

With funds provided by persevering French businessmen, and Ehrenberg going along as Spanish translator, surveyor, and mining expert, Poston led a party of twenty-five tough adventurers to examine land grants for sale inland from the Gulf of California. Going ashore near present-day Los Mochis, they recognized the fertility and promise of that delta area, but decided not to buy there. Today that area provides the United States market with most of its winter tomatoes, bell peppers, and other fresh vegetables. The party traveled on northwestward through Sinaloa and Sonora, surveying mineral and farming lands with general disfavor. Mexican officials at Guaymas were testy, but Poston convinced them his party bore arms and maintained military discipline solely as defense against Indians.

They paused at Magdalena and at Real de Arizonac, site of the Planchas de Plata silver discovery which in 1736 had extended the Spanish mining frontier northward, and which eventually gave Arizona its name. At Sonoita on the present border they crossed into United States territory where another party of Americans had elbowed aside Mexican miners at the copper deposit at Ajo. Here they collected a bag of ore samples that excited the commanding officer at Fort Yuma on the Colorado, where they emerged from the dread desert following the route called El Camino del Diablo. Major Samuel P. Heintzelman had mining fever combined with business instincts. After joining Poston and a few of his companions in surveying a townsite at the location of modern Yuma, where already he was a partner in the ferry at Yuma Crossing, Heintzelman worked with Poston in organizing the Sonora Exploring and Mining Company. They obtained strong financial backing in Cincinnati, a flourishing Ohio River railroad center, where promoters already had thoughts of pushing a railroad all the way to the Pacific. A Sonora base might provide traffic and at the same time expedite that bold enterprise.

PIONEER MINING EFFORT

Ehrenberg spent the two following years in Sonora in mineral exploration and drew the first professional map of the Gadsden Purchase and northern Mexico; meanwhile Poston supplied and led an expedition that marched through Texas and New Mexico to Tucson, where Ehrenberg rejoined him in August of 1856. They subsequently moved their workmen and equipment into the old fort at Tubac, about eighteen miles from the Mexican border, making the abandoned garrison buildings the headquarters for the company's ambitious plans. During the next four years the mining firm opened about eighty mineral claims, attracting widespread attention and many investors (including the famous gunmaker Samuel Colt) through a steady outpouring of promotional material in the eastern press and Ehrenberg's frequent descriptive letters to the daily *Alta California* in San Francisco.

Mining efforts of the firm included purchase from two Mexican brothers of a ledge called the Cerro Colorado, some twenty miles west of Tubac, where they built a mill and renamed the site the Heintzelman Mine to honor the company president. Rich silver ore produced there was converted into fancy tableware by Tiffany's for display in New York City to further advertise Arizona's riches.

American prospectors, adventurers, and speculators by the score flocked into the area under the stimulus of the Gadsden Purchase and the Sonora company's promotion. One of the company's subsidiaries established the first Arizona newspaper, the *Weekly Arizonian,* at their makeshift capital of Tubac. It too became an oracle of Arizona's promising future.

SEPARATION STRATEGY

The Gadsden Purchase fattened the New Mexico Territory, which stretched from the high plains of Texas to the Colorado River, with its capital in Santa Fe. Residents of the lower Rio Grande Valley oriented toward the market and farming center of Mesilla (modern Las Cruces, New Mexico) immediately saw their isolation from the northern capital as a handicap. While passing through there en route to Tucson, Poston had attended a convention at which a petition urged that the Congress divide New Mexico Territory and assign the name Arizona to the southern portion bordering Mexico. Soon after Poston arrived in Tucson, residents there held a similar convention. A petition signed by 260 residents (including Ehrenberg but not Poston) notified Congress that Arizona had "no law, no courts, no vote, no representation in any legislative body," and was "cut off among savage tribes." Among the participants was Frederick A. Ronstadt, pioneer ancestor of rock singer Linda Ronstadt. Petitioners asked for the protection of separate government, speedy adjudication of land titles, survey of public lands, protection of mining interests, establishment of postal routes, subjugation of hostile Indian tribes, and admission to Congress of a delegate (Nathan P. Cook) elected at the Tucson convention.

Despite the myth perpetuated by western novels and movies that the frontier was dominated by lawless criminals and fugitives, here is indubitable evidence that on the Arizona frontier advocates of law, order, and justice were in control. The Gadsden Purchase had created many opportunities for orderly settlement and development that pioneers did not wish to lose through neglect or lack of proper institutions of government. Southern interests meanwhile advocated congressional approval in support of early railroad construction across the Gadsden Purchase. It would be some time before these two forces would be united in this common interest of developing the inland Southwest.

Here too was the beginning of a local separation movement, based in good part upon the Anglo-American leadership's distaste for the dominant Hispanic control and character of the Santa Fe government.

TRANSPORTATION CORRIDOR

California's rapid development created a need for transportation speedier than the wagons of immigrants, ocean travel around South America, or land passage across Panama or Nicaragua connecting the Atlantic and Pacific sides. Important business and pressing personal mail, above all, had to be hurried along. By midsummer of 1856 a passenger-and-mail stage operated twice monthly between San Antonio and San Diego, shortening travel time for passengers and mail by more than two weeks between coasts. Because Congress subsidized the mail, it acted to protect it by sending American troops into the southern part of the Gadsden Purchase. These soldiers replaced the Mexican garrison that had remained in Tucson until March of 1856 to provide residents with protection against Indian attacks.

Generally following Cooke's wagon road, the San Antonio & San Diego Mail Line built a string of relay stations across Arizona that was to have a major impact upon the area. Each station was a microcosm of a pioneer settlement. The station building was headquarters and home for the stationkeeper and his hostlers and herders, and a place to feed passengers. A blacksmith shop offered facilities for shoeing animals and repairing equipment. A corral nearby held teams of relay animals. A water supply was developed, and fields were planted in hay and corn for livestock and gardens to augment the diet of crews and passengers. Stations also offered a haven of security and supply for prospectors, who were swarming everywhere, opening mines whose basic needs often were supplied from the stations. Not surprisingly, the stations were also magnets that attracted Indians.

Curiosity was the first reaction of Indians to the white settlers. Learning quickly that they could exchange bundles of wild grass and dry firewood for flour, tobacco, coffee, sweets, geegaws, and liquor which the stationkeepers had in abundance, the Indians became involved in a work relationship that returned material benefits to them, no matter how strange, time-consuming, and unlike their own patterns of life it was.

RAIDING REDUCED

The Apaches also realized that these stations stretching across Arizona offered them a new life-style with a lower risk factor. For the previous two centuries, and especially the last generation, they had been making their living by raiding settlements on the Spanish-Mexican frontier. Bloody hatred had grown between Indian and Mexican in recurrent reprisals for raids and punishment. Stage stations provided a new source of the basic necessities of life closer to their favored homeland, free from many hazards of raiding.

Why endure the tiresome travel across endless deserts to harvest cattle and horse herds deep in Mexico when an adequate substitute had been brought so near? To the Indians it was simplicity itself to lower corral bars and take what was needed without the hardships of travel, flight from pursuit, gunfights, and the tragic casualties and mourning that came of raiding into Mexico. Bands of Chiricahua and Mimbres Apaches in particular crowded closer to the stage stations. While their women were induced to labor for trade goods, the warriors watched and waited for safe raiding opportunities. With the growth of farming and ranching along the streams and valleys in southern Arizona and the opening of mines in surrounding hills, attacks on isolated travelers, settlers, stage stations, and miners were inevitable. Just as unavoidable was the abuse and murder of Indians, whose very presence pioneers perceived as a threat, conditioned as they were to extermination policies in the trans-Appalachian dark and bloody ground.

The early curiosity of Indians toward Anglo-Americans, best characterized by Mangas Coloradas's willingness to join the United States Army in its war on Mexico ten years earlier, was now deteriorating into hostility. The transformation in Indian attitudes toward the whites followed a typical pattern. Initial Indian curiosity about newcomers was a normal human trait, very often leading to the exchange of token gifts of minor value. Wonder and delight frequently followed as the native people acquired new amenities of life thanks to fodder and fuel traded to the stations. They moved closer, performing household and herding chores. Generous and fairminded settlers sought to buy peace with a potential enemy by giving the Indians gifts. Their gratitude for such gifts, however, frequently was only temporary, gradually dissolving into greed for more of the same, and ultimately to surprise, shock, and blood vengeance when familiarity irritated abrasive members of both societies, especially when Indians were subjected to punishment for seizing what they had so quickly learned to like.

When James Birch of Sacramento, founder of the San Antonio &

San Diego Mail Line, was lost at sea, a more potent firm won a government subsidy of $600,000 a year, four times that provided for Texas–California mail service, to operate twice-weekly stage and mail service to San Francisco from the railroad's end west of St. Louis and from Memphis. Stations and stock of the first mail line in Arizona were absorbed into the Overland Stage Company, owned by John Butterfield and William Fargo. Late in 1858 this Butterfield Mail made its first westward run in a half-hour short of twenty-four days, a full day ahead of schedule. The station agent at Tucson was William S. Oury, who had fought beside Ehrenberg at the First Battle of the Alamo and now was one of the most prominent Anglo cattlemen and citizens in southern Arizona. Twenty-two years later Oury was serving as mayor of Tucson when the first railroad reached that city.

As travel, trade, agriculture, and mining activity increased in Arizona, so did Indian raids and complaints of Indian depredations. The total number of cattle and horses being stolen by Apaches probably had not increased a great deal, but the raids now were concentrated within American territory. American stock was being stolen, and American victims suffered losses. To Anglo pioneers, government officials, and military personnel this was exceedingly more serious than the raids into Mexico that had been the Apache way of life for centuries.

8

Stopped at Stanwix Station

Population and political problems of the Gadsden Purchase increased steadily in the decade of the 1850s, as did traffic of all kinds on the California road, including cattle drives of magnitude comparable to the later and better-known herds trailing northward from Texas to Kansas. In this decade Texas longhorns were driven to California to meet the hunger of its booming population.

It was a fitful period for the entire nation. The peculiar institution of slavery was intensifying sectional disputes which often were expressed euphemistically as noble principles in which national unity stood in balance against states' rights. Although slavery never became a problem within the Gadsden Purchase, abolitionists worried that if a railroad were constructed via the southern route to the Pacific, slavery might accompany an extension of civil government.

Efforts of a growing group of supporters to establish Arizona apart from New Mexico Territory invariably failed in one house of Congress or the other because of the highly emotional sectional issues.

Residents of the Gadsden Purchase sought civil administration for internal safety and to enlarge opportunities for orderly development. Railroad promoters, mainly in the South, recognized the merit of the railroad route along the borderland and supported local aspirations in recognition that the Gadsden Purchase was a geographical province quite different from northern New Mexico. Politicians and entrepreneurs had their own obvious reasons for supporting the area's struggle for self-identification.

By mid-1860, as the national election warmed up, more than fifteen bills had been considered in Congress to establish Arizona either as a separate territory or as a judicial, military, or surveyor general's district. Two bills proposed naming the area "Arizuma." A few passed one house or the other. Each bill acquired a constituency that felt almost anything would be preferable to the stifling neglect that was first blamed on Hispanic officials in Santa Fe, later attributed to an indifferent federal government, but finally, with Abraham Lincoln's emergence as the candidate of the new Republican party, the scapegoat for Arizona's frustrations became "black Republicanism."

There were strong southern and Democratic currents in the area, although demographically the Gadsden Purchase had more roots in the North than the South. New Mexico, responding at last to the clamor of residents of the Gadsden Purchase, had tossed them a political bone by creating Arizona County, comprising the area from the Rio Grande to the Colorado south of the 34th parallel. This same area formerly had been part of Doña Ana County, but now Tubac was named county seat. The new county, however, was little more than a token on paper and was reincorporated into Doña Ana County within a year.

ARIZONA NOT "SOUTHERN"

The 1860 decennial census of Arizona County, taken prior to the fall elections, listed about 2,300 whites, 21 blacks, and some 4,000 Mexicans and "tame" Indians. Analysis of the origins of the Anglo residents reveals that Arizona was not "southern" in composition— people from the northeastern states, attracted by jobs with stage lines and at mines, outnumbered those from below the Mason-Dixon Line. Regardless of their origins, however, most of the white residents shared common aspirations that inclined them toward the secessionist wing of national sectionalism. Neither slavery nor other economic determinants of the secessionist movement cast Arizona in that direction. It was, rather, belief that the federal government had neglected Arizona, coupled with a shared geographic expansionist interest in a transcontinental railroad emerging from the South, that drew Arizona toward new southern friends.

SEPARATE BUT NOT EQUAL

In 1860 there also appeared the first vision of Arizona separated from New Mexico by a north-south line. Prior concepts of separation had involved an east-west division along the 34th parallel, thus producing a long or flat Arizona reaching from the Colorado to the Rio Grande, or, in some versions, all the way to the New Mexico north-south line with Texas at 103° West longitude.

Hoping to goad Congress into speedier action, a provisional government was formed at a Tucson convention in April 1860. Delegates drew up a constitution they believed would accommodate the area until the federal government created an official Arizona Territory. They were not yet in open revolt against federal authority, since an oath of allegiance to the United States Constitution was required of officials. Dr. Lewis S. Owings, a young physician turned goldminer, was elected the first governor of Arizona at this convention. He was to achieve greater distinction later as the mayor of Dennison, Texas.

The provisional convention reasserted Arizona's unyielding effort to send a delegate of its own choosing to Congress. This effort had been initiated four years earlier, in 1856, when, feeling that the New Mexico delegate ignored the southern area's special interests, its residents had named Nathan P. Cook as delegate in a rump election, and sent him to Washington. Congress rejected him, but the Arizonans stubbornly persisted. Three times unofficial balloting designated politically ambitious Sylvester Mowry of Rhode Island as Arizona's delegate. A graduate of West Point and successor to Samuel P. Heintzelman as commander at Fort Yuma, Mowry spent most of three years—1857 into 1859—in Washington in attempts to catch the ear and attention of Congress.

The national legislature simply viewed Arizona as part of New Mexico, which had representation by a legally chosen delegate. Although Mowry could not wheedle official recognition from Washington, he energetically, ingeniously, and relentlessly promoted Arizona's dream. In 1857 he published a promotional pamphlet at his own expense, *Memoir of the Proposed Territory of Arizona,* which increased knowledge of the area, but did not garner enough support. Having resigned his Army commission and with his personal purse growing thin, late in 1859 he accepted a post as special agent for the Gila Indians in Arizona, supervising a survey of their reservation and distributing $10,000 in tools and goods—the federal government's first recognition in Arizona of an obligation to educate and civilize Indians rather than merely control them militarily. A few months later Mowry began to survey a new border between California and Nevada, but soon thereafter purchased an old silver-lead mine near the Mexican border and attempted to work it despite constant Indian depredations.

Rebuffed in Washington, the Anglo residents of Arizona found themselves drawing closer and closer to advocates of secession, simply because Arizona found more sympathetic ears in the South. Indeed, some Arizona advocates of separate territorial status were southerners; the bulk were opportunists—miners, merchants, many lawyers, and other professionals who hoped to profit by patronage and clients on the new frontier.

When secession finally became a reality as President Lincoln took office and a rebel Texas volunteer force marched up the Rio Grande, the troop was warmly welcomed at Mesilla by Anglo leaders, although the Hispanic population along the Rio Grande was cool toward the Texans.

REIGN OF TERROR

The outbreak of hostilities brought suspension of the Butterfield Overland Mail, which ran through war zones in Arkansas and Texas. Its stock and rolling equipment were moved northward to a new route running west from St. Louis through Salt Lake City to San Francisco and Los Angeles. Three military posts in the Anglo mining areas of Arizona—Forts Buchanan and Breckenridge in the southern part and Fort Mohave on the Colorado River—as well as Fort Defiance in the Navajo country were closed. Supplies at southern forts were destroyed to keep them out of hostile hands. Troops were reassigned to more strategic areas of conflict. Southwestern Indians almost immediately responded to this weakened white presence, increasing their raids upon farms, mines, and settlements until the horizon was marked with smoke pillars from burning haystacks and habitations, and with blood-stained earth as Indian rapacity forced abandonment of most ranches and mines and all settlements except Tucson. Charles D. Poston's younger brother, James Lee Poston, was killed at the Heintzelman Mine. Accompanied by a prominent visiting mining engineer, Raphael Pumpelly, Charles Poston fled across the Papago Indian country to Fort Yuma.

By July 20, 1861, when the bitter First Battle of Bull Run served notice that the Civil War would not be over in a few months, residents of Arizona also reconciled themselves to war's tragic arrival. One week later the strongest military post along the Rio Grande, Fort Fillmore, fell to Confederate Lieutenant Colonel John R. Baylor, who led a group of volunteer Texas Mounted Rifles into the area, taking charge as Union troops withdrew northward to join in a spirited defense of Santa Fe and Fort Union, supply center for southwestern military contingents.

Confederate strategy called for a Texas army to seize all military stores in New Mexico and then invade the new goldfields of Colorado, while a second army was to make a dash for the Pacific, where it was anticipated that members of the secret Knights of the Golden Circle would lead an uprising to capture cities and ports for the Confederacy.

Having forced Union soldiers from all but one southern post, Colonel Baylor, on August 1 at Mesilla, proclaimed the formation of the military Territory of Arizona within the Confederacy, with himself as governor. Within a few months another Tucson convention had elected Granville H. Oury, brother of William S. Oury of Alamo fame, as delegate to the Confederate Congress meeting in Richmond, Virginia. Through his presence, on February 14, 1862, that government created a civil Territory of Arizona as part of the Confederate States of America. That event took place exactly fifty years to the day before Arizona was admitted as a full partner in the United States of America.

Colonel Baylor persuaded citizen militia companies, made up of miners and ranchers organized to defend Mesilla Valley settlements against Indian attack, to join the Rebel forces en masse. They were assigned mostly to local duties as Confederate General H. H. Sibley led an army of more than 3,000 Texans northward in pursuit of the

Union forces, which had been augmented by Hispanic volunteers with a deep-rooted antipathy for Texans. Sibley won a substantial victory at Valverde on the lower Rio Grande and pushed on rapidly into Albuquerque and Santa Fe, forcing the Union army back to the main supply depot at Fort Union, where volunteer reinforcements had arrived from Colorado. Rebel and Union advance forces became engaged in a sharp fight in Glorieta Pass east of Santa Fe that loomed as a pivotal battle for control of northern New Mexico. During the fighting in the pass a fast-moving party of Colorado horsemen circled to the Rebel rear and destroyed most of Sibley's wagon train and supplies. Cut off from his source of supply by a long road flanked with unfriendly Hispanics engaged in guerrilla tactics, Sibley started a tragic retreat back home to Texas, losing more than half of his army in the process.

THE ARIZONA CAMPAIGN

During this rapid rise and fall of the Texas army in New Mexico, a militia company known as the Arizona Guards under the command of Confederate Captain Sherod Hunter, a rancher from the Mimbres Valley near present Deming, New Mexico, penetrated the Apache country and raised the Texas flag over Tucson on February 28, 1862. Hunter demanded an oath of allegiance to the Confederacy from all Anglo residents. A few enlisted in Hunter's company, but others sought sanctuary in Sonora, while a braver few faced hazards of Indian assault to make their way eastward and sit out the duration of the war with friends in New Mexico. A Confederate colonel rode with a cavalry escort to Hermosillo, Sonora, to purchase needed food supplies left behind at abandoned stage stations. Southern sympathizers heading home from California to join the Rebel cause—notably Albert Sidney Johnston, who as a general commanding Texas forces was to die a hero at Shiloh—had brought word that a Union army had been recruited in California to attack Texas from the west.

This Union counterattack was to be made by the Column from California, under the command of Colonel James H. Carleton. Thus Arizona was to become the westernmost battleground of the Civil War. An earlier Union contingency plan to attack Texas across Mexico from Mazatlán or Guaymas had been abandoned because of the paucity of roads in northern Mexico and lack of sufficient wagons, animals, forage, and food for such a campaign.

Carleton had collected volunteer militia companies from northern California towns and mining camps, forming an army of 1,800 men at Fort Yuma, a staging area where equipment was overhauled and troops were sent forward, a company at a time, to reverse the westward march made by Colonel Cooke and the Mormon Battalion fifteen years earlier. Carleton's army marched toward the Rio Grande in small units because of the limited supply of water and grass.

At an old Butterfield Overland Stage stop known as Stanwix Station on the Gila River about seventy-five miles east of Yuma, scouts of the probing Confederate party encountered outriders of the Union force. One of the rebels opened fire at long range, wounding a Union soldier from Sacramento in the shoulder. That contact was the most westerly bloodshed of the Civil War. The Confederate thrust for the Pacific stopped at Stanwix Station.

Knowing that the Union army was advancing in strength, the Rebels trotted back to Tucson to report to Captain Hunter. He posted pickets at Picacho Peak, on the main road about forty miles northwest of Tucson. They too engaged in a skirmish with Union advance riders on April 15, 1862. The first volley killed a Union officer and two enlisted men, but two Confederates also died and several were captured in this so-called Battle of Picacho Pass, often incorrectly described as the only contest of the war in Arizona. Actually, neither the earlier skirmish at Stanwix Station nor the firefight at Picacho Pass can be dignified as a battle. Each encounter involved only a few men from either side, both lacking the formality, planning, and numbers generally associated with battles.

Rebel refugees from the melee at Picacho Pass carried word to Captain Hunter that the Column from California now had collected several hundred men at the Pima villages on the Gila, preparatory to attacking his headquarters at Tucson. Captain Hunter decided a judicious withdrawal of his hundred or so volunteers was indicated. Apaches boldly attacked the Confederates as they retreated toward the Rio Grande, killing several, probably identifying them as enemy from knowledge that Baylor several weeks earlier had issued an extermination policy concluding with the order "Allow no Indian to escape." This harsh edict led to Baylor's removal from command of his dual posts as governor and military commander. At that time the Confederacy was seeking favors from Queen Victoria, who had abolished slavery in the British Empire. Because Baylor's genocidal policy might be considered offensive to Her Majesty's concern for backward people, Baylor was demoted and returned to Texas, where before the war's end he redeemed himself and again achieved military command and civil positions.

TUCSON "RECAPTURED"

In the early morning light of May 20, 1862, three Union columns, two of cavalry and the third mounted infantry, were positioned and ready for the recapture of Tucson, which the southerners had held since February. As the sun came over the Rincon Mountains, lighting fluttering guidons and the Stars and Stripes, a bugle sounded "charge." In a scene that lacked only John Wayne, the dashing, whooping troops converged on the center of the city. The excitement of attack dwindled into embarrassment as amused residents explained that the Rebels had withdrawn a week earlier, giving the Column from California a total but hollow victory.

Carleton himself arrived in Tucson on June 8, simultaneous with word he had been promoted to brigadier general. He proclaimed martial law, made himself military governor of Arizona, imposed heavy taxes on local business, dispatched soldiers to protect outlying mines, and ordered the arrest of an alleged Confederate sympathizer, Sylvester Mowry. Brought to Tucson with Mowry from the Patagonia or Mowry Mine were a number of his employees, who gave conflicting testimony about the former officer's activities. This ardent advocate of civil government for Arizona contended he had not given aid and comfort to the southern cause, but had asked both armies for protection against Indian attacks. True, he had provided ammunition to Sherod Hunter's troops, but only under the duress of leveled rifles, he insisted. A board of officers, obviously with predetermined bias, ordered him confined for an official court-martial at Fort Yuma, where Mowry was held in parole as a popular former commander.

By November he had been cleared of all charges, but his mine had been sequestered and looted by Carleton's friends. Mowry sued for recovery of the mine and a million dollars, but, after a long delay, obtained only a pittance in compensation for the illegal seizure. When the first Arizona territorial legislature convened in 1864, it passed a resolution supporting Mowry and censuring Carleton for seizure of the mine.

Since Indian depredations had increased greatly in the absence of military patrols along the California road, Carleton invoked a repressive Indian policy nearly as harsh as the directive of total extermination proposed by Baylor. As Carleton directed his men toward the Rio Grande, the aroused Chiricahua chieftain Cochise collected 700 Apaches to contest the column's advance through Apache Pass. Two mountain howitzers, fired into granite boulders hiding the natives, devastated and routed the ambush. Thereupon Fort Bowie was built near the head of the pass to protect its line of communication and a vital spring, the post becoming the hinge of military control of the border for a quarter-century.

THE BASCOM AFFAIR

Virtually unnoticed until late 1860, Cochise had been vaulted to prestige among Indians by a notorious incident in the same locality just prior to the war. Following the kidnapping of the stepson of an Anglo farmer in a raid upon his ranch at Sonoita Creek, a young army officer, Lieutenant George Bascom, led a scouting party from Fort Buchanan to recover the stolen cattle and the boy. Cochise approached the army camp curiously, but denied all knowledge of the particular assault. Tradition indicates that the captured Cochise cut his way to freedom from a tent where he was confined by Bascom, who held three relatives of Cochise among six other Apache hostages. Cochise then went on a rampage, capturing, torturing, and killing several innocent travelers, and dragging a stationkeeper to death before white troops. Following the advice of a senior officer, Bascom hanged the hostages.

The Apache Indian wars and the loss of several hundred white lives have sometimes been attributed simplistically to this incident, on the assumption that previously Cochise had been an innocent and peaceful child of nature, and that Bascom's error had transformed him into a ruthless warrior. No evidence has been presented that Cochise was an angel prior to the Bascom Affair. Apache character did not require vengeance as a motive for assaults upon the whites. Neither was Indian action normally stimulated by political aspirations or by ecological, environmental, or geographical concerns. The Apache was by tradition and training a raider and a warrior, taking his sustenance and other useful things anywhere they might be found. He did not differentiate between hunting wild animals and seizing domestic livestock; both were desirable food items. He had little interest in objects other than his clothing and weapons, roaming the Southwest in search of consumable or functional booty. He readily fought for the things he wanted—food, women, guns, clothing, animals, and, as they became known to him, items such as coffee, sugar, flour, whiskey, and soap.

Major conflict between Apaches and Anglos became inevitable when the California road intersected Apache raiding routes to Mexico and subsequently stage lines, settlers, drovers, and military posts introduced livestock in such abundance as to provide an attractive nuisance, one too tempting to leave alone. Two aggressive peoples could not occupy the same territory without conflict. While the Bascom Affair inflamed and popularized Cochise, it was not a major cause of the Apache wars; it was simply an unfortunate, explosive incident involving volatile forces.

Once Carleton had moved his Column from California to the Rio Grande and had driven Texas Rebel forces southward beyond Fort Davis, he turned north to assume command of the new military Department of New Mexico. His major task was subjugation of hostile Indians, whatever the cause of their discontent. The first task was to eliminate the Apache threat to travelers, miners, settlers, and freighters in the south and to subdue Navajo raids on New Mexico settlements, which had intensified when Fort Defiance was closed for the duration.

CAPTURE OF MANGAS

An Indian reservation was established on the Pecos River at remote Bosque Redondo, later to be called Fort Stanton, and the roundup of Mescalero and Mimbres Apache bands began. This led to the capture of Mangas Coloradas, the Mimbres leader who sixteen years earlier had offered to join General Kearny in the War with Mexico. Pioneers considered Mangas the chief culprit in a reign of terror Apaches had thrown over the Mesilla Valley and the eastern half of the Gadsden Purchase. The interception and capture of Mangas was engineered in part by Jack Swilling, who had entered the Civil War as a lieutenant in Mastin's Company, a militia unit that had defended New Mexico mines, ranches, and freighters against Indian assaults before Baylor mustered it into the Rebel force.

Swilling undoubtedly led the southern troop that scouted westward along the Gila from Tucson, drawing Union blood at Stanwix Station. Some weeks later, after escorting military and political prisoners to the Rio Grande, Swilling deserted the Rebel forces to prospect in the Pinos Altos region near present Silver City, New Mexico. One of the prisoners he had escorted to New Mexico was Captain William McCleave, close friend of General Carleton, who shared a passion for goldmining with the Union commander. Captain McCleave not long afterward employed Swilling, the Rebel deserter, as a civilian messenger, scout, and guide for Union forces.

After the capture of the aged chief Mangas as he slept beside a campfire, heartless guards touched heated bayonets against his bare feet. When the chief awakened in alarm, they shot him dead under the pretense that he had attempted to escape. The guards had heard an officer say he wanted Mangas "dead." After thus serving the Union Army in this sanguinary pacification of the area, Swilling guided a prospecting party westward toward Tucson and the mountains of central Arizona. This group was the so-called Joseph Reddeford Walker party, comprised largely of southerners who had left California to join in the Civil War, but, being barred from the California road at Yuma by Union troops, had circled northward into Colorado and then down the Rio Grande. Disheartened by the turn of the war, they decided to hunt for gold in Arizona, which Walker had crossed as a mountain man and trapper, and which Swilling knew more intimately than anybody else in the group.

Swilling had arrived in the Southwest about six years before as a member of the Leach party improving a wagon road along the Gila River route and had penetrated as far west as Gila City (only eighteen miles east of Yuma) during the brief gold boom there between 1858 and 1860. Always willing to fight Indians, he had led a party of Arizona Rangers from the Pima villages to punish raiding Yavapai Indians, and in following them up the Hassayampa River, a branch of the Gila, he found traces of gold in the stream. He led the Walker party into Arizona, unerringly up the Hassayampa to the pine-clad mountain area, where their easy discovery of rich placer gold deposits came close to fulfilling General Carleton's hope of becoming a mining magnate while serving also in the military. Swilling's talent for being near the scene of vital action and his nose for gold, which together had brought him back into Arizona, made him perhaps the most significant individual in determining Arizona's destiny during the following decade.

9

~

New Home in the West

Union victories on far western battlefields in the spring of 1862 brought Arizona its long-awaited success in Congress within another year. Six years of anguished pleading for civil government and protection ended happily, not alone because of the triumph of northern arms, but also because Confederate interest in Arizona advertised its strategic location and rich mineral potential. The agitation to make Arizona a separate territory had been pushed vigorously by Cincinnati investors in the Sonora Exploring and Mining Company and the affiliated Santa Rita Mining Company. That a million Ohio dollars were invested in Arizona mines was dramatized by a debater holding aloft in the House of Representatives a specimen of silver ore from the Heintzelman Mine.

Even in the din of wartime, during which he was wounded at Bull Run and had a mangled arm dressed without even dismounting from his horse, Heintzelman continued to lobby for Arizona's establishment. As a brigadier general commanding an Alexandria sector in the defense of Washington, he was in communication on almost a daily basis with members of Congress and other friends of Arizona lobbying for its separation from New Mexico.

Samuel P. Heintzelman's journals, personal papers, and military records in the Library of Congress disclose his unending effort to win votes for Arizona. His dedication to that goal was total and personal. Heintzelman's life savings were invested in Arizona mines. He had obtained financial investment in the mines among Cincinnati residents, and was determined to prove that what was good for Arizona was good for Cincinnati also.

STRONG OHIO SUPPORT

Two southern Ohio congressmen and one of its senators were to have key roles in drafting and winning approval of Arizona's organic act. James M. Ashley in the House and Senator Benjamin F. Wade concurrently were chairmen of the committees on territories in the two bodies of Congress. For Arizona it was a stroke of luck. Their associate, Congressman John A. Gurley of Cincinnati, lost his seat in the 1862 election, but not until after he had helped pass the Ashley bill, which cleared the House May 8, 1862. Thereafter Gurley continued as an ardent lobbyist for Arizona, garnering a reward Fate did not allow him to collect.

Although the Republican party had been excoriated in conventions in Mesilla and Tucson as the "black foe" of Arizona's aspirations, the Ashley bill moved through the Congress with overwhelming Republican support. After passing the House, the bill gestated in the Senate for nine months until February of 1863. Senator Wade by then had acquired significant support from Senator James A. McDougall of California, a Democrat who said he had explored Arizona extensively, explaining that many Californians who had moved there to develop mines had been driven out by the Indian scourge. Together Wade and McDougall resisted sharp opposition arguments based largely on the sparse population of the area, with Wade thundering to his colleagues that the mining wealth of territories should be developed even during wartime.

During the war, Charles D. Poston had joined Heintzelman in Washington and also worked enthusiastically as a lobbyist. His firsthand acquaintance with Arizona and his recent narrow escape from Indians had telling effect as he provided information and arguments to friendly congressmen. William Wrightson of Cincinnati, a financial supporter and, with his brother, publisher of the *Railroad Record,* an early advocate of Arizona's organization, also roamed Washington corridors supporting the effort.

THE FIRST OFFICIALS

On February 24, 1863, President Abraham Lincoln signed the organic act creating Arizona Territory.

Former Congressman Gurley, who had scurried around soliciting support for Ashley's bill, was the president's first choice for governor of Arizona, but died at his home in Cincinnati on August 19, 1863, as territorial officials prepared to depart for their new posts. There was a scramble for succession, with the honor going to John N. Goodwin of Maine, another former congressman, who first had been appointed to the territorial supreme court. Justices of the territorial court were Joseph P. Allyn, a health seeker from Connecticut, William F. Turner of Iowa, and William T. Howell of Michigan. The president appointed Levi Bashford of Wisconsin as surveyor, Milton Duffield of New York, Ohio, and California as United States marshal, and Almon Gage of New York to be district attorney.

Probably Lincoln's wisest appointment to an Arizona office was that of Richard C. McCormick of New York as secretary of the territory, a position Poston later complained McCormick had elevated to the level of premier by establishing a political "ring" that endured for nearly twenty years. A former journalist and government clerk, McCormick was talented, nimble, and articulate. En route to Arizona he purchased a printing outfit to establish the *Arizona Miner,* which became his mouthpiece and the most influential newspaper in Arizona for a decade.

In his journalistic memoirs, which sustained him at an advanced age when his other enterprises crumbled, Poston recalled fretfully that he was being left out of the division of spoils at an oyster supper until he asked: "What is to become of me?" and Gurley reportedly answered: "Oh, we will make you Indian agent." Poston reported that the exchange took place at an event he arranged for "lame duck" or defeated congressmen to spread political patronage among persons no longer employed. Evidence reveals that Heintzelman actually was the host at the oyster supper, which was held considerably before there were jobs to pass out. Moreover, only one guest, Gurley, was a defeated congressman. Poston frequently stretched the truth. With his knowledge of Arizona and his unquenchable zest for political fulfillment, he probably coveted the office of superintendent of Indian affairs as an ideal launching pad (as it turned out to be) for his intended campaign for delegate to Congress. He already had asked to be appointed governor, but could not muster the support that Gurley and Goodwin received.

Poston did not accompany the other appointees on the long journey to Arizona, but went ahead by overland stage to San Francisco to plead with Army officials for more troops and posts to protect Arizona and also to purchase farming tools, clothing, blankets, tobacco, trinkets, and other gifts to distribute to his Indian charges. The other officials gathered at Fort Leavenworth, Kansas, and traveled from there with an Army escort to Fort Union, New Mexico, where they were met by General Carleton, overflowing with news, advice, and offer of a fresh escort to Arizona.

HEADED FOR TUCSON

The original destination of the territorial officials had been Tucson, the only town in Arizona known to Congress. Carleton degraded the Old Pueblo as a den of Secessionists and urged that the temporary capital be located instead at or near the military post he had ordered built in central Arizona. He directed them to Fort Whipple in Chino Valley about twenty-five miles north of the gold placers being worked by the Walker party and a growing swarm of goldseekers from New Mexico and California.

During more than five weeks spent in New Mexico the entourage of eighteen men grew enormously as word spread that placer gold and a myriad of profitable business opportunities were to be found in Arizona. When it crossed the border from New Mexico into Arizona on December 27, escorted by Missouri and New Mexico volunteer troops, many fortune seekers, from musicians to miners and merchants, had joined up. The party moved as a caravan of some twenty loaded wagons, many coupled to ox teams, accompanied by drovers with herds of horses, mules, and cattle, as well as a number of riders with pack outfits.

On December 29, 1863, well inside Arizona at Navajo Springs, the party paused to raise the Stars and Stripes, hear a speech from Secretary McCormick (which the Reverend Hiram W. Read translated into Spanish), sing "The Battle Cry of Freedom," fire salutes, and drink toasts to Arizona's civil government as the officials took their oaths of office.

Progress from Albuquerque onward had been leisurely; now it slowed even more. The governor did not reach Fort Whipple until January 22, 1864. He found the site open and windswept, but with an abundance of grass and water for stock. Timber for firewood and building was many miles away, near the placer mines where 300 men, despite low water, were attempting to wash creek sands for gold.

Inadequacies of the temporary capital site were apparent as Governor Goodwin with a military escort departed on a survey of other proposed centers of government. The Organic Act authorized him to make the ultimate selection. Goodwin visited Tucson, the leading town, but strangely bypassed La Paz on the Colorado River, which had grown quickly due to discovery of placer gold nearby. The confluence of the Verde and Salt rivers had been touted as a capital site to be named Aztlan, but upon arriving there the governor's party found it uninhabited except for Tonto Apaches who followed and harassed the survey party. While Goodwin was on tour, Army inspectors had visited Fort Whipple and decided the military post must be moved to a more protected site. They selected a sheltered basin on Granite Creek, bordering the huge pine forest that covered the Bradshaw and Sierra Prieta mountains, about eighteen miles closer to the goldfields stretching along Lynx and Big Bug creeks and the nearby source of the Hassayampa River. The Army was needed nearby because the rapid influx of miners and settlers had quickly incited Indian resentment, resistance, and attacks. So on May 18, 1864, Fort Whipple was moved to a new permanent location.

PRESCOTT AS CAPITAL

Secretary McCormick, a man of action and decision, already had filed on a 160-acre homestead west of Granite Creek for Goodwin and himself. Robert Groom, former surveyor of San Diego County in California, was employed to lay out a townsite on a flat adjacent to the McCormick-Goodwin homestead about a mile west of new Fort

Whipple. This townsite McCormick named Prescott, honoring the popular historian William Hickling Prescott. When the military post was moved, McCormick supervised transfer of the territorial offices and officials, establishing at Prescott in the heart of the pine-clad hills of Yavapai County the political machine that he was to dominate, withal beneficially, for more than two decades.

Following the process and pattern for creation of new territories provided by the Northwest Ordinance of 1787, Governor Goodwin directed United States Marshal Duffield to make a census of the territory, which temporarily was divided into three judicial districts with courts established at Tucson, La Paz, and Prescott. There were 4,573 settlers counted in the territory, a figure that included a few blacks, a handful of "tame" Indians, and soldiers at military posts. The immediate establishment of courts—contrary to the myth that the frontier was lawless—was a tour de force by Governor Goodwin, establishing the moral tone by which the Arizona territorial government operated from the very first. Each justice presided over the district court in his own area, and they came together to sit as the territorial supreme court.

Governor Goodwin also designated voting districts and set July 18, 1864, as the date for the election of a legislature and delegate to Congress. Four candidates were quickly in the field for the seat in Congress, but Charles D. Poston was far ahead of his opponents in preparedness. While in San Francisco purchasing goods for distribution to Indians and pleading with the military to establish Army posts in the territory to protect the rush of settlers from Indian hostility, he also hired a personal press agent. This individual was his old friend J. Ross Browne, who wrote for the San Francisco *Bulletin* and was a former secret agent for the federal treasury.

CLASSIC DESCRIPTION

Browne came to Arizona with Poston on a tour of Indian reservations and the mines in which Poston was financially involved. Browne's descriptive articles and sketches in the *Bulletin* were reprinted in *Harper's Weekly* and eventually were collected for a book called *Adventures in the Apache Country: A Tour Through Arizona and*

Sonora, which has been reprinted several times and remains the classic description of southern Arizona at the time. That Browne was paid initially on government travel vouchers (perhaps illegally) to publicize Poston's endeavors and political aspirations did not diminish the author's perceptive, often amusing comments, including the following:

> With millions of acres of the finest arable lands, there was not at the time of our visit a single farm under cultivation in the Territory; with the richest gold and silver mines, paper-money is the common currency; with forts innumerable, there is scarcely any protection to life and property; with extensive pastures, there is little or no stock; with the finest natural roads, travelling is beset with difficulties; with rivers through every valley, a stranger may die of thirst. Hay is cut with a hoe, and wood with a spade or mattock. In January one enjoys the luxury of a bath as under a tropical sun, and sleeps under double blankets at night. There are towns without inhabitants, and deserts extensively populated; vegetation where there is no soil, and soil where there is no vegetation. . . . Politicians without policy, traders without trade, storekeepers without stores, teamsters without teams, and all without means, form the mass of the white population.

There was more hyperbole than fact in this evaluation of Arizona. Although illness in his family called Browne home to Oakland before the campaign ended, Poston won handily with 514 votes, helped by a substantial lead from the southern and western parts of the territory, where he was well known. Off he went to Washington by way of Panama, at a cost of $7,000 to taxpayers.

As delegate, Poston worked enthusiastically during his short term in Congress, which ended in March of 1865. Confident that he would be re-elected for a full two-year term, he remained in the national capital, promoting Arizona's need for roads and postal routes (one of the latter went to his brother Sanford) and pleading for increased military forces. He persuaded Congress to fund an irrigation project on the Colorado River Indian Reservation above La Paz, the nation's

Freight teams arrive in Prescott with goods from Ehrenberg. 1870s.

Pearce, Arizona: Mine mill and town, late nineteenth century.

Desert cooler, nineteenth–early-twentieth century.

Commercial Hotel, Phoenix. 1890.

Mule teams pulling supplies up the Roosevelt Road (later named the Apache Trail). Seen here at Government Wells, the last watering place on the low desert before entry into the heavy grades along the Salt River Canyon.

The *Charles H. Spencer* at Lee's Ferry. Late fall, 1911.

Campaign display for Nathan Oakes Murphy's successful bid for election as territorial delegate to the U.S. Congress. Prescott, 1894.

G. W. P. Hunt, first governor of the state of Arizona.

Carl Hayden during his first campaign for election to the U.S. House of Representatives. 1911.

Bisbee, Arizona. 1950s.

Present-day Phoenix.

Senator Barry Goldwater.

first budgetary commitment to irrigation. He did not return to Arizona to campaign, since he believed Secretary McCormick had promised him the support of the *Arizona Miner*.

Surprisingly, Governor Goodwin became a candidate for delegate with McCormick's avid support, winning easily with 717 votes, while Justice Allyn received 381 and Poston was humiliated with only 206. Poston screamed "fraud" in a huge advertisement he placed in a New York newspaper; then he dropped out of the Arizona scene for a dozen years. Three years later, when Browne was appointed a special envoy to China, Poston went along to study Oriental agriculture. During his long absence from Arizona he embraced Zoroastrianism in India, and when he returned to Arizona as receiver for the federal land office at Florence in 1877, he attempted to build a Temple to the Sun on a hill near the Gila River which he called Primrose Hill. This touch of nostalgia reflected several years spent in London, where an eminence in Regent Park bore that name. Eventually Poston's remains were entombed on the hill, now called Poston's Butte.

CIVIL WAR FORGOTTEN

The first election votes counted, legislators convened at Prescott, only to learn they had no meeting hall. On the north side of Gurley Street construction of a long building that was to serve as territorial capitol had been started. Congress had not provided funds to Arizona Territory for public buildings, but authorized rented quarters. A local pioneer building contractor, Van Christie, agreed to construct and rent a building suitable for territorial purposes, but it was delayed while his crew hastened to complete a private house a few blocks to the west contracted by McCormick and Goodwin. This so-called Governor's House was finished before the capitol, so the initial caucus meeting of legislators was held in the dwelling. Wind whistled through unchinked cracks of the downtown capitol building where on September 26, 1864, Arizona's first territorial legislature convened. The log structure was without a floor other than Mother Earth.

Elected president of the Council or upper house was Coles Bashford, former governor of Wisconsin, who came to Arizona with his brother Levi, the surveyor general. Coles Bashford was the first attorney licensed to practice in territorial courts, and he, more than Justice William T. Howell, was principal author of the code of laws which always has been called the Howell Code.

Chosen as speaker of the lower house was a fiery frontier lawyer and politician, W. Claude Jones, listed as a resident of Tucson but formerly of Mesilla, where only two years earlier he had denounced President Lincoln and urged residents of the Gadsden Purchase to join the Confederacy. Members of the lower house included two Tucson men, Francisco S. León and Jesús M. Elías, who spoke only Spanish. A third native of Mexico, José María Redondo of Arizona City or Yuma, also had been elected, but since he was still a Mexican citizen, he could not serve. Upon completing citizenship requirements in a few years, he was elected to later legislatures and enjoyed a distinguished public and private career in the pioneer territory, where individual merit then mattered more than nativity.

The past southern partisanship of Speaker Jones and a half-dozen other members from below the Mason-Dixon Line was of little consequence. Northerners outnumbered southerners two to one in the legislative body, but, more important, the Civil War was a closed issue in Arizona, set aside in consideration of immediate local problems on which nearly all settlers were in agreement. Foremost was escalating Indian trouble. The Arizona legislature asked Congress for $250,000 to arm and supply militiamen to punish hostile Indians, while requesting another $150,000 to buy tools, gifts, and food for friendly tribes. Postal service and wagon road construction were given high priority, railroads and toll roads were franchised, and four counties were organized—Pima, Yuma, Mohave, and Yavapai.

CAPITAL MOVED TO TUCSON

Goodwin's election to replace Poston dropped the office of governor into the expectant, capable hands of McCormick, whose private life soon was saddened by the death in childbirth of his young wife and their baby. For this reason, although Prescott had brought him high office and welcome opportunity, McCormick was not opposed to the transfer of the capital to Tucson in 1867. As long as he chose, he dominated the Arizona political structure, naming his successors and doling out federal patronage with clout and acumen that demonstrated his political talent and influence.

In 1867, the year that the capital on wheels was hauled off to Tucson by the ox team of Charles Trumbull Hayden for a ten-year stay before returning to Prescott for twelve years, 1877–89, a new community was emerging in the Salt River Valley near the junction of the Salt and Gila rivers that would displace Prescott and Tucson from their early roles as economic, political, and population centers. Responding to the pleas of settlers, the Army had built a row of military posts across Arizona on a northwest-southeast axis, east of which lay Apacheland and to the west busy mining settlements which required strong military protection against Indian warfare.

Among these posts was Fort McDowell, built in 1865 on the Verde River, several miles above its junction with the Salt. Troops stationed there took the field against the Tonto Apaches who had joined Yavapais (a non-Apache group) in raids on central mining and farming settlements.

SWILLING'S INFLUENCE

During a lull in mining caused by Indian warfare and the recession following the Civil War, idle miners, farmers, and merchants formed the Swilling Irrigating and Canal Company to farm lands in an area soon called the Phoenix Settlement. The Salt River Valley was a center of population in aboriginal times, and was to become that again, because of its abundant, fertile alluvial lands blessed with the steady flow of the Verde, Salt, and Gila rivers.

This enterprise had been created by Jack Swilling with an eye to profiting by supplying grain for the Army animals at Fort McDowell and foodstuff for the troops as well as miners and residents of Wickenburg and other mining camps that the post was to protect. Swilling was an ebullient goldseeker and restless pioneer whose activities during the Civil War period probably influenced Arizona's destiny more than any other person's, including Poston's. Swilling frequently appeared at the scene of critical decisions in Arizona for two decades after he arrived as a teamster with the Leach Wagon Road party in

1857. Swilling had no compulsion to hoe corn and grow crops, nor was he the first Anglo-American to observe the network of ancient Indian canals in the huge Salt River Valley and realize they could be cleared of debris and silt to support crops again by diverting into them water from the nearby river. This idea had been undertaken tentatively on a small scale a year or two before by Army personnel below Fort McDowell, but they did not persevere.

Despite his unpredictable personality, Swilling brought together in the canal company energetic men looking for new opportunities. He fired their interest in clearing land to grow grain and other crops that could be sold profitably. Much of the high cost of importing grain was the expense of freighting. By growing the crop locally, logic suggested, the saving on transportation could be converted to profit. Swilling and his associates overlooked the basic law of supply and demand. When their first fertile fields of grain and sweet potatoes ripened, the selling price of farm products dropped substantially. But their enterprise did thrive, proving the practicality of irrigated farming in the central valley, and soon made Phoenix the breadbasket and agricultural center of the territory.

Swilling built his family a large adobe house on the eastern edge of the new settlement, where on June 15, 1869, he became the valley's first postmaster. Restless, quarrelsome, a heavy drinker, also addicted to opium because of a head injury, Swilling did not stay long at one place or calling. Ten years later, having moved through fresh cycles of mining and ranching along the Agua Fria River at the southern foot of the Bradshaws, he died in the Yuma jail, accused of stage robbery. His guilt or innocence in that episode is still debated. However mercurial his attitudes and unplanned his activities as he drifted about, during the two decades that Swilling lived in Arizona Territory he had a tremendous influence in determining pioneering policies.

Agriculture grew in importance in the central valley, supportive of the territory's overwhelming involvement in mining. The search for precious metals continued to attract newcomers to the territory, an irresistible force in the years of readjustment following the Civil War despite an increase of Indian hostilities in pace with the growth of population. After the first flash of excitement that accompanied every placer gold discovery, lode mining eventually would exceed the output of the gravel fields, whose production was perpetually limited by the water shortage in most of Arizona. The ledges and outcrops of the hard rock of surrounding hills required investments for mills, water systems, roads, and other necessities of development.

To stifle Indian depredations, the Army built more military posts, whose need for supplies led to local cultivation of farm products and cattle ranching, and attracted a stable population. The combination of mining, protective military establishments, and supportive agriculture stimulated a persistent growth pattern in the young territory.

10

~

Settling
the Indian Question

Arizona Territory could not achieve the place in the sun its founders desired for it so long as Indian hostilities impaired the advance of mining and of full development and production in newly irrigated river valleys. Indian terrorists made travel in Arizona hazardous, settlement precarious, and life itself often temporary. Murder and pillage increased in proportion to gains in the white population.

The presence of more troops at new Army posts did not restrain determined Indians in their fatalistic effort to destroy the white horde they saw as an overwhelming threat to their life and lands. Remarkably adaptable, the Indians exploited the troops massed against them. More soldiers, more camps, and more supply trains meant more targets and more booty from raids. As soldiers fell, their captured guns increased the firepower and deadliness of Indian resistance. Domestic mounts acquired from whites made the Indians more mobile, thus better hunters and more dangerous warriors. Cattle and sheep imported by whites provided a basic dietary need as the already limited game was decimated.

Warfare between the native population and the incoming settlers had been inevitable since the Spanish withdrawal from the Southwest. Through three centuries the Spaniards had attempted to educate and propagandize the natives for subservience to Spanish kings and for obedient faith in the Roman Catholic Church. Civil and ecclesiastical efforts, while often more beneficent than harsh, were rejected by Indians, who cherished the freedom and ease of their primitive life-style over the constricting demands of the foreign intruders.

Pacification of Indians had been every colonizer's insoluble problem. Spain failed through three centuries. The young Republic of Mexico lacked expertise and resources either to conquer or to win over the Indians in the scant quarter-century it had domain over the Southwest. At the end of the War with Mexico the United States acquired a vast territory and inherited the tangled problem of Indian raiding and resistance. During the years of expansion and development in the 1850s and 1860s Anglo miners, merchants, settlers, soldiers, and civil servants alike poured into the Southwest, all groping for some way to survive and to achieve their productive goals despite the ingrained Indian resort to war.

POOR COMMUNICATION

Simple misunderstandings of intent between travelers and Indians often led to bloodshed, followed by vengeful retribution and more bloodshed. Not infrequently, the curiosity of naïve Indians toward the wagons, outfits, and strange appearance of the newcomers, abetted as well by the gnawing hunger of people usually living on the brink of starvation, led them to visit the camps of travelers. If the Indians did nothing more harmful than beg for a little food or tobacco, and such requests did not bring unkind, harsh, or mischievous reactions from the whites, the incidents might pass harmlessly and even lead to agreeable trading between the parties. Such encounters with Pima and Maricopa Indians were particularly characteristic of travel on the Gila Trail. Petty thievery did sometimes cause trouble, but none that could not be rectified by cool heads.

On the other hand, Anglo travelers often entered Arizona with prejudicial attitudes toward Indians based upon traditional notions, or on accounts of episodes that had received sensational treatment in newspapers or in the inflammatory dime novels and penny dailies that flourished after the Civil War. Put on edge by exaggerated stories of atrocities and widespread belief in the "good Indian–dead Indian" syndrome, travelers were frequently trigger-happy, shooting harmless visitors induced to enter white camps by curiosity or hunger. Occasionally thoughtless or frightened travelers wantonly attacked peaceful Indians, even when the innocents had in their possession "good conduct" identification issued by Army officials or other parties with whom they had enjoyed friendly relations. It must also be said, however, that there were cruel Indians as well as cruel whites; ample documentation exists of murderous native attacks upon a lone traveler to obtain as booty nothing more valuable than the traveler's clothing.

An almost universal belief in manifest destiny permeated the great western migration; one of its central tenets was that Indians were subhuman, a canard that contributed to the myopic acceptance of the national removal policy that had been a factor in early-nineteenth-century efforts to occupy the great interior plains of the nation. As late as 1881 Arizona's fifth governor, John Charles Frémont, whose reputation as a great pathfinder had been derived to a large degree from following and mapping Indian trails through the passes of the Rocky Mountains, involved himself in public controversy when he endorsed such a heartless and impractical plan. Although most Arizona tribes by the 1880s were settled upon reservations, where fully ninety-five percent of the natives lived peacefully and never caused serious trouble, disturbing outbreaks that year led Frémont to propose that Congress purchase or lease Baja California from Mexico and forcibly round up and remove all Arizona Apache bands to that stark area.

Ultimately the Indian wars in Arizona were concluded with a slight modification of the untenable removal policy. Conditions of Geronimo's final surrender to General Nelson A. Miles in September of 1886 provided for the exile of the Chiricahua Apaches to Florida. Acceptance of these terms of surrender and punishment had been delayed several months by General George Crook's vigorous protests and his resignation. Crook insisted that nonbelligerent Chiricahuas, especially his friendly scouts, should not be forced into exile along with Geronimo's small hostile band. The innocents were shipped away with the worst of Geronimo's warriors despite Crook's resistance. The national consciousness had not been clarified even as warring between Apaches and whites ended in Arizona.

Within a decade of the creation of civil government in 1863 Indians began to recognize and accept the inevitable consequence of the white nation's superiority in numbers, firepower, and resources. By successive stages they gathered at feeding stations or reservations. But contradictory national policies were to precipitate constant turmoil, leading often to outbreaks, murder, and pillage.

GRANT PEACE POLICY

As a general practice before 1871 the few reservations in existence were administered by Army officers with a military presence intended to keep the Indians from the warpath. Sometimes they were given partial rations. With the advent of the so-called Grant Peace Policy in 1871 the administration of Indian affairs was divided between civil and military institutions. This division meant a multiplication of trouble. Indian agents now were civilians employed by the Bureau of Indian Affairs, chosen for their jobs upon recommendation of church groups. In Arizona the Dutch Reformed Church was assigned critical territory, although that denomination invariably designated as agents persons who were not of its sect. This situation was typical of many anomalies inflicted upon Indians in an era when strong Christian moral influence had brought the Quaker-dominated Board of Indian Commissioners into prominence. Ignoring or unmindful of the valiant Catholic effort to bring peace to the frontier through the church mission as a colonizing institution in Spanish times, the United States failed to take full advantage of the Catholic experience and effectiveness in many areas. Equally neglected was the fine record of the Mormon church in dealings with Utah natives. So long as Indians remained on reservations peacefully, they were under benign supervision of the Christian agents. Most of these Indian agents were sincere, but most were woefully untrained for their tasks. Some few were patently dishonest, disgracing the churches they had to thank for opportunities to cheat and steal from the Indians as well as the federal government.

Once trouble broke out—when Indians fled reservations because their rations were inadequate or of very poor quality—responsibility shifted to the military, which was expected to take the field immediately to return the Indians to the reservation. Too often the process was repeated a second or third time, bringing civilian and military officials into hopeless conflict. Indians learned to play one side off against the other, while wavering federal policy and budgeting added new woes to the frontier situation.

PIONEERS' HARSH ATTITUDE

Pioneer attitudes added another element of discord. Generally, Anglo and Hispanic settlers were predisposed to hostility toward Indians. Even those with fair attitudes became excited when neighbors and relatives were killed or wounded during Indian outbreaks. Frequently settlers railed against the feeding policy on reservations, not realizing the Indians were provided—or promised, as the case might be—beef, flour, and other necessities because reservation life denied them their natural freedom as hunters and gatherers. Insufficient or poor rations often provided Indians an excuse to leave their assigned camps to obtain needed food by gathering indigenous plants, bulbs, seeds, and nuts, or to revert to raiding. In addition, the growing temperance movement, closely linked to church organizations, frequently led to bans on brewing of a corn beer called tizwin, which the Indians insisted had ceremonial importance to them.

Settlers frequently complained that civilian control of the Indians was altogether unrealistic and soft, and that military officials, when they were active, did not deal as severely with the native people as the depredations and bloodshed of outbreaks warranted. Federal officials were invariably wrong, it seemed. Settlers supported removal and harsh treatment, but were the first to suffer when Indians rebelled and raided because of unfair treatment on reservations.

Indian genocide was never the official or implied policy of the federal government, although extermination was frequently advocated by pioneers, and in the heat of battle, as their comrades fell, it often became the result in practice. Had the United States ever firmly decided to seek the genocide of its Indian population, as Hitler did to six million innocents in Europe, it had the strength to achieve such a goal. The halls of Congress did sometimes hear advocates of such gross, total inhumanity, but the lawmakers rejected such ignominy.

At no time in our national life were Indians without their defenders and friends. Modern times have no monopoly on goodwill, compassion, and tolerance. Quaker Vincent Colyer's dominance of federal policy through the philanthropic Board of Indian Commissioners was the result of an organized movement for the protection of Indians. This concern was to lead in 1882 to formation of the powerful Indian Rights Association and even earlier, in 1879, to the Women's National Indian Association. Neither group came into existence in time to have any important influence in Arizona. Both emerged after the denominational selection of agents had proved a failure. Natives could not find much comfort in such a high-minded purpose of the Indian Rights Association as the "civilization" of the Indian, for that obviously meant the Christianization and Americanization of the Indian and possibly to a much lesser extent his protection from overt mistreatment. Such group efforts did not peak until 1886, when the major crisis in Arizona had been settled by force rather than justice.

While reform organizations with Indian protection as their goal were very popular in the East, from which they obtained funding and membership, and where they interacted with Congress and federal agencies, they were little understood or appreciated in the Far West, where obituaries and claims against the government for Indian depredations molded public opinion in favor of a heavier hand in Indian matters. The East was the home of the doves and a loving attitude toward Indians, but the hawks, as well as most Indians, lived in the West, where mutual contempt and hatred were commonplace.

TEMPTING TARGETS

Prior to and during the Civil War period the principal Indian disturbers of the peace in Arizona had been Apache bands in the south, flanking the Gila River stage-and-wagon route across the country. With the establishment of mining and civil government in the central mountains, the new adversaries were the nomadic Yavapais, who also had a hunting-gathering economy and a propensity for raiding only slightly less intense than that of the Apaches, to whom their origins and depredations were frequently attributed. Under impact of the rapid Anglo immigration, Yavapais decimated the horse and cattle herds of the intruders and, in turn, themselves suffered as the prey of irresolute pioneer attacks. Tonto Apache bands which roamed the eastern slopes of the Bradshaw Mountains and the Verde Valley likewise attacked outlying white mines and settlements and themselves were hunted as predators.

Supplies for central mining districts were brought from Colorado River landings by wagon trains and pack outfits which were too tempting and vulnerable to be overlooked by Hualpai and Mohave bands that lived between the central highlands and the river. The life-style of the Hualpais was also a hunting-gathering combination, while the Mohaves practiced crude irrigation farming after spring flooding of lower river terraces, supplementing these crops with desert gathering and hunting. They too knew the feel of hunger, and so were impelled to destroy and loot wagon trains hauling supplies toward the interior.

Before the Army could establish and man new posts to curb Indian hostilities, in 1864 three expeditions of volunteers led by King S. Woolsey and provisioned by merchants and citizens of La Paz, Wickenburg, Tucson, and Prescott followed the trail of Indian raiding parties toward the Salt River Valley and across the Verde River eastward into the Sierra Anchas and Pinal mountains. They destroyed *rancherías* and killed Indians wherever encountered. Woolsey, who owned farms at Agua Caliente on the Gila and at Agua Fria on the stream by that name near present-day Humboldt, believed in a policy of total extermination. After he persuaded a band led by Chief Big Rump to sit down for a parley in a mountain canyon south of the Salt River, probably beside present-day Fish Creek, Woolsey at a prearranged signal directed his companions, armed with concealed guns, to kill the Indians. The site is now known as Bloody Tanks in sorrowful remembrance of the violence that many pioneers believed was the only proper response to Indian raiding.

The federal government authorized Governor John N. Goodwin to organize local volunteer organizations after the first legislature petitioned Congress for assistance against increased Indian depredations. Five companies of volunteer militia, two formed of Pima and Maricopa Indians and the others largely of Mexicans, took the field against hostiles in 1865 and 1866, brutally destroying Yavapai and Tonto Apache villages before formal Army forces were ready to provide security for the new territory. A dozen military posts were operative by the end of 1865, but Congress in the post-Civil War period reduced the armed forces and limited arms and equipment to surplus Civil War materiel. Continuing strong pressure from Arizona citizens and their friends increased the military strength to eighteen posts by the end of the decade, and a separate military Department of Arizona was formed in 1870 under the command of General George Stoneman, who as a lieutenant had served with the Mormon Battalion in the march across Arizona in 1846. Later he was to be governor of California.

Federal policy toward Indians changed as Stoneman took charge. Military activities in Arizona largely were limited to construction of camps and trails connecting the military posts and reservations being established near or around forts. Washington officials had decided Indians were to be trained as farmers, to instill in them the Puritan ethic of useful work as well as to augment their food supply. While they learned to sow and till, the Indians were fed. Feeding Indians was believed to be less costly than fighting them. A choice had been made in favor of peace with subsistence rather than extermination. Humanitarians had managed to be heard, pleading for justice and mercy for the Indians.

CAMP GRANT MASSACRE

Residents of the Tucson area were not persuaded that establishment of feeding stations, plus the farming program introduced at Camp Grant on the San Pedro River northeast of Tucson, guaranteed peaceful results. The Indians were rationed every ten days, without a daily muster. Farmers and ranchers along the Santa Cruz said this procedure allowed the Aravaipa Apaches at Camp Grant ample time to raid to their hearts' content, then return in time for roll call and rations. General Stoneman was unable to halt the raiding, but foolishly hinted that pioneer residents should protect their own interests. Thus a massacre was conceived.

Tucson's most popular citizen assumed leadership of the tragic episode that resulted from General Stoneman's thoughtless advice. He was William S. Oury, pioneer cattleman and former Butterfield Stage agent, survivor of the First Battle of the Alamo, who had been named mayor of Tucson by Governor Goodwin in 1864. Enlisting a party of 146 men, mostly Mexicans and Papago Indians and only six Anglos, on the night of April 28, 1871, Oury led them in a dawn raid on sleeping Aravaipa Apaches at Camp Grant. This war party killed 85 Apaches, of whom 77 were women and children and 8 old men. They brought 27 or 29 children back to Tucson as captives. The Aravaipa warriors were absent. The Camp Grant Massacre stunned the nation. General Stoneman, who earlier had recognized that the Indians "must starve, steal, or be fed," was removed from command for failure to prevent the raid and also for operating from headquarters at Drum Barracks at San Pedro, California. (Southern California had been made part of the military Department of Arizona.)

The public outcry against the horrendous bloodbath brought an inquiry by a grand jury at Tucson, which indicted 104 members of the party, but at the same time expressed open sympathy for pioneer attitudes toward Indians. Oury, his co-captain, Jesús Elías, and their followers never denied their part in the raid, but insisted it was justified to protect civilization in Arizona. They were quickly acquitted by local jurors who agreed with them.

The massacre heightened pioneer ire. When Vincent Colyer arrived in Arizona on a tour of inspection at the request of President Grant, a Prescott editor only half-jestingly suggested he should be thrown down a mine shaft. Governor A. P. K. Safford called for calmness and fair play, but most Arizonans made Colyer uncomfortable. Arizonans objected to the Grant Peace Policy, complaining that it catered to Indians, and asserted that their friends and relatives in the territory's cemeteries were crying for blood vengeance.

To resolve the Indian problem in Arizona the War Department sent an experienced and successful Indian fighter, Colonel George Crook, to Arizona in 1871 as commander of the Arizona department. While assigned responsibility for establishing peace, Crook was una-

ble to act for more than a year while idealists in Washington remained in full control. Biding his time, Crook trained and prepared
his forces for action. He believed Colyer's peace effort was a "humbug
that would soon come to naught," yet he patiently stood aside, allowing federal officials and Indians to explore all their paths of peace
before taking the field. In a series of talks with Indian leaders he
explained that revised federal policy called for food instead of guns
as the weapon of reconciliation. Indians who gathered on reservations
would be fed and taught to farm; if they declined that invitation, they
would be treated as hostiles, hunted down, and forcibly confined.

Colyer originally wanted to concentrate all Apaches at Camp
Grant, but after the massacre he decided it was located too close to
Tucson, the most populous and most aroused area in the territory.
Thereafter he chose a site where the small San Carlos entered the
larger Gila River in east-central Arizona. He would make it the major
reservation, despite warnings that many Indian bands and tribes in
Arizona had lived in almost perpetual conflict with each other, which
might be intensified if they were forced to live in continuous close
proximity.

CROOK'S STRATEGY

Not until November 1871, after a stagecoach was attacked by Indians
west of Wickenburg and six of eight passengers were killed (one of
them a prominent Boston journalist), did the War Department allow
Crook to move. He had prepared well: recruiting scouts from many
tribes, organizing pack trains to supply troops in a roadless land, and
marching mule-mounted infantrymen long distances to condition
them for tough campaigning. After Crook set February 15, 1872, as
the date on which Indians must report to reservations, he had to
postpone his D-day while the Indian office rushed a second peace
commissioner to Arizona to extend an olive branch to the restless
native peoples. General O. O. Howard, respected Civil War hero and
head of the Freedmen's Bureau, managed to meet with Cochise, the
Chiricahua leader, and convinced him to settle his tribe on a reservation in the southeast corner of the territory bordering upon Mexico.
Cochise agreed because the site proved a convenient location for raids

into the neighboring nation. Howard subsequently endorsed Colyer's plan to gather all the natives at San Carlos, thus economizing by eliminating small reserves.

Despite the gentle ministrations of the two peace commissioners, the pace of Indian hostilities had resumed, causing terror and bloodshed almost as severe as that inflicted during the Civil War absence of restraining troops.

Finally relieved of the restraints upon him, on November 15, 1872, Crook sent nine columns into action against Indians north of the Gila River, sweeping most of the country from the Colorado River to the Sierra Anchas and destroying habitations, crops, and food supplies at the advent of winter. By April his intense campaign brought the remnants of hostile northern bands into Camp Verde to surrender. Most native bands had accepted peacefully the offer of reservation provisioning and restraints. The few who chose to resist were treated severely. The success of Crook's campaign was widely applauded, and he believed the war days were over. Farming tools, seed, livestock, cash payment for labor, and tillable lands were extended to Indians collected at San Carlos and at Fort Apache, some sixty miles to the northeast.

By the time, however, when Crook, with a deserved promotion for his even-handed resolution of the Indian problem, left for the Dakotas to aid Custer with Sioux troubles, the euphoria of his achievement had been reduced by other nagging problems. The Yavapais collected at Camp Verde were marched to San Carlos during winter without adequate food supplies, blankets, and supportive transportation. At San Carlos, tribes with ancient rivalries were fighting over minor incidents. The Chiricahua Apaches of Cochise refused to take up the plow, hoe, and scythe, but resumed assaulting Mexican villages. Their reservation became a rest-and-recruiting point for murderous Indians who fled other reservations. The Christian agents sent to Arizona to administer the reservations fared poorly in most instances, owing to lack of training, conflicting federal policies, inadequate funding, and in some cases outright dishonesty and incompetence. There was one remarkable exception.

JOHN P. CLUM:
VIGOR AND COMPASSION

John P. Clum, chosen by the Dutch Reformed Church and assigned to San Carlos at age twenty-three, brought vigor, intense determination, compassion for Indians, contempt for military methods, and honesty to his assignment; but he was also so aggressive and arrogant that he rarely obtained full cooperation from other officials. Following the lead of Crook and others who had enlisted native police—although Clum claimed and erroneously has been credited with the first use of native police—he enjoyed spectacular success for almost two years. His greatest achievements were the orderly transfer of most of the Chiricahuas to San Carlos and the capture of Geronimo after that distrustful successor to the dead Cochise fled into Mexico and from there to the Ojo Caliente (Warm Springs) Reservation in New Mexico.

Clum's early magic was dissolved by his arrogance and the Apaches' inherent love for freedom. The daily muster required by Crook had been abandoned when Clum maneuvered removal of troops from the vicinity of feeding stations. Indians returned to drunken ways with tizwin bouts. They broke out on hunting expeditions that became bloody raids. They tired of digging irrigation ditches and farming. When their terms of enlistment ended, Clum's Indian police reverted to hostile ways, using rifles and ammunition they had hidden but reported lost or stolen. One disappointment following another, Clum resigned as Indian agent, to be replaced by men less controversial but also less honest and not so dedicated to the Indians' welfare. Clum remained in Arizona, becoming first a lawyer and then a newspaper editor. As founder of the Tombstone *Epitaph* after the discovery of silver in southern Arizona, he became the center of new political controversies and was blamed by some critics for local discord that led to the infamous gunfight at the O.K. Corral.

In June of 1881 a ghost-dance cult emerged at remote Cibicue Creek. Misguided efforts to suppress it by a display of force led to a sharp fight in which the prophet of the mystic sect and several soldiers and Indian scouts were killed. A general uprising of White Mountain Apaches followed, with months of frenzied raids and a frontal attack upon Fort Apache. The turmoil finally was ended by a massive campaign that resulted on July 17, 1882, in the Battle of Big Dry Wash above the Mogollon Rim, the bloodiest and last major conflict of the Indian wars in Arizona, with twenty-two Apaches killed and a larger number taken prisoner.

With the Arizona reservations in trouble, General Crook was called back from the Department of the Platte, where his fame had been tarnished in battle on Rosebud Creek but luckily he had escaped the fate of Custer shortly thereafter. Military control of Arizona Indians had now been deemed essential, although they still were being fed and offered facilities to develop self-sufficiency.

Each recurrent disturbance at San Carlos provided an excuse for the restless, untamed Chiricahua Apaches to flee. Generally they turned south, raiding Arizona ranches and Mexican towns before hiding among inaccessible canyons in the Sierra Madre between Sonora and Chihuahua. Necessity finally led Mexico and the United States to diplomatic acceptance of a "hot pursuit" agreement so the mobile Indians could be driven from hiding places on both sides of the border by either Mexican or American troops.

CROOK'S RETURN AND RESIGNATION

In an effort to quell Indian raids General Crook donned his canvas field uniform and pith helmet, mounted a mule, and plunged into Mexico, accompanied by 193 Indian scouts and 45 cavalrymen. He returned a public hero with Geronimo and his band. Further attempts to pacify the jumpy Chiricahuas failed. Geronimo's pledge of peace was ruptured by the Indians' insistence that the Apaches should be allowed to brew tizwin at will. They insisted its manufacture was a holiday festival, not unlike the whites' Thanksgiving. Because prolonged drinking bouts usually ended in melees in which husbands often killed wives and family members, even the tolerant Crook objected to the use of tizwin.

For a second time Crook's scouts and troops took the trail into Mexico in pursuit of Geronimo's band. Again Crook brought Geronimo back to the border. At a conference at Cañon de los Embudos on the Mexican side of the line, Geronimo agreed to surrender one moment, only to lie outrageously a minute later about his past behavior and misdeeds. Before he could be returned to San Carlos, he and his band became drunk on whiskey sold to them by a white trader. The Chiricahuas again reeled toward a hiding place south of the border.

The conditional surrender having been aborted, Washington officials demanded unconditional surrender of the Chiricahuas and their permanent exile outside Arizona. Crook protested that his loyal scouts included many Chiricahuas, who deserved praise and reward rather than punishment for themselves and their families. The federal pendulum swung to the opposite arc: a dozen years earlier the dove of peace had fluttered along the Potomac; now the cooing changed to harsh demands for imprisonment of the entire tribe. For the safety of the white community, some innocents would be confined with the bad actors.

After Crook's steadfast, even-handed pressure upon the Apaches brought the Indian wars in Arizona near an end, a restrictive mantle of leadership fell to General Nelson A. Miles, a vain and pompous man. Two Chiricahua Indian scouts, who ironically were rewarded by exile, led Lieutenant Charles G. Gatewood to Geronimo's camp near Fronteras, Sonora. The scouts and Gatewood convinced Geronimo that his days of freedom had ended. Weary and hungry, his band greatly reduced, he submitted on September 4, 1886, at Skeleton Canyon within Arizona. Several days later he was shipped into exile from Fort Bowie, wearing a new pair of cavalry boots he had admired. Arizona citizens honored Miles at a huge celebration in Tucson, while Crook aided reformers in seeking fair play for the Chiricahuas and their New Mexico cousins, the Warm Springs Apaches, who also were deported to Florida. From that damp climate, where many succumbed to tuberculosis, they were moved to nearby Alabama, which was somewhat better, and eventually to Fort Sill, Oklahoma.

Although selected Indians were permitted to return home after several years, Geronimo knew of a murder indictment awaiting him in Arizona, so he chose to remain in the safety of Oklahoma. He became a great tourist attraction, posing for photographs for a fee, selling his "last" bow-and-arrow set and "last" headdress adorned with buffalo horns to countless tourists, and even made a pretense of embracing Christianity. In 1903 he rode in Teddy Roosevelt's inaugural parade.

With Geronimo's exile, peace settled over Arizona after twenty-five years of recurrent (but not constant) warfare since 1861. Hundreds of settlers, travelers, and Indians had died violently. Man's inhumanity to man was evident on both sides of the conflict. In retrospect, it appears that ninety-five percent of the Indians never did any harm to whites. At the same time, and contrary to the mythology of Western movies, the Indians were not always innocent, nor did white men break every treaty and harry the red people unmercifully. That these two enemy forces have learned to live largely (but not perfectly) in harmony and peace since 1886—almost a full century—is again proof that men can be brothers when they endeavor conscientiously to understand and tolerate each other's imperfections.

11

~

The Wheel in the West

A steamboat and camels were hardly to be expected in the middle of the Arizona desert, yet there they were, staring at each other, on the damp morning of January 23, 1858. They met at the Colorado River near the point where Nevada, California, and Arizona come together some fifteen miles north of Needles, where I-40 now hurdles the river.

Edward F. Beale, former Navy officer now surveying a wagon road from Fort Defiance near the future New Mexico–Arizona boundary to the Pacific, and leader of the United States Army Camel Corps, described the scene rapturously:

> Here, in a wild, almost unknown country, inhabited only by savages, the great river of the West [the Colorado], hitherto declared unnavigable, had for the first time borne upon its bosom that emblem of civilization, a steamer. The enterprise of a private citizen had been rewarded by success, for the future was to lend its aid in the settlement of our vast western territory. But alas! for the poor Indians living on its banks and rich meadow lands. The rapid current which washes its shores will hardly pass more rapidly away. The steam whistle of the *General Jesup* sounded the death knell of the river race. Accompanying Captain Johnson was Lieutenant White of the United States Army, and fifteen soldiers as an escort, which, with as many rugged mountain men, and the steamer as a fort, made a dangerous party to meddle with.

In his enthusiasm Beale had jumbled facts and made an unreal-
ized prediction. The *General Jesup* was not the first steamer on the
Colorado. The *Uncle Sam,* more a tug than a cargo vessel, had come
up the river in 1852, two years before the sidewheeler *General Jesup,*
104 feet long and seventy horsepower, was put in service. Steamboat
captain and owner George Alonzo Johnson also had a larger stern-
wheeler, the *Colorado,* hauling profitable cargo downstream as he
witnessed the meeting with the camels at this point far north of all
settlements. Johnson was more elated and excited than Beale, for the
meeting of his steamer with the camels climaxed his private victory
over the United States government, from which he had grown prosperous and with which he was feuding. Congress had appropriated
$75,000 to explore the Colorado River and find the head of naviga-
tion. Johnson offered to undertake the task for $3,500. The offer was
rejected because a relative of the secretary of war had been assigned
to assemble a small iron steamer at the mouth of the Colorado River
and conduct the investigation. In January 1858 Lieutenant Joseph C.
Ives had the *Explorer* operational and, with a pilot borrowed from
Johnson, was following the wake of the *General Jesup* northward.
Actually, Ives was to steam to Black Canyon (site of present-day
Hoover Dam), farther north than Johnson's penetration to El Dorado Canyon, seventy miles north of Fort Mohave. But Johnson had
gone far enough to humiliate Ives. Satisfied that he had reached the
practical head of navigation (basically, he was correct), Johnson had
started the return trip when he met Beale. Later he bought the
Explorer at an Army surplus sale and controlled commercial traffic
on the Colorado River until 1877, when a larger, more grasping
transportation combine, the Southern Pacific Railroad, made him an
offer too good to turn down. Wealthy, he retired to San Diego to live
out his eventful life.

Beale's prediction that steamers would bring an end to the
Mohave Indians living along the stream was far off. Accretions of
civilization enabled the tribe to grow in the following century, despite
tribal wars, epidemics, white intrusions, government meddling, and
injustices to which it had been subjected.

CAMELS AND STEAMERS YIELD

This spectacle of a steamboat meeting camels on the Colorado was a paradox of pioneer transportation problems in the Far West. Here resourceful American technology met a military dream. Science represented by the steamer supplied essential transportation needs of the frontier, bringing in manufactured goods, equipment, and personnel for mining camps and their protective military posts until railways displaced steamboats coming 'round the bend. The military dream was that since camels had proved durable and dependable in Africa, Asia, and the Middle East, they could supplant horses and mules as beasts of burden and fast messengers for military purposes on southwestern deserts. The secretary of war supported the camel experiment, but it never reached fulfillment, interrupted by the Civil War and hampered by the chaos and confusion the smelly beasts created among Army packers and wagoneers and their animals.

When Beale's party met the *General Jesup* and hitched a ride to the east bank of the Colorado for his baggage and staff while mules and camels swam the chilly river, he was already convinced of the effectiveness of the camel experiment. He was on his return trip, having made an easy westward journey from Fort Defiance to Fort Tejon a few months earlier. The camels carried heavy loads, survived on the shabby forage of the arid land, endured extremes of heat and cold without complaint, and managed well enough with widely spaced draughts of water from the stingy waterholes of the high desert plateau of northern Arizona. Beale surveyed and marked a practical military road from Fort Defiance to Fort Tejon and Los Angeles, a route which became substantially the line of the second transcontinental railroad across Arizona. The Indians that he fancied were doomed made his route too inhospitable for civilian wagon travelers.

The camel experiment conducted by Beale was an Army project paralleling private efforts to import camels from Asia for use in California; it failed in part because the technology of steam and iron rails advanced faster than men and mules could adjust to the huge beasts. Circuses and zoos acquired some of the Army's camels, while others were turned loose on the deserts to disappear finally to hunters and natural causes.

This meeting of steamer and camels was witnessed by a large group of Indians residing in the area, and a few friendly ones accompanied Johnson's and Ives's steamer crews as guides and interpreters. By this time the Indians of Arizona had become accustomed to shocking innovations in transportation.

EL CAMINO REAL

Arizona Indians probably did not ever see a wheel until the late eighteenth or early nineteenth century, when ox-drawn *carretas* with squealing, greaseless, solid wooden wheels came up the Santa Cruz Valley from Mexico with heavy items used in construction of the missions of San Xavier del Bac and Tumacácori. The Spanish civilians, soldiers, and priests who followed Coronado through Arizona in the first three centuries of exploration traveled afoot or mounted on burros, mules, or horses. Royal roads actually followed trails the Indians had made in their traveling and trading between tribes. Generally these trails paralleled streams where any existed or connected river valleys, since water was indispensable for any journey of more than a few miles in the arid Southwest. When mountains had to be crossed or the travelers moved across dry desert stretches from one stream or waterhole to another, the distance that could be covered was limited by the amount of water that could be carried in a clay canteen. When the Spaniards introduced domestic animals, they brought with them kegs and skin waterbags that could hold sufficient water to extend travel over greater distances.

Kino, Garcés, Espejo, Oñate, and Anza made their significant journeys across Arizona without wheeled vehicles, depending solely upon pack outfits and animal energy. In many instances the highways of today closely follow the trails they marked, traveling the shortest distances between available water supplies.

Wheeled vehicles were rare in Arizona until after the War with Mexico. A few traders' carts reached Tubac and Tucson with supplies for the missions and presidios in Spanish times, and during the Mexican period *diligencias* or stages followed north-south trails that were dangerously close to the plunder trails by which Indian raiders sought booty and slaves on the Sonoran frontier.

The first Anglos in Arizona were streambound trappers who hauled their gear and pelts on pack animals as they plundered the Verde, San Francisco, Salt, and Gila rivers for Sonoran beaver after the bountiful Rocky Mountain streams had been depleted.

COOKE'S WAGON ROAD

Until the War with Mexico there is no precise record of Anglo wagon travel in Arizona. General Stephen Watts Kearny on his dash for California with a hundred dragoons had two mountain howitzers which had to be dismounted and carried on muleback through rough canyons along the Gila River. Not until the following Mormon Battalion crossed Arizona in the winter of 1846 did Arizona actually see a full-fledged wagon train. That group of intrepid soldier-colonizers built Cooke's Wagon Road as an extension of the Santa Fe Trail from New Mexico to San Diego.

For more than thirty years thereafter, until the Southern Pacific reached Fort Yuma in the early summer of 1877, river steamers and wagons supplied the commercial import and export needs of Arizona, bringing in manufactured goods and settlers, hauling out ore, refined minerals, wool, and animal pelts.

The 1848 discovery of gold in California greatly increased the east-west traffic pattern, and in a few years considerable eastbound traffic developed as successful and failed goldseekers returned along Cooke's Wagon Road to their homes east of the Rockies. Fort Yuma on the California side of the Colorado became an important supply point for travelers moving in both directions, as well as a pacifying element to restrain Indian depredations. River steamers began operating in 1852, initially to supply the needs of Fort Yuma, but eventually provisioning all the interior. This resulted in heavy eastbound traffic from Yuma and other river landings to interior communities as mining and agricultural growth spawned population centers.

SAN ANTONIO & SAN DIEGO MAIL

Scheduled mail and passenger service on stagecoaches across Arizona began on a twice-monthly basis in June 1856 on the San Antonio & San Diego Mail Line. A daily stage running from San Antonio to Indianola, near present Houston, connected with semiweekly steamers for New Orleans, providing the fastest coast-to-coast transport available. In the Southwest the line was known inelegantly as the Jackass Mail, because sand dunes on the California side of the Colorado River were crossed by the passengers on muleback.

Operation of the stage line across Arizona led to construction of relay stations at intervals of twenty to forty miles, usually at a spring or stream where water would be available. There the horses and mules were herded, fed, and rested for their dash to the next station. Around each such station a small farming community developed, growing feed for the animals and foodstuffs for the station crew and passengers. These stations frequently attracted Indians, who cut wild hay or firewood and did other useful tasks in their introduction to barter and trade with Anglos. This proved a means of establishing rapport, on the one hand, and a source of trouble, on the other, when Indians began to covet and hence to steal material goods belonging to the station crew and passengers. Private travelers frequently stopped at such stations to replenish food supplies or seek repairs to equipment, since most stations necessarily featured blacksmith shops.

BUTTERFIELD OVERLAND MAIL

The San Antonio & San Diego firm was to lose its United States Mail subsidy in 1857, when the Congress granted a $600,000 annual subsidy to a new line to carry the mail from Memphis and St. Louis to San Francisco on a faster schedule than the earlier line could provide. The new contract was obtained by John Butterfield and William Fargo, experienced stagecoach operators in the eastern states. Taking over the stock and equipment of the earlier line west of the Rio Grande, the Butterfield Overland Mail bypassed San Diego for Los Angeles, then continued northward along the mission string on the California coast to provide service in twenty-five days from

Tipton at the end of the railroad west of St. Louis to the city by the Golden Gate.

The Butterfield stages, with six racing horses or mules pulling brightly painted Concord thoroughbrace stages, remain the glamorous vision of nineteenth century travel in the Far West. At the same time less glamorous stage lines with plainer, functional equipment and fewer animals branched off from the main line at Tucson to serve smaller communities developing within the Southwest. These branch lines at times owned no equipment other than a buggy or farm wagon that could carry some merchandise, the mail, and a few passengers. Two important supplemental stage routes entered Arizona from California by ferries at Ehrenberg and Hardyville, on more direct routes to the interior mining regions.

Steamer landings became depots for shipments into the interior and for the loading of ore, wool, and other products destined for smelting and trade centers on the Pacific Coast. San Francisco, western terminus of the first transcontinental railroad in 1869, was the major supply center for Arizona. Sea-going vessels sailed from there to the mouth of the Colorado River, where cargo and passengers were transferred to steamers and the barges they towed upstream to major river stops at Yuma, Castle Dome Landing, Ehrenberg, Liverpool Landing (now Havasu City), and Hardyville, as well as at several intermediate stops. From these depots freight outfits pulled by ox teams or mules made the long, slow journeys to the interior. It was dangerous business, as Indians coveted the booty the freight outfits hauled and exploited their vulnerability. Still, Arizona became covered with a cobweb of trails and wagon roads radiating from the river ports, immutably linking Arizona to California economically and demographically.

This combination of steamboats and wagon transportation dominated Arizona trade until the first train whistle was heard at Yuma (formerly called Arizona City) in May of 1877, marking the arrival of the Southern Pacific Railroad on the California side of the Colorado River. Thereafter steamer traffic was in decline as the iron rails pushed across Arizona, giving rise to many shipping points along the railroad.

Shortly after the discovery of gold in California and the Mexican

Cession, Congress ordered a survey of railroad routes to the Pacific, seeking the most economical and best route to join the oceans. These studies clearly indicated that the route across southern Arizona on the 32nd parallel was ideal. At a commercial convention in Memphis in 1845 James Gadsden of Charleston, South Carolina, who later was to negotiate the Gadsden Purchase, had proposed construction of the South & Pacific Railway to link the Cotton South with the Pacific via El Paso and this low desert route. Geography definitely favored Arizona.

The Civil War delayed western railroad expansion, following which the decision of Congress to support building the first transcontinental line through Nebraska, Wyoming, Utah, and Nevada into California was reached on political rather than rational or economic grounds.

In 1866 the Congress chartered the Atlantic & Pacific Railroad to build along the 35th parallel—Beale's camel route—and authorized a federal land grant of ten square sections of public domain plus a cash subsidy for each mile of line completed. Thereafter the Texas & Pacific obtained a similar land subsidy on the 32nd parallel route across New Mexico and Arizona. This latter line with eastern financial backing started building westward from Marshall, Texas, but fell into bankruptcy after it had built halfway across Texas. Since Texas had retained all public lands when it became a state, the line did not have the double advantage of a federal land subsidy.

PRIVATE INITIATIVE TRIUMPHS

Meanwhile, builders of the Central Pacific (the western half of the first transcontinental line), the infamous Big Four—Crocker, Huntington, Hopkins, and Stanford—had forged a rail monopoly in California and now were reaching toward the Gulf of Mexico and the Atlantic with a line called the Southern Pacific. Hoping in good time to acquire the Texas & Pacific land grant, they began building eastward with private funds. At Yuma their advance was halted in May of 1877 by last-ditch political efforts of Texas & Pacific lobbyists. More than a year passed before the Southern Pacific could obtain permission to build across the quartermaster depot grounds within the town of Yuma. By October of 1877 a railroad bridge had been built to the Arizona side of the river, but armed soldiers barred the puffing engines from crossing until November 18, 1878, a full year later, when approval came from Washington that allowed work to continue.

A construction crew of 200 Anglos and 1,100 Chinese pushed the tracks eastward, suffering from severe heat as summer arrived. The rails became so hot they could be handled only with tongs. On May 19, 1879, work was halted when the rails reached Casa Grande. No progress was made for eight months, but material was collected for the next big push eastward. Most of the Chinese workers scattered, finding jobs in the booming mining camps in the Globe and Clifton areas, opening laundries and restaurants, and some becoming truck farmers. In January of 1880 when a call went out to resume work, only 300 Chinese workers responded. The weather was sunny and balmy when the new crew moved toward Tucson. Three miles of track was put down in three days, but that fast pace was slowed by a rare snowstorm and then by a shortage of rails. Running three days behind schedule, the Southern Pacific reached Tucson on March 20, 1880, to be greeted by a feverish public festival with banquets, heavy drinking, grand hopes, and a special train that arrived from San Francisco bearing owners, investors, and prominent politicians. Charles Crocker drove in a silver spike to hail the event.

East of Tucson there were fewer interruptions. Supplies had been stockpiled and the weather was less severe. The San Pedro River was reached at a new town called Benson on June 22. On July 30 the tracks climbed over Dragoon Summit, reached San Simon on September 15, and a week later crossed the border into New Mexico— three years after the smoke from a diamond-stack Southern Pacific locomotive left the banks of the Colorado River.

RAILROAD AIDS SILVER BOOM

Completion of the railroad was a triumph for the hard-fisted Big Four, who soon arranged rail connections into New Orleans. It also came at a fortuitous time for the Arizona mining industry. During the construction period a great silver boom developed at Tombstone, about thirty miles south of the natural rail junction at Benson on the San Pedro River.

Meanwhile the Atlantic & Pacific was building from east to west across northern Arizona, assisted by federal land and cash subsidies, but encountering geographical and management problems. Great difficulty was experienced in recruiting dependable labor forces and in bridging Canyon Diablo between Winslow and Flagstaff. One of Brigham Young's sons rounded up newly arrived Mormon colonists to expedite construction (as his father had done for the Union Pacific a dozen years earlier in Utah), so the track was pushed on to the Colorado River, there to face a more serious stalemate. California lacked extensive federal public domain to provide subsidies for railroad construction. The Big Four had acquired control of the California legislature and thus obtained right-of-way at its will. After reaching the Colorado River at Yuma in 1877, the firm built a line from Bakersfield and Mohave eastward to the only other good river crossing at Needles. Thus, when the A&P approached the river, it found the Southern Pacific owners barring access to southern California and Pacific ports.

This barrier was averted by a clever move engineered by the young Atchison, Topeka & Santa Fe Railroad, which had invested heavily in the A&P and eventually would acquire all its assets when the A&P failed. Seeking a Pacific outlet for its lines, which had proliferated in Kansas, Missouri, and Oklahoma and had pushed southward to the Gulf of Mexico at Galveston, the Santa Fe entered Colorado, built a line over Raton Pass into northern New Mexico, touched Albuquerque, followed the Rio Grande southward, and angled off to the west, only to meet Southern Pacific survey crews at Deming. This work was undertaken by a Santa Fe subsidiary called the New Mexico & Arizona, which was headed for salt water at Guaymas, Sonora, on the Gulf of California.

Realizing they had been outmaneuvered, the SP owners granted the Santa Fe transit rights on their track between Deming and Benson, where the Santa Fe affiliate followed the San Pedro to Fairbank, there turning westward along Sonoita Creek to the Santa Cruz, reaching the Mexican border at Nogales to connect with another rail subsidiary built from Guaymas northward as the Sonora Railroad.

Ultimately the Southern Pacific and the Santa Fe made an effective trade: the Southern Pacific acquired the line into Mexico, thus obtaining a long-time monopoly on the west coast of Mexico with its Sud Pacífico de México. In exchange the SP yielded to the Santa Fe its right-of-way from Needles on the Colorado River westward to Mohave, thence over Cajon Pass to San Bernardino, providing access to Los Angeles and the port of San Pedro.

By 1884 Arizona had two transcontinental railroads, the first western state so favored, and turned to developing inner ancillary lines. On July 4, 1887, a branch of the Southern Pacific built northward from Maricopa reached Phoenix, opening the rich Salt River Valley to trade. Later that year the Prescott & Arizona Central built southward off the Atlantic & Pacific from Seligman to Prescott, a line of Toonerville Trolley inefficiency that failed in a few years. By 1895 this had been replaced by the Santa Fe, Prescott & Phoenix, giving the valley connections to two main-line railroads as the Santa Fe branch came cowcatcher to cowcatcher with the SP's Maricopa & Phoenix branch at Phoenix. Four years later the capital followed the iron rails into Phoenix, fixing its destiny as the commercial and political center of Arizona.

The linkage of the two transcontinental railroads by branches serving Phoenix effectively marked the end of the pioneer period for Arizona, closing out dependence on interstate wagon and stage transportation. Phoenix was now within a week by rail of every population, wholesale trade, and manufacturing center in the nation. The Old West was near its end in Arizona.

During the next quarter-century, until transportation by automobiles and motor trucks began to offer serious competition, nearly a thousand miles of railroads were built in Arizona, joining the rich mining districts, forests, and rangelands to the main-line railroads and to the dual commercial centers of Tucson and Phoenix, with the latter cementing its dominant role by 1900.

After the Wright brothers in 1903 perfected their flying machine, sunny Arizona soon was to be on the route of daring airmen seeking to cross the continent by air. Their route was strikingly close to the all-weather and low-altitude crossing of the Rockies that had attracted wagon pioneers to the Gila route sixty years earlier. In 1911,

Arizona helped to usher in the age of commercial aviation when the city of Tucson built the first municipal airport in the United States.

During World War II, Arizona's ideal flying weather made the state a high priority choice for training sites for pilots, heralding another phase in the area's development, sharply stimulating the huge population boom that followed the war and brought Arizona to the forefront as a key area in the dynamic Sun Belt of the late 1960s and 1970s.

12

~~~

Hidden Wealth
Revealed

Searching for the fabled Seven Cities of Cíbola, Coronado's legion marched through Arizona valleys rimmed by mountains hiding billions in mineral wealth. As they followed the San Pedro River valley northward in 1540, on their right flank were the Mule Mountains, within whose bosom fabulous copper deposits waited for the invention of the electric generator and widespread commercial and household lighting to create an insatiable market for the red metal shortly before the coming of the twentieth century.

A day's journey northward, had the party turned to the right into Mule Pass and followed it several miles to higher ground, they might have walked where Ed Schiefflin defied a warning in 1877 that he would find his tombstone among hostile Indians, but instead found riches. Spaniards, instead of an American, might have stumbled onto ledges of soft silver of amazing richness that by 1880 had opened one of the most stirring chapters in western mining history. Tombstone became a bonanza punctuated with the angry fire of handguns, so is a mining camp remembered most for a gunfight rather than for its stirring, positive effect upon the economy of the region.

As they crossed the Gila River several more days' journey to the north, the sunset silhouetted the Pinal Mountains, on whose slopes great silver and copper lodes of the Globe-Inspiration-Miami district were to create new millionaires and fortunes at the end of the nineteenth century. Rays of the morning sun slanted through spires of the Gila Range, on whose sunrise side in 1874 prospectors more practical than these conquistadors of Spain were to begin exploiting silver-capped copper deposits of the Morenci-Clifton district, thus launching the billion-dollar Arizona copper industry.

Those first Spaniards came in quest of riches that existed only in imaginative folklore, ignoring beneath their feet and on either side of their historic trail an unparalleled treasure in gold, silver, copper, and trace metals that had been distributed through a flaming mass of magma which in the creation cooled into the earthen sphere.

Although Indians occupied this land, they lived in a simple Stone Age society in which the properties and values of metals were unknown; with the coming of Europeans to the Southwest began the unending, passionate, death-defying search for this hidden wealth of the earth. After Coronado's failure and retreat into Mexico the Arizona frontier was largely forgotten for most of two centuries. Two exploring parties from New Mexico, named for their patrons Espejo and Oñate, crossed Arizona and recorded the presence of metals, but these were seen in barren lands, among hostile peoples, far from paths of trade, roads, and sources of supply and market. Forgetfulness descended again upon the land.

With the coming of Spanish missionaries late in the seventeenth century the Jesuits' search for pagan souls to win to God took priority over mundane and materialistic matters, except for such essential needs as bread, oil, candles, and wine. Much, much later Mexican romantics would whisper of hidden Jesuit mines and treasure troves and of Kino's lost bars of silver, but these were words of sheer folly, more stuff of folklore, separated only by time from Coronado's dream and equally lacking in substance and reality. The Jesuits were poor, even if a restless few pecked at ledges where rain and erosion unmistakably revealed stains of mineralization. There is, however, no authentic record of productive mission mining in Arizona.

PLANCHAS DE PLATA

Not until a third of the eighteenth century had passed was there any mineral discovery in Arizona worthy of documentation. In tangled hills some twenty miles southwest of Nogales an astounding discovery was made: native silver of great purity, deposited in loose, decomposed strata in slabs or sheets, as if molten silver had been poured over mounds of stone and gravel. The Real (mining district) de Arizonac startled Spanish officials, who had seen such riches only once before, in the main body of the Sierra Madre at Guanajuato. Would Spain once more need to form an armada to escort newfound treasure home to Cádiz? The simple herders who discovered the *planchas de plata* (sheets of silver) were prepared to surrender the normal king's share of one-fifth of the wealth *(el quinto),* but the viceroy insisted this mine was so rich it had to be considered the patrimony of the king. The king and the viceroy (at least, their greedy minions) claimed it all. Tradition has it that one chunk of silver weighing more than 1,500 pounds was taken to Mexico City. Unbelievable! It would have been impossible to transport such a mass by the only means of carriage available, muleback or on burros. Hyperbole and exaggeration certainly clothed the stories of richness found in the Real de Arizonac. Such tales brought hundreds of Spanish-speaking prospectors to this new mining frontier. Soon the prime discovery was exhausted, the wealth drained and dissipated by officials. Only one element persisted: from that mining district Arizona derived its name, a word that originally was a Papago Indian phrase which meant "small spring."

Nothing to match the sheets of silver was found during the Spanish-Mexican occupation. Not that men did not relentlessly scour the hills in search of instant wealth. On the desert to the south and west, along streams sloping toward the Sea of Cortés, a few gold placer deposits were worked before the Anglos came to occupy the Southwest. These placers provided only tortillas and frijoles for a few laborers, nothing of magnificence. The *planchas de plata* were an isolated find, separated by about 400 miles from the honeycombed hills around Alamos, on the west slope of the Sierra Madre, which half a century later became a colonial silver-mining center of significance in Sonora.

After Arizona was acquired through the Mexican Cession and the supplemental Gadsden Purchase as a railroad route and bridge to California, the lure of minerals was to be a major stimulus in its early development. With the initial impetus provided by Charles D. Poston's (unwarranted) conviction that a fortune awaited him here, the land was explored and exploited for its metals as rapidly as Indian resistance could be curbed.

PLACER MINING

As in California precisely a decade before, Arizona's first gold strike was a placer field. The eternal pattern of erosion finds rain, wind, earth movements, temperature changes, and time wearing away waste rock in which particles of gold were deposited during the creation and cooling of the earth. While the elements reduce the rock to dust and sand, heavier gold bits gradually settle at the bottom of streams against bedrock. The art of mining placer gold has historic roots in Africa, whose Moors transported the skill to Spain, from whence it came to the Americas, to be introduced into California by Chilean and Mexican miners. The Anglos acquired the art from them. Working with *bateas* of wood, which the Americans called gold pans, they washed waste from their pans with a twirling motion, leaving the heavier gold nuggets, or *chispas,* behind. From the simple, one-man operation of a gold pan, partners and teams of workers utilized cradles, long toms, dams, and hydraulic jets and dredges to work sand deposits more efficiently. In the absence of sufficient water, gold-bearing dust was tossed into the air on blankets or pieces of canvas, utilizing the wind as primitive farmers long have separated chaff from grain. This "dry-washing" was a common scene at the first Arizona gold discovery at Gila City (1858–60) on the Gila River about eighteen miles east of the Yuma Crossing. That first Arizona gold boom coincided with opening of the Butterfield Overland line, which carried the news on to California, accelerating the arrival of more miners.

Before its demise Gila City produced well enough to advertise Arizona as a new golden land adjacent and second to California in its promise of quick riches. Placer mining took no capital, only muscle, determination, and luck.

During the Civil War southern California's economy was severely disrupted by successive droughts and floods, so disgruntled citizens in the vicinity eagerly responded to news of another Arizona gold strike. Early in 1862 an old mountain man and trapper, Paulino Weaver, turned up at a store near Yuma with a goose quill filled with golden flakes and *chispas* recovered from a sandy wash on the east bank of the Colorado River 150 miles upstream. He and friends who soon flocked there called it La Paz, dating its discovery on the Feast Day of Our Lady of Peace (La Paz) in January 1862. Since California was locked in depression, a wild stampede of miners, merchants, and even a few mendicants soon had gathered at the river. The mayor of Los Angeles, Damien Marchessault, staked a mining claim in Arizona, the first incident supporting that city's later claim of far-flung city limits. Among early merchants at La Paz was Michel Goldwater, Polish-born grandfather of United States Senator Barry Goldwater.

The new mining district gained prestige in mining news as nuggets from La Paz as heavy as twenty-two ounces were delivered to the Wells Fargo express office in Los Angeles. A second exciting placer find in Arizona soon added to the importance of the goldfields in Arizona. With a good steamer landing and as a terminus of the Bradshaw Road stretching across the desert from San Bernardino, La Paz became the supply and outfitting center for miners and traders hurrying toward the headwaters of the Hassayampa River and Lynx Creek in the mountains of central Arizona.

At the close of the Civil War campaign in Arizona (see Chapter Eight) a former Confederate officer and deserter, Jack Swilling, guided a party organized by the well-known mountain man Joseph Reddeford Walker on a prospecting trip into Arizona. Word of their gold finds along mountain streams had been relayed through General Carleton in New Mexico to Washington to become a contributing factor in the creation of Arizona Territory in February of 1863; the excitement spread as well to California to accelerate the rush of adventurers to the Arizona promised lands. Goldseekers and other fortune hunters were now converging on Arizona from east and west.

Placer mining required an ample supply of water, a resource rarely available in Arizona. During dry seasons many miners prospected, attempting to follow gold float upstream to the eroded ledges from which nuggets and dust had been separated. Soon the sound of miners' drills and blasting powder echoed through the hills. Promising new discoveries followed in the mountains south of the Walker

District and on the desert stretching westward toward the Colorado River. An Austrian prospector and his companions found a fabulous ledge they called the Vulture Mine. The town near it was called Wickenburg for the principal discoverer, Henry Wickenburg.

LODE MINING TAKES OVER

The establishment of civil government and troops assigned to curtail Indian attacks created a more favorable climate for widespread exploration. It soon became apparent that almost everywhere in Arizona there were outcrops and ledges rich in minerals. Because of its value, gold was the first metal sought, but prospectors quickly learned that silver was more abundant in Arizona, frequently being found as a cap on large but then unprofitable deposits of copper ore.

Most of the two decades following the Civil War was a period of extensive mineral exploration. The liberal federal mining law of 1872 and concurring territorial laws allowed the filing of hundreds of thousands of mining claims, which were bought and sold as merchandise. Despite the severe danger from Indian attack, scarcely a square mile of the 113,909 in Arizona was not probed for mining prospects. Before it became a federal reserve and a national park, the Grand Canyon itself was invaded by copper, gold, and asbestos miners.

During the decade of the 1870s, despite the inadequacy of wagon roads and the widespread Indian troubles, several important silver mines and one major copper district came into production, intensifying interest in Arizona mining and attracting venture capital needed to finance extensive underground workings and the mills required to prepare the ore for market.

The Peck Mine and the Tip Top in the mountains south of Prescott were compelling operations by 1876. On the desert to the west the McCracken and Signal mines were profit makers in 1874 as silver was supported by federal programs. Discovery of silver at Globe, perched atop a vast copper deposit, opened that region in 1874. A year later the McMillenville and Richmond districts twenty miles north were in production, leading unscrupulous federal officials to modify the boundary of a nearby Indian reservation to benefit their speculator friends. And in 1877 the fantastic riches of Tombstone were exposed by Ed Schiefflin. Twenty years earlier a German prospector, Frederick Brunckow, had opened a mine nearby, but Indians had killed him before he could profit from it. Tombstone had an astoundingly brief productive spasm, producing as much as $50 million in silver in five or six years, and thereafter achieving fame for violence and the fiction that it was "a town too tough to die." All efforts to resuscitate its mines have ended in failure as water from the nearby San Pedro River continues to flood underground workings.

Attracted originally to the San Francisco River by gold placers, Henry Clifton and others by 1872 were staking out extremely rich copper deposits adjacent to the stream. These lode mines were acquired two years later by the Lesinsky brothers, New Mexico merchants, who built an adobe smelter at Clifton and a narrow-gauge railroad to handle ore between the Longfellow Mine and the smelter. The Morenci-Clifton district became the first major copper-producing area in Arizona.

GREAT CAPITAL NEEDED

A mountain of rich copper ore was discovered northeast of Prescott in 1876 in the Black Range. Requiring coke for smelting, it was not until 1882—when the westward progress of the Atlantic & Pacific brought Colorado coke within easy reach by wagon road—that many scattered claims on the east slope of the mountain could be joined to form the United Verde Copper Company. The camp was named Jerome for Eugene Jerome, a New York financier who was treasurer of the United Verde (and, incidentally, a cousin of Jennie Jerome, Winston Churchill's American mother).

Arizona had now reached the point in mining development where the colorful prospectors with their patient burros were outmoded, except as discoverers of lodes and leads. No longer could even a small group of men pool labor and a few thousand dollars to develop a small gold or silver property with crude and often home-built machinery. Great capital demands were squeezing out small operators, even though for twenty years after the Panic of 1873 the federal government attempted to support such individual efforts by pegging the price of silver to that of gold, a factor that in the end extended uncertainty rather than security to western mining.

The age of mechanization came to Arizona mining as the nation rode the iron rails toward irreversible industrialization. The agricultural age in which Jefferson idealized the husbandman and individual effort was in decline. More and more the giants of Wall Street became involved in group activities. A number of Scottish corporations invested in Arizona mines. The belching steel mills of Pittsburgh, and the railroads reaching from coast to coast which they frequently financed and controlled, presaged the coming age in which mining profits would be assured only through the investment of millions of dollars. Sweat and willingness to work could not alone provide the means to build wagon roads or branch railroads to mineral deposits, to dig shafts thousands of feet into mountains, to erect costly mills and smelters and dam streams to provide them with water, to build power plants, and to buy out the small miners whose courage and initiative in the face of untold danger had made major development possible. The corporate age had arrived.

One feckless pioneer, George Warren, who shared the glory of discovering the great copper deposits at Bisbee, in sodden revelry wagered his share of one rich claim on his skill as a foot racer—and lost to a man on horseback. Tradition has it that a mine developed on that claim later was worth millions.

THE RISE OF PHELPS DODGE

As the market for copper grew stronger with increased use of electricity on the industrial eastern seaboard, and the Southern Pacific completed its line across Arizona while the Atlantic & Pacific still was working westbound, the most dynamic personality in Arizona mining history arrived in the territory.

James Douglas, a Canadian physician, set aside dual medical and ministerial training for an avid interest in the chemistry of copper ores after his father made an unwise investment in a Quebec copper mine. Young Douglas and another medical doctor developed a new process for extracting copper from difficult ores. This discovery led

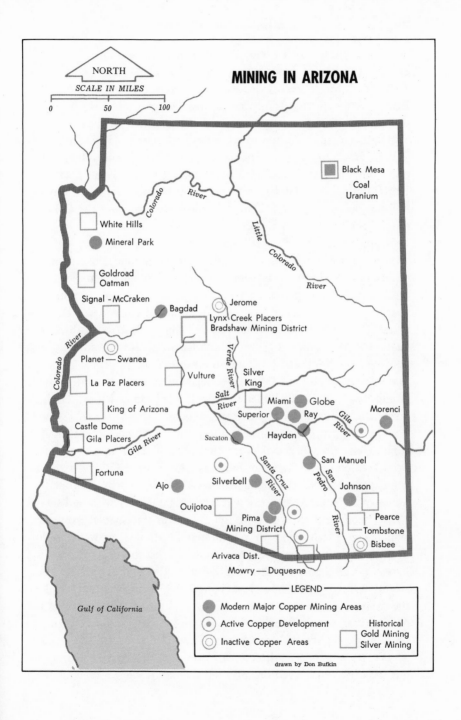

NORTH

SCALE IN MILES

0   50   100

MINING IN ARIZONA

Black Mesa
Coal
Uranium

White Hills

Mineral Park

Goldroad
Oatman

Signal - McCraken

Bagdad

Jerome

Lynx Creek Placers
Bradshaw Mining District

Planet — Swanea

Vulture

Silver
King

Miami   Globe

Morenci

La Paz Placers

Superior   Ray

King of Arizona

Castle Dome

Hayden

Gila Placers

Sacaton

San Manuel

Fortuna

Silverbell

Johnson

Ajo

Pearce

Ouijotoa

Pima
Mining District

Tombstone

Bisbee

Arivaca Dist.

Mowry — Duquesne

Colorado River

Little Colorado River

Verde River

Salt River

Gila River

Gila River

Santa Cruz River

San Pedro River

Gulf of California

─ LEGEND ─

Modern Major Copper Mining Areas

Active Copper Development

Inactive Copper Areas

Historical
Gold Mining
Silver Mining

drawn by Don Bufkin

him into contact with a national firm of metal merchants, later to become the Phelps Dodge Corporation. The company sent him to Arizona in 1880 to survey deposits reported at Jerome, Morenci, and Bisbee. After visiting the three camps, Douglas advised immediate investment at Bisbee, which was close to the new railroad, assuring economical transportation to refineries and markets. His recommendations led to organization of the Copper Queen Consolidated Mining Company, and later to Phelps Dodge's purchase of the Old Dominion Mine at Globe, the Arizona & Detroit Copper Company holdings at Morenci, the United Verde at Jerome, and the Calumet & Arizona at Ajo and Bisbee.

Dr. Douglas and his son, "Rawhide Jimmy" Douglas, were to be presidents of Phelps Dodge and guide it to a dominant position as the richest and most influential mining firm in Arizona. When the Southern Pacific failed to provide Phelps Dodge with favorable freight rates to transport concentrates from its reduction mills at Ajo and Douglas to a smelter at El Paso, Dr. Douglas built the El Paso & Southwestern Railroad as a competing line. Later Rawhide Jimmy adroitly maneuvered the Southern Pacific into an untenable position, forcing it to purchase the El Paso & Southwestern and at the same time provide "main line" service to Phoenix, a demonstration of Phelps Dodge's masterful political influence in the state.

The Ajo property was the earliest known copper deposit in Arizona. Mexicans worked it when that part of Arizona was acquired from Mexico in the Gadsden Purchase. Later John C. Greenway developed it as the New Cornelia Mine, one of the first profitable open-pit mines in Arizona. Greenway was a mining engineer who had served with Theodore Roosevelt's Rough Riders in the Spanish-American War and in the Marines in World War I. After Greenway's widow became Arizona's representative in Congress in 1933, succeeding Lewis W. Douglas, grandson of Dr. Douglas and son of Rawhide Jimmy, Greenway's statue was erected in National Statuary Hall in the capitol as a hero of Arizona in war and peace. This honor shows how pervasive the influence of the copper industry had become in the economic and political life of Arizona. Lew Douglas retired from Congress to become budget director for President Franklin D. Roosevelt, but they soon disagreed on financial policies. Douglas resigned that position and became president of Mutual Life of New York. During the Truman administration he served as ambassador to Great Britain.

COPPER SURPASSES PRECIOUS METALS

The year 1888 was the watershed of the Arizona mining industry. Prior to that the focus was on two precious metals, gold and silver, with Arizona favoring free silver during federal efforts to regulate the national economy by linking the price of silver to that of gold. By 1888, as a strong industrial market for copper developed, the value of copper mined in Arizona exceeded that of all precious metals. That leadership has never been surrendered, although the value of silver and gold—now recovered only as by-products of copper mining— enormously exceeds the yield of the late nineteenth century when numerous silver and gold mines dotted the Arizona hill country.

In 1887 Arizona gold and silver production was $3.7 million. In 1977—a year in which not one predominantly silver or gold mine was in operation—Arizona copper producers shipped more than $46 million worth of the two metals, acquired as trace metals in copper production. At the same time a new trace metal, molybdenum—used in hardening steel and aluminum—brought Arizona mines a return of $117 million. By the late 1970s the annual sale of copper yielded $1.3 billion, and Arizona mines produced more than 65 percent of United States output and about a third of the world's supply.

At beer halls in mining camps, when there is time to relax, the myth prevails that the trace metals in Arizona copper pay the total production costs of the mines. Myths often are nonsense, especially this one; the payrolls of Arizona mines in 1978 were close to $400 million, with the average annual wage of Arizona miners standing at $19,264, markedly higher than in any other business or industry.

BLUE-SKY PROMOTIONS

As copper became king in Arizona mining at the turn of the century, the territory aspired to statehood and was attempting to present a positive and responsible image to Congress. This was somewhat tarnished by a rash of blue-sky mining promotions.

Uncounted bundles of worthless mining stock in nonproductive and even nonexisting properties were peddled to gullible investors who were attracted to buy Arizona stocks by the selective news of good profits earned in several new and successful mines, notably the Congress, Fortuna, King of Arizona, and Commonwealth mines. Although these mines for a while early in the century boosted gold production to $6 million, that was less than a third of the new peak achieved by copper. Some stock promoters made a pretense of opening their ledges and building some surface works. This activity created a false impression of sincerity and production, but in time these false fronts fell apart, leaving ghosts of forlorn hopes and bad investments.

LABOR DIFFICULTIES

Obtaining the bulk of its labor needs from neighboring Mexico and skilled hardrock miners from Cornwall and the Balkans, Arizona copper mining boomed in the years before World War I.

The Ray-Hayden field became a major producer. The old Silver Queen at Superior was enlarged under new ownership as the Magma Mine. Many new shafts and ore bodies were developed at Bisbee to supplement the Copper Queen. A second major mine, the United Verde Extension, boosted Jerome production. The Inspiration Mine between Globe and Miami boosted development in that area. Morenci-Clifton made more gains, and the Silver Bell became a copper producer of merit. Meanwhile mines under American ownership in Mexico at Nacozari and Cananea were pouring their output across the line into Arizona for milling.

As the Populist movement gained adherents in national political circles, unionization of mine workers increased substantially. The Western Federation of Miners organized many districts, but soon faced aggressive challenge from the radical Industrial Workers of the World. Recruiting avidly as good wages were paid in Arizona mines, the IWW struck for higher pay and improved working conditions at Globe, Jerome, and Bisbee. The strike at Globe never got out of hand. Strikers were banished from Jerome at the insistence of Rawhide Jimmy Douglas, without any great reaction or outcry.

At Bisbee passions had been inflamed by the notorious Zimmermann Affair, in which a telegram sent by the German ambassador to Mexico was intercepted and published, revealing that he had offered Mexico the return of Arizona and other border territory after a German victory, which Mexico was expected to support by remaining neutral, thus allowing harassment of the United States frontier by German agents. Two men were killed during the strike. At Douglas's suggestion, a committee of citizen patriots was organized, and at the direction of Sheriff Jim Wheeler, on July 12, 1917, armed men loaded 1,286 workers—mostly IWW strikers but some unorganized workers and a few innocent citizens and bystanders as well—onto freight cars and deported them to Columbus, New Mexico. News of the Bisbee deportation caused a national uproar and brought Felix Frankfurter, later to be a United States Supreme Court justice, to Arizona as a federal investigator. In the prevailing atmosphere of war excitement, this violation of civil rights was equally defended and deplored in Arizona.

WORLD WAR II PROSPERITY

Like other industries, mining in Arizona floundered during the depression years of the 1930s, with several large mines closing, but it began recovering lost ground at the beginning of the World War II boom. Under the pressure of wartime demands for copper, the Bagdad Mine (known in the 1870s as the Hillside Mine) became a major producer. In the Miami area the open-pit Castle Dome was developed, and preliminary exploration and construction were undertaken at the San Manuel Mine in the San Pedro Valley, although it did not become fully productive until after V-J Day. Exploration for new mineral deposits had been encouraged by the federal government. Soon thereafter the Copper Cities Mine north of Miami came into production.

Along the Santa Cruz River valley, where numerous claims had been staked and some high-grade ore extracted ever since the 1856 development of the Heintzelman Mine in the nearby Arivaca Valley, aerial surveillance with geophysical instruments indicated there were large ore bodies beneath the gradual western slope of the valley. Core drilling confirmed the disclosures, leading to development work that has made Pima County the state's largest mineral producer, a role formerly enjoyed by Cochise, Gila, and Greenlee counties. The Twin Buttes Mine in that area is third among Arizona's top copper producers (exceeded only by the Morenci and San Manuel mines), and the Sierrita Mine is the fifth-best copper mine in the nation. Arizona lists eleven of the fifteen leading copper producers in the United States, three of them new mines south of Tucson.

TRIUMPH OF EFFICIENCY

The remarkable gains in Arizona mining production in the past century may be explained by the utilization of energy in increasingly efficient forms and by ingenious developments in means of handling ore and extracting minerals from waste materials. Placer miners and the first lode mining on ledges depended largely on human energy, after which burros and mules contributed animal power. Steam engines and then internal-combustion engines provided the motive force as deep shafts sought underground ore bodies. Power plants fired by oil and coal introduced electricity to underground works. With the completion of the Theodore Roosevelt Dam in 1911, hydroelectric power became available at the Magma Mine and at Gila County operations. Steam shovels first made open-pit mines productive, to be displaced for an interim by electric shovels and trains. Efficient diesel haulage and excavating equipment now has further reduced the expense of removing waste or overburden and of delivering ore to mills for the beginning of the complex refining process. Nuclear power and solar converters have not yet appeared at Arizona mines, but they are included in future development plans.

Treatment of ores to recover a greater proportion of the mineral content has brought milling, flotation, leaching, and electrolytic extraction processes to new levels of efficiency. Superior extraction and handling techniques have increased the available ore reserves in the state despite record production. Prior to 1900 ore mined underground had to yield at least 5 or 6 percent copper to be profitable, while by 1920 ore with 2 percent metal content could be handled profitably. Development of open-pit mines lowered the range to 1 percent profitability. A great leap forward was accomplished by 1980, when major copper mines in Arizona operated profitably with ores containing as little as 0.5 percent copper. That means that a ton of rock must be dug from the earth, ground to the fineness of flour, mixed with water, and run through chemical, drying, and smelting processes in order to yield ten pounds of copper, a chunk no larger than a brick.

13

~

Cowboys, Cattle, and the Law

There can be little dispute that the American cowboy has been our nation's greatest contribution to world literature and the strongest character in the universal popularity of American movies.

A personal example: The author once drove an automobile across the Austrian border into a dismal customs office in Yugoslavia. Reading our Arizona license plates, the guards enthusiastically cocked their thumbs and pointed forefingers in boyhood's universal sign of the six-gun, shouting warmly: "Cowboy! Cowboy!" They did not bother to check our luggage in their delight at meeting what they believed to be genuine American cowboys, not realizing that neither my wife nor myself nor our daughters had an affinity for horses. We like our horsepower wheeled. But what else but "cowboy" does Arizona mean to half the world?

Lo, Father Kino's name leads all the rest in the Cowboy Hall of Fame at Oklahoma City. Because he brought domestic cattle into Arizona in 1700 as life support for his beloved Papago Indian converts, the cattle industry and western history buffs consider him a cowboy. Since cowboy, cattleman, professional rodeo performer, and the western sheriff generally dress much alike, in slender denims, cowboy boots, and big hats, most Americans persistently identify all of them as cowboys. Moviegoers and western buffs have a real identity problem.

Such is the myth; now for the rest of the story.

The discovery of gold and instant growth of population in California in the mid-nineteenth century led to the trailing of huge herds of

Texas longhorn cattle across Arizona to feed the goldseekers and their friends. Professor Joe B. Frantz, doyen of Texas historians and President Lyndon Johnson's consultant on historic matters back home in Texas, has said that more cattle may have been driven across the Rio Grande bound for California than made the journey north to Kansas cowtowns at the end of the railroad.

No significant cattle industry developed in Arizona during the period of Spanish rule. The seed stock Kino provided the Papago Indians helped feed the missionaries and their military escorts, but no surplus was produced. Following the Spanish withdrawal in 1821 Mexican colonists established sizable herds of cattle and sheep on the abundant grasslands south of the Gila. The livestock frontier extended well beyond the mining settlements, reaching to the *despoblado,* enticing Indians to hunt and herd kine with their newly acquired horses.

Despite the establishment of stock-raising haciendas and a cordon of military presidios across this northwest frontier of Mexico, the young republic was unable to check rapidly increasing Indian raids. Cattle and horses and mules and sheep were temptations too alluring for native restraint. In the Apache reign of terror (Chapter Five) preceding the War with Mexico, most of the frontier stock ranches were abandoned.

BATTLE OF THE BULLS

Cattle left behind when the colonists retreated into Mexico multiplied in freedom until the War with Mexico brought an army into present-day Arizona. As the Mormon Battalion marched westward in the winter of 1846–47, building Cooke's Wagon Road from Santa Fe to San Diego, it unexpectedly encountered a herd of wild bulls. The battalion had moved southwestward from the Rio Grande along the northern fringe of present Sonora until reaching the San Pedro River not far from present Bisbee, where it turned northward, following the stream toward the Gila.

At the approximate location of the community of St. David the ox train was attacked by a herd of wild bulls. These animals evidently perceived the oxen pulling the military wagons as likely recruits for their bovine harems, so they charged in to get acquainted. A few wagons were overturned in the excitement, resulting in a broken finger for one man. Several wild cattle were killed, adding welcome fresh meat to the menu of the travelers for a few days.

When the war ended, the discovery of gold in California stimulated cattle drives from Texas across Arizona. New opportunities in mining and trade again brought permanent settlements to southern Arizona. A number of cattle ranches were established along the Santa Cruz River and its tributary creeks between Tucson and Sonora. Remnants of herds driven westward found good grazing along the few perennial streams in the area, furnishing welcome fresh beef for miners and for military posts that soon were activated as Anglos began to outnumber the earlier Hispanic colonists and Arizona moved toward territorial status. Major travel routes across Arizona were marked intermittently with small cattle outfits. Almost invariably each arriving party of settlers drove a few cattle, sheep, or goats with them into the new land. While the settlers built cabins and planted crops or picked at ledges for hidden metals to mine, their animals foraged for themselves.

As the land filled with settlers and miners, and as civil and military officials grappled with Indian hostilities, the cattle industry became a key factor in the reservation system. Hostile Indians were confined so the bulk of the territory could be safely exploited for mining and agriculture. Responsible military leaders recognized that Indians herded into reservations would starve if not fed, and sales of beef to feed Indians and soldiers on reservations provided the major market for range herds until the coming of the railroads in the 1880s. With the advent of the railroads the Arizona cattle industry entered a new phase of export prosperity. Marketable cattle could be shipped either to midwestern slaughter centers or to Pacific Coast markets, whichever was more favorable at roundup time. The favorable profit cycles of the late nineteenth century resulted, however, in widespread overgrazing of the rangeland, with serious damage resulting from erosion as grass was cropped too closely. Heavy growths of mesquite in the desert and hill provinces and juniper at higher elevations followed overgrazing.

The expansion of reservations during the 1870s and 1880s had a positive influence on native life-styles. Ordinarily, beef was the favored item in native rations supplied to heads of families in a portion based on a ration of three or four pounds per individual each week or ten days. Some enterprising Indians with large families persuaded government agents to give them live animals in lieu of slaughtered beef, contending that needless expense and waste could thus be avoided. Tightening their belts, the Indians eked out their existence with indigenous foods plus their flour ration, nurturing the live animals to develop herds of their own. As a result, Apaches on the White River (or Fort Apache) Indian Reservation and Hualpais living in northwest Arizona, as well as the Papagos to whom Kino introduced cattle, developed cattle industries which continue to be an important part of their adaptation to the white economy.

BARBED WIRE AND WINDMILLS

The invention of barbed wire and the development of low-cost windmills revolutionized the cattle industry in Arizona as they did in the Mountain West. Initially, barbed wire was popular with homesteaders or nesters, who used it to keep stray cattle out of their planted crops. Very soon barbed wire fencing was used widely to give stockmen greater control over their herds on expansive ranges. Fencing minimized the need for enormous roundups, which frequently stirred up disputes over the ownership of unbranded stock. Fencing allowed herds to be worked with fewer hired hands. Windmills placed strategically reduced the loss of stock during rainless periods.

With these innovations came herd improvements and the pen feeding of stock after they had grazed for two years on grass. Cattle "finished" with grain and other supplements brought a greater dollar return than rawboned range cattle. Selective breeding with Hereford bulls produced heavier beef animals which also commanded higher prices at the turn of the century. The practice of finishing cattle in pens shifted the marketing of cattle from remote ranch locations to towns in irrigated valleys along railroads, and helped integrate the stock industry into the territorial economy. Feeding pens often were located near or adjacent to flour mills in farming areas.

The early concentration of the cattle industry on the lush grasslands of southeastern Arizona, which is blessed with two distinct rainy seasons each year, coincided with the mining boom in that area. The location adjacent to the Mexican frontier and easy-money conditions of the mining boom fostered persistent rustling from one side of the border to the other. Mexican stock was stolen and driven into the San Pedro Valley for sale to butchers of uncertain ethics at Tombstone and Bisbee. In turn, Arizona cattle were driven into Mexico for sale to ranchers whose herds had been depleted.

This kind of criminal activity became so intense that in 1901 the territorial legislature created the Arizona Rangers to war on range crime, especially along the Mexican border. Experienced cowboys and peace officers, some of them veterans of the similar Texas Rangers, were armed and authorized to cross county lines and even the international border in pursuit of criminals in general, not cattle thieves alone. They were overwhelmingly effective. In only seven years the Rangers had established new respect for legal processes in Arizona. The force was dissolved because of the growing jealousy of sheriffs who resented its popularity and flexibility. The exploits of the Arizona Rangers were romanticized and, naturally, greatly exaggerated in the 26 Men television series and in several books.

By the turn of the century similar changes were taking place throughout the western cattle country. The spread of railroads, barbed wire, irrigation projects, and windmills brought greater stability to the stockraising industry even as forces of conservation were gathering to urge tighter control of the public domain that had been virtually open country for stockraisers until homesteading was sharply curtailed in 1895. The creation of forest reserves and imposition of grazing fees by the federal government constricted cattle outfits and raised new barriers to the romance that had enveloped and glamorized the industry.

MYTH AND REALITY OPPOSED

The cowboy stood tall in the saddle as the knight of the western grasslands, a folk hero idolized in printed literature and soon to be magnified and glorified even more by the emerging moving-picture craze. High adventure was pictured in print and on film as the cowboy's principal role. His adoring biographers generally ignored the realities and drudgery of cowboy life, surrounding him with fictional exploits and adventures that insulated readers from a clear vision of rangeland activities.

What insanity it would have been to include in a romantic novel the protesting bellows of cattle and the cursing and revulsion of workers dehorning and castrating cattle during roundup. Writers did not bother to represent the boredom and weariness of building and mending fences, cleaning out springs, and pulling frantic cattle from bogs. Lovers' murmurings would be grossly interrupted by windmills that demanded grease, and infested cattle that needed doctoring. Who would believe that the brilliant scenery could have periods of thick clouds of dust when breathing was polluted, and that living outdoors in extremes of weather meant sandy bedrolls, tasteless or poor food, labor from daylight to dark in hazardous terrain—all this for a scant few dollars a month? Yet, despite the demeaning hardships, ranch life attracted vast numbers of young men whose dreams of being cowboys had been stirred by lurid novels and romantic fiction of the wonderful Wild West.

ZANE GREY IN ARIZONA

Prolific writers of western adventure stories—foremost among these being Zane Grey, who wrote a number of novels while living in Oak Creek Canyon and later in a cabin east of Payson close to the Mogollon (not Tonto) Rim—served as unwitting employment agents for the cattle industry. Rarely did they describe the mundane side of cowboy life, accentuating instead the love interest, adventure, and positive gratifications, and the striking beauty of the Far West. It was glorious and less crowded than other parts of the nation. In the generations following the completion of the first transcontinental railroad in 1869 manifest destiny was to find its recruits in young men seeking adventure, fame, fortune, and everlasting love as cowboys.

Many of the stereotypes of western lore originated in such novels, to be further embellished in the movies. An obvious distortion is the canard that sheep and cattle will not drink at the same trough or waterhole. On the contrary, many major livestock operations in Arizona traditionally have maintained flocks of sheep as well as herds of cattle, sometimes grazing and watering them together. The narrow snouts and sharp front teeth of sheep allow them to forage and fatten among rocks where cattle cannot swipe up the grass with their broad tongues. Neither sheep nor cattle are fastidious about the purity of the water they need.

While cattlemen and sheepmen sometimes competed for access to range, that was based not on any inbred antipathy in their livestock, but rather on a natural desire for economic advantage. Grey exploited and enlarged upon a local family vendetta in Tonto or Pleasant Valley, some twenty-five miles from his cabin, to produce the book called *To the Last Man.* The Graham and Tewksbury families, both barely existing by stockraising in a marginal environment, became embroiled in armed conflict. Sheep and cattle grazed in their valley, although contested possession of animals instead of territorial dominion created the family feud. Grey and a coterie of following writers who have rehashed and enlarged the yarn for pulp magazines have failed to clarify the basic issues or prove that it actually was a war between sheepmen and cattlemen.

Once the movies had seized upon the cowboy as a distinct American character, it took very little time to consolidate the cowboys, peace officers, ordinary drifters, criminal types, and rodeo performers into a single embodiment of western life. This conglomerate westerner defies all rational efforts to view his varied components in the separate and distinct roles each acts out in the rangeland drama. The common use of the horse as personal transport before the automobile reached its ascendancy is compounded by the popularity of boots, wide-brimmed hats, and denim jeans. To this uniform of the West the movies have added the omnipresent six-gun and cartridge belt.

CRIME NOT CONDONED

An added distortion of truth emanates from the related myth that Arizona and, indeed, all the cowboy West in pioneer times was inhabited almost exclusively by crooks, gunmen, and other assorted maldoers. To the contrary, the earliest Anglo arguments for creation of a separate Arizona territory were that under the prior New Mexico administration courts of law did not meet with regularity. Citizens wanted public officials and institutions to record their purchases and sales of mining claims and stock, lots and other parcels of land, their marriages and other vital statistics. They wanted law and order up front, applied as a scale of decency to govern orderly development of their new settlements and business enterprises.

One of the most respected sheriffs in Arizona history was Carl Hayden, Arizona's first congressman and a United States senator who served in the Congress for fifty-seven years, longer than any other person in our national history. As sheriff of Maricopa County before going to Washington, Carl Hayden had an enviable record for arresting criminals and enforcing the law, yet he never once wore a pistol or carried a rifle.

Jails were among the earliest public buildings in many communities because the pioneer communities were allied against criminals and insisted that ordinary maldoers and felons alike should receive a poor local reception as a deterrent to antisocial behavior. Lynch law, which rarely functioned in Arizona and then basically on a judicial and not a racial theme, was a manifestation of the public's desire to punish criminals quickly rather than endure legal delays and maneuvering.

Western law officers often were drawn from the ranks of cattlemen. A notable example in Arizona was a small, hardbitten Texan, John Slaughter, who had trailed his bawling longhorns into Cochise County after drought in Texas had threatened his life's accumulation. Slaughter was elected sheriff, accepting the post because he found southeastern Arizona plagued with rustlers. Armed with a shotgun and a passion to create a countryside in which honest citizens could ride, work, and live in peace, he rid the county of cattle thieves. Yet he was a tender-hearted husband and father who rescued an orphaned Apache Indian waif and treated her as a daughter.

RODEO COWBOYS

As for rodeo performers, they are trained athletes who have adapted the cowboy's basic workaday skills of roping and riding to professional entertainment. Many are drawn from families associated with the cattle industry, and aspire to use their earnings to acquire ranches of their own. But two of the most popular rodeo acts—bulldogging and calf roping—would never be allowed with arena intensity on working cattle ranches where livestock is treated gently in realization that a hard fall or bad bruises can ruin sirloins that bring the rancher high prices at the slaughter pen.

During the late nineteenth century, when the cattle industry operated less formally and in Arizona was handicapped by Indian depredations, it was common practice for a cowboy to have a rifle on his saddle and even wear pistols while riding. This was for protection against Indian attacks, to kill predators such as skunks, coyotes, or snakes, and to bring a humane end to injured stock. Most frontier communities—knowing the predictable volatile result of mixing gunpowder and booze—had ordinances requiring that arms not be carried or worn in town. Travelers and cattle workers were expected to deposit their guns at a livery stable, hotel, home, or some other safe place while in town for rest and recreation. Upon leaving town, returning to the danger zone outside the urban area, they retrieved their guns.

The most publicized of western shooting episodes, the gunfight at the O.K. Corral in Tombstone in October of 1882, was an aftermath of such an ordinance. The McLaury brothers and Billy Clanton, victims of the fight, were leaving town and had not yet armed themselves when they were assaulted by the Earp brothers and Doc Holliday, erstwhile gamblers and pimps who had been recruited as town officers in an ongoing political battle that was a cover for stage robbery.

At the end of the nineteenth century, cowboy raiment had become the uniform of western and later southern law officers, being comfortable, practical, and distinctive. No movie has ever shown cowboys in the true working garb found only on old glass plate negatives and in ancient albums. Bib overalls were far more practical than the jeans popularized in this century by Levi Strauss.

For a full century or more the stockraising industry in Arizona has added to the color and charm of a land of extensive vistas and almost limitless grasslands distributed between desert and forest areas. The range aspects of the industry are dependent upon grazing permits issued by the federal government under multiple-use concepts of the public domain and forest reserves. State lands also are leased to cattlemen for grazing. Only a small proportion of the native grass and natural water upon which the industry is supported is privately owned in a state where roughly three-fourths of the total area is under federal control.

The fine line of separation between the cowboy and the cattleman or ranch owner is one of upward mobility and ownership—in other words, experience and financial success. The cowboy usually begins as a hired hand, aspiring to acquire his own outfit and become a cattleman. To accomplish that end, he may enliven his apprenticeship in ranching skills and savvy with a period of fun and games as a rodeo performer. If he survives the accidents of that highly competitive entertainment field, he may acquire a nest egg to allow him to own his own ranch and hire younger cowboys to continue the ongoing tradition.

The dress and the image of the cowboy have been superimposed upon the entire West, and in the past generation cowboy boots and wide-brimmed hats have permeated the Southeast until only a trained ear can distinguish between the "you-all" of Georgia and the "Howdy, partner" of Montana. But it always has been thus, if you are willing to go along with the experts in American literature who insist that the first genuine novel of the cowboy West was written by Owen Wister of Philadelphia. Published in 1902, the book described Wyoming from 1874 to 1890, at the apex of the cattle industry in the Far West, and was dedicated to President Theodore Roosevelt, the sickly New York youngster, educated at Yale, who retrieved his health and acquired his "bully" attitude on a cattle ranch in the Dakotas. The book was called *The Virginian, a Horseman of the Plains.*

Who is to say the cowboy is not a truly American type, a product of the ethnic and geographical melting pot of a nation that clasps this image to its heart in total defiance of all logic and rationality. Why worry? We all enjoy a moment or two of playing cowboy. Sometime each year nearly every Arizona community holds some kind of western celebration in which urbanites and pastoral types dress in jeans and boots and for a few harmless days emulate those guardians of the Yugoslavian frontier who greeted our touring family party so effusively with "Cowboy! Cowboy!"

To the movies goes full credit for making the American cowboy the best known and best loved of all New World personalities. It matters little in Stockholm, Lyons, Milan, or Athens that Roy Rogers is a native of Duck Run, Ohio, that Gary Cooper was from the mining camp of Helena, Montana, and that Gene Autry came to manhood as an Oklahoma telegraph operator. They are recognized the world over as cowboys. Likewise, it did the author no hurt to be confused with them one rainy afternoon.

14

~

South from Zion

The pendulum of public feelings about Indian conditions in Arizona was to swing all the way from horror to euphoria in the mid-1870s, following the scandal and disgust of the Camp Grant and Wickenburg massacres. General George Crook's conquest of the northern nomadic bands in the winter campaign of 1873–4 was followed by the concentration of the Yavapai and Apache groups at San Carlos and Fort Apache. The new era of peace and settlement was highly publicized, stimulating colonization interest in the sunny new territory.

While Arizona attracted a few utopian colonizing groups, most immigration efforts directed toward the territory were basically pragmatic rather than idealistic. Not that dreamers did not give it a try.

In the tumultuous years after the Civil War, many disillusioned abolitionists believed that the resettlement of freed slaves would bring faster and more humanitarian results than their acceptance by a society grieved and suffering from the heavy losses of the war. Milton B. Duffield, the first United States marshal for Arizona Territory, had been involved with a group of abolitionists in an effort to colonize former slaves in Nicaragua, and after that failed he accepted the law enforcement position and came to Tucson with the quiet hope that Arizona might become a haven for freedmen. His children by a companion of African descent were described as "chocolate-colored" by a Tucson editor who obviously did not share Duffield's empathy for blacks. Duffield, a violent man, was shot to death in 1874, the result of a personal quarrel, before he could undertake a serious campaign in that direction.

Several years later, Territorial Secretary John J. Gosper aroused editorial criticism by advocating the colonization in Arizona of freed slaves from the Chicago area. Gosper had lost a leg in the Civil War while leading black Union troops into battle. Nothing more was heard of his colonization plan after the negative editorial comment. As a mining investor, partner in the first Phoenix newspaper, horse and cattle rancher, secretary of the territory, and acting governor during frequent absences of Governor John C. Frémont, Gosper became involved in more than one man's quota of controversy.

The publication of a book called *The Marvellous Country* in 1874 in Nova Scotia, and two years later simultaneously in Boston, London, and Paris, romantically and extravagantly recalled three years' adventures in Arizona and New Mexico of Samuel W. Cozzens, who had been a member of the Boundary Commission twenty years earlier. He dedicated his book to pioneers of Arizona, and "especially to those sons of New England who have sought, and who may seek, homes beneath her sunny skies."

Cozzens was among the chief promoters of the American Colonization Company, which recruited about a hundred residents of Boston to accompany him to the "marvellous" valleys of northern Arizona. When the expedition reached the Little Colorado River near modern Winslow in the spring of 1876, a substantial group of colonists from Utah had already diverted water from stream to newly planted fields. Undaunted by the pre-emption of the area he had hoped to cultivate, Cozzens led the Boston party westward. Beside a flowing spring at the present site of Flagstaff a pine tree was stripped of its branches and, according to tradition, on July 4, 1876, the centennial of American freedom, members of the party raised the American flag and put down the roots of northern Arizona's most important city. There was little arable land in that forested area, so the party moved south to Prescott, where many became businessmen and entered mining. Others continued farther south to become pioneers in the development of Phoenix and Tucson.

EXPANDING ZION

The farmers who had pre-empted the tillable land along the Little Colorado River were Mormons called by Brigham Young, president of the Church of Jesus Christ of Latter-day Saints, to establish agricultural settlements south of the Colorado River as part of Young's inspired plan to extend the Mormons' land of Zion into Mexico. To Jews of the Old Testament, Zion was the idealized national homeland for the ingathering of the Diaspora; to Mormons, Zion symbolized the refuge found in the Rocky Mountains after Young, in midwinter of 1846, led the Mormon exodus from oppressive persecutions at Nauvoo, Illinois.

In the thirty years since the Mormons reached the valley of Great Salt Lake, their concept of Zion had expanded to absorb the astounding results of their proselytizing efforts in the southern states, in England, and in the Scandinavian countries. Zion was also an everyday term for the Kingdom of God, which encompassed both spiritual and physical boundaries that Mormonism aspired to in preparation for the latter-day return of Christ to earth. President Young saw Mexico as a new frontier of Zion, a way station to the eventual inclusion of all South America in the Kingdom of God.

Mormons believed that American Indians were descended from a lost tribe of Israel called the Lamanites, and that they were destined to rejoin the church before the Millennium. Hence, in church doctrine Central and South America, with their substantial Indian populations, were a field of ordained education and obligation for Mormon missionary endeavors.

All of Arizona north of the Gila had been included in Young's proposed State of Deseret—a political substructure of the spiritual Zion—that Congress had been asked to create before it gave approval to smaller Utah Territory in 1850. It had taken twenty years for Young to bridge the Colorado River with an emigrant road to link the mother colony of Utah to Mexico, where at some date not far in the future outposts had to be created to accept plural families.

During the War with Mexico the Mormon Battalion skirted the northern edge of Mexico, and some participants noted lands where irrigated agriculture would thrive. Representatives of the church later contacted Mexican officials, who were not hostile to peaceful colonization on their northern frontier; neither were they aroused by the polygamy problem which concerned the authorities of the church, who were under mounting pressure from the United States government.

The Colorado River also had been studied as a possible avenue of immigration for Mormons arriving at Pacific Coast ports from all over the world, especially during the Civil War when the heavy flow of converts from Europe had been choked off by the battling eastern armies of North and South.

Mormon feelings of spiritual kinship with the American Indians or Lamanites had set a pattern for friendly relations between the colonists and the Indian population. As early as 1854 missionaries visited Navajo and Ute bands on the northern border of modern Arizona. Beginning in 1858, Jacob Hamblin led several parties on peacemaking and exploring missions into Hopi, Navajo, and Paiute lands flanking the Grand Canyon. Largely through his patience and leadership, an era of friendly association with Indian bands resulted, providing a calm interlude for extensive colonization efforts undertaken first in 1873 and, after that initial failure, again in 1876.

CORRIDOR OF SETTLEMENTS

The southwestern corner of Utah and adjacent lands of the Arizona Strip north of the Grand Canyon had been settled by Mormons in a thrust toward the Pacific Coast along the Old Spanish Trail. This Dixieland of Utah with St. George as its center was a land filled with cotton and tobacco fields, vineyards, and orchards, watered from the Virgin and Muddy rivers. At nearby Cedar City was an incipient iron industry. Soon after the creation of Arizona Territory in 1863, Congress attached to Arizona Pah-Ute County, the extended triangular corner of the desert south of the Utah line, north of the Colorado River, and west to the diagonal border between Nevada and California. Congress finally transferred Pah-Ute to Nevada in 1866. This "lost" county of Arizona now comprises most of modern Clark County, Nevada, centered on Las Vegas, which originally was a meadow where freight trains paused en route from the Mormon outpost and wheat-growing center of San Bernardino to central Utah. John Doyle Lee, the most controversial figure in the Mormon story of Arizona, established a difficult yet functional ferry crossing of the Colorado River within the deep canyon at the mouth of Paria Creek, at a site first used by Hamblin. Lee was an early soldier of the church whose involvement in the nefarious Mountain Meadows Massacre in southern Utah in 1857 had led to his self-banishment to the few acres of arable land where the Paria emptied into the Colorado. In the refuge he called Lonely Dell he built a crude ferry that allowed determined travelers to cross the river at any season. Avoiding federal marshals, Lee also developed a small farm west of the Hopi village of Oraibi and adjacent to the small valley of Moenkopi, and Mormon travelers later made it an important way station, watering place, and center of missionary activity which won them the goodwill of the Hopis but only one important convert, Tuba. These developments marked a start on the corridor of settlements leading toward Mexico that Brigham Young envisioned and put into motion when he wintered at St. George, Utah, in 1873. A party he assigned to plant crops on the Little Colorado ventured into Arizona at his bidding, but turned back to Utah, defeated by the harsh environment and their own lack of fortitude.

In the early spring of 1876, again on orders from Young, another fiery soldier of the church, Lot Smith, led a major and better-prepared Mormon colonization effort into Arizona which tenaciously established four villages along the Little Colorado between modern Holbrook and Winslow. The present hamlet of Joseph City is the sole survivor of the four. Brigham City, Sunset, and Obed succumbed to the seasonal (often summer) floods that afflicted the arid Little Colorado settlements, washing out dams and canals faster than farmers could build them.

In the late 1870s the Mormons pushed upstream along the Little Colorado and built settlements at Woodruff, near the mouth of Silver Creek, and at Snowflake, Taylor, and Show Low along that tributary stream. In 1880 they purchased holdings from Mexican settlers at St. Johns on the Little Colorado. They expanded this foothold with the towns of Springerville, Eager, Nutrioso, and Alpine. Smaller settlements at Erastus, Hunt, Forest Dale, and Greer rounded out the

Little Colorado settlements. Scattered along the Mogollon Rim were a number of other tiny Mormon hamlets—Heber, Wilford, Overgaard, Clay Springs, Linden, Vernon, and Pine—that were linked to the Little Colorado settlements within the church structure and by familial relationships.

Unfortunately, this area was marginal farming country. The growing season was short, the water was often too salty for crops (and distasteful besides), the topsoil frequently was thin, but the Mormons hung on with fierce determination, inspired and driven by religious conviction and the belief that better days lay ahead.

The settlements survived in isolation, despite the severe environment, in part because the area became a refuge for polygamists from Utah. For one period it was the underground home of Wilford Woodford, whom the church in 1889 called to be president, and who issued the 1890 Manifesto by which plural marriages were forbidden as the church moved closer to accepted American mores in Utah's quest for statehood, which Congress finally granted in 1895.

Mormon settlers in Arizona, living within an agricultural economy, occasionally under communal precepts of the United Order, struggled against fierce odds. With limited farmlands and a hazardous water supply at best, they grazed cattle and sheep on neighboring grasslands and in the forests, developed a large dairy operation at Mormon Lake (near modern Flagstaff) to manufacture butter and cheese, and earned cash by freighting supplies to Army posts and mining camps. To supplement this agricultural income, they worked on construction crews of the Atlantic & Pacific Railroad, operated sawmills, and took jobs as cowboys on the huge cattle ranches of their non-Mormon neighbors. No task was too menial or arduous for these devoted settlers.

COMPLETING THE AGRICULTURAL CHAIN

In 1877 a second southward thrust into Arizona began from a base at St. George. Colonists took up virgin lands along the Salt River east of Phoenix and Tempe in a community first called Jonesville but soon to be named Lehi. The next year more Mormons arrived from Utah and Idaho, crossing the Colorado River by Lee's Ferry, and created a neighboring community a few miles south of Lehi. Again there was a pattern of changing names. Its founders first called the settlement Hayden, then Zenos, and finally settled on the permanent name of Mesa. The name of Hayden had been used in appreciation of assistance (both in supplies and jobs) given the colonists by Charles Trumbull Hayden, the miller at nearby Tempe and father of United States Senator Carl Hayden.

The Salt River Valley settlements fortunately were in an area with deep alluvial soil, a plentiful water supply, and an ideal climate. Although floods often destroyed the early brush-and-rock dams for diverting water into canals, the Lehi and Mesa settlements rarely lacked water. Differences in the community's attitude toward Lamanites (Indians) at Lehi caused an early rift among settlers, during which P. C. Merill, one of its most ardent founders, led several dissatisfied families away from Lehi. This splinter group helped develop a new farming community called St. David on the San Pedro River, very near the site of the comical Battle of the Bulls during the Mormon Battalion's march to California in 1846.

Directed by church authorities to reinforce the Arizona settlements, new parties of colonists recruited in Utah and Idaho continued to enter Arizona. Mormon converts from the southern states who had never been to Utah began to arrive in Arizona as immigration was directed to this new frontier. Many converts from the South —especially Arkansas, Alabama, and Mississippi—settled with the Mesa and Tempe colonists and then cultivated virgin farmlands along the Gila River in eastern Arizona.

Settlements at Central, Pima, Thatcher, Bryce, Safford, Eden, Fairview, Hubbard, and Solomonville resulted from this third significant wave of Mormon immigration into Arizona. Several of the smaller hamlets in time lost their separate identity by amalgamation into the valley complex of which Safford emerged as the principal trading center and seat of government of Graham County. As in the Salt River Valley, this farming area was favored with rich soil, good climate, and sufficient water.

The four centers of Mormon colonization in Arizona—the Little Colorado, Salt River Valley, upper Gila Valley, and San Pedro Valley settlements—all were relatively close to major mining districts, where their farm produce found welcome markets. Despite the opportunities the mining camps provided for freighting and occasional day work, Mormon settlers rarely became investors or speculators in mining, which had been the strongest single element in attracting population to Arizona. Mormon church leadership in the hierarchical system that led from headquarters in Salt Lake City to every local ward emphatically guided the Arizona missions into agricultural channels. In planning colonies to reach from central Utah into Sonora, President Brigham Young deliberately sought a chain of farming communities that could support new colonists moving southward with their wagons and livestock. An agricultural economy and large families were compatible; within this framework Young envisioned the orderly strengthening of the church with accompanying economic stability and success for individual members.

MORMON COMMUNALISM

The ward meetinghouse or local church was the heart of every new Mormon settlement, the hub of its many-faceted religious, social, and recreational activities, often its schoolhouse as well as the center of local government revolving around the Mormon bishop, who functioned as spiritual leader of the religious community and performed many of the functions assigned to mayors in nonsectarian communities. The Mormon church had no professional clergy; the church called all leaders from the ranks. Frequently the bishop and his counselors held the offices of justice of the peace and constable in the civil government. The bishop and his counselors were chosen by the church hierarchy, but their local neighbors sustained or approved them as a matter of formality. With this dual backing they exercised wide authority within a theocratic system that provided a safety valve of participatory democracy at the ward level flexible enough to achieve the resignation of extremely severe or dictatorial leaders.

The church was involved in the daily lives of the entire community. New settlements frequently began with a highly communal structure, often including a common dining hall, cooperative construction of dams, canals, and central buildings, and in many instances the establishment of cooperative stores. Such general stores operated for many years at St. Johns, Snowflake, Holbrook, and Mesa. Organized as stock companies, they were not owned by the church itself, but frequently enjoyed patronage only a hairline short of official church blessing.

By pooling resources, at least in initial times of hardship, the settlements were able to overcome problems beyond the reach of individual effort. Within the church organization, tithing (one-tenth of income, given in goods or cash) has been a moral and religious obligation, directly strengthening the mother church and the bishop's storehouse as a continuation of the cooperative thrust. This method provided the substance for local assistance to needy families in preference to governmental welfare programs. Even with strong emphasis upon cooperative programs in pioneer and difficult times, free enterprise flourished in a moral atmosphere in which leadership and acceptance of personal responsibility were encouraged.

Education held a high priority in all Mormon communities. Graded school classes generally convened in the ward meetinghouse on weekdays; in the evenings the buildings were utilized for general civic and auxiliary church activities, and on weekends for religious worship. In a sparsely settled territory with very few public high schools, the Mormons established seminaries at St. Johns, Snowflake, and Thatcher that taught religious subjects as well as a core educational curriculum. These seminaries trained young men for missionary assignments—personally funded two-year stints devoted to advancing the proselytizing program of the church. The seminary at Thatcher eventually evolved into Eastern Arizona Community College.

Wholesome group activities, centered on the ward organization, enlivened Mormon communities with drama, music, libraries, athletics, debating, and numerous homemaking and farm-improvement programs. The universality of such organized church and community programs led Mormon towns to the incontrovertible boast that juvenile and criminal problems were less prevalent in their communities than in non-Mormon towns.

HOSTILITY TOWARD PLURALITY

The isolation of Mormon towns in Arizona, particularly in the 1880s and 1890s when colonists poured into the territory to escape prosecution for polygamy, occasionally created friction between the dominant Mormon population and a minority of "gentiles," or non-Mormons. Several years of ugly acrimony, for example, developed in Apache County, resulting in the imprisonment of several Mormon leaders for illegal cohabitation. The territorial assembly, in wavering partisan efforts to secure or nullify the presumed bloc vote of the new settlers, often considered measures restricting the voting privilege of Mormons. Generally, however, most gentiles considered the Mormons peculiar in their doctrinal precepts, but not necessarily criminals.

Marriage custom encouraged members of the church to have nuptials solemnized or "sealed" in a temple, an edifice of greater holiness than the "ward" or "stake" structures. Until the Mormon Temple at Mesa opened in 1928, the closest temple where marriage ordination could take place was at St. George, Utah. Consequently, from 1877 until 1928 couples made the long trip from the Arizona settlements to St. George Temple, mostly by wagon or buggy, camping out for the two or three weeks required for the trip over what became known as the Honeymoon Trail. This trail followed in reverse the tracks of Mormon migration into Arizona, usually crossing the Grand Canyon at Lee's Ferry, and traversed the Arizona Strip north of the Grand Canyon on a westward course through the isolated settlements of Fredonia, Pipe Springs, and Moccasin en route to the temple for the holy endowments.

During the period of Mormon trials in 1885 and 1886 for plural marriage and illegal cohabitation many families fled to new Mormon colonies established in Chihuahua and Sonora as refuges for the faithful. Some leaders left some wives and parts of families behind in Arizona while taking some spouses and offspring with them to the Mexican settlements. It was a trying time for divided families, and a period when the bishops' storehouses and assistance programs within the church met the test of their purpose. The 1890 Manifesto barred additional plural marriages, but did not require that established families should be dissolved. The Mexican colonies were successful, but had to be abandoned during Pancho Villa's revolutionary seizure of the northern border areas of Mexico in 1911 and 1912. Many of the Mormon families then returned to Arizona communities. Time had eroded much of the hostility toward polygamy, and since family heads among the refugees from the Mexican hegira were along in years, their return to Arizona communities did not elicit any further prosecutions.

While the official church has steadfastly opposed plural marriage since 1890, some splinter groups have followed earlier principles and attempted to continue the practice in remote places. One such colony at Short Creek, in the Arizona Strip near the Utah border, attracted a dramatic raid by Arizona state officials in 1953. State highway patrolmen rounded up women and children and brought them to high school gymnasiums in Flagstaff while other officers vainly attempted to arrest the heads of families. After legal skirmishes the county released the mothers and children on humanitarian principles, and the colony resumed its lonely vigil, changing its name to Colorado City in the hope that the sensation-seeking public would forget the episode and allow its residents to practice their customs in solitude.

15

Perils of Partisan Politics

Arizonans impatiently endured the long period of territorial status from 1863 to 1912. During these years men of determined political ambition migrated to the growing territory. In their new surroundings they sought to launch or to enhance political careers; while awaiting personal opportunities, they often voiced unwarranted criticism and exaggerated the faults of territorial officials appointed by the incumbent president in faraway Washington.

Appointed executives were a fixed liability of the territorial patronage process. They were a trial to be suffered during the waiting period until a territory's population and economy and, most importantly, the mood of Congress gained it admittance to full and equal status as a state. On the whole, appointed Arizona territorial officials were an acceptable lot, basically equal in qualifications and reliability to later elected officers. Only a few demonstrated the incompetence and venality traditionally attributed to carpetbag rulers.

The territorial governor, secretary, federal district attorney, marshal, and justices of the Arizona supreme court were appointed officials. Each owed his job (and usually meager pay) to the president and dominant political party in Washington. The governor was allowed a modicum of personal patronage, selecting (often with the advice and counsel of local party political chiefs) officials such as territorial treasurer, auditor, attorney general, adjutant general, and other minor functionaries.

Citizens of the territory elected the territorial legislature and the delegate to Congress, often in spiteful determination to counterbalance the policies and actions of the appointed carpetbag officials. Rarely did the elected and appointed officials enjoy political harmony or adherence to the same party standard.

During most of Arizona's territorial period the Republican party held control of Congress and the presidency. Only three of Arizona's sixteen appointed governors were Democrats, while the populace in Arizona favored Democratic candidates with increasing pluralities as time passed and frequently elected as delegates to Congress Democrats who had the special talent of adding fuel to the combustible criticism of Republican appointed governors. But miracles did happen: in some cases Republican governors worked agreeably with Democratic legislatures, and even more often the chief executive and the delegate found common cause in an issue or problem that transcended partisan political considerations.

In the early years of the territory the fierce resistance of Indians to white control was a unifying issue, so threatening to the Anglo settlers that the antipathies of the ongoing Civil War rarely surfaced in Arizona, as adherents of both North and South united against the common red enemy in the West. The second unifying issue of the first decade was the need for roads and postal service, and soon afterward party differences were softened by the quest for financial capital required for the development of mining. After the banishment of Geronimo and his Chiricahua Apaches in 1886 resolved the major Indian problem, Arizona residents—realizing how they were suffering under a colonial regime imposed by politicians on the distant Potomac—began to clamor for home rule. This simple desire to manage their own affairs evolved surprisingly rapidly into a demand for statehood. Arizonans of both parties jointly asked for the privilege, and blamed others for its denial; the guilty party was the one in power, and the promise of deliverance from the evil was the hope of all political tomorrows. With the desire for home rule, paradoxically, came a call for more federal aid in all its generous forms: public lands for homesteads and millsites and in support of public schools, land-grant colleges with cash emoluments as well as blocs of forest and public domain, military posts, branch mints, and federal works of all sorts, as well as, first and last and always, jobs in the form of federal patronage for faithful party workers. Late in the nineteenth century, when William Jennings Bryan preached that gold was a crown of thorns on the richest nation on earth, Arizona was unified in the forlorn quest for free silver coinage.

To the degree that Arizona's appointive governors embraced or rejected some of these unifying or divisive issues, they faced the perils of partisan politics in a century when men in politics lived and died by the sword that swept swiftly from side to side, rarely sweeping cleanly as it cut into men who sought public favor and fortune in the political arena.

John N. Goodwin: Goodwin, the first Arizona territorial governor, a former chief executive and congressman from Maine, was uncomfortable and miscast in the pioneer environment of Arizona, especially after a long horseback trip through the southern part of the territory in search of a better capital location than original Fort Whipple, during which his military escort had several encounters with hostile Indians. Neither was he favorably impressed by the elected lawmakers who met as the First Legislative Assembly in Prescott in September of 1864. On balance, the first secretary of the territory, Richard C. McCormick, was completely confident and politically astute. McCormick soon encouraged Goodwin to run for delegate, offering him the support of his newspaper, the *Arizona Miner.* Goodwin's easy victory over Delegate Charles D. Poston, who had not returned to Arizona for the campaign, and his departure for Washington—never to return to Arizona—cleared the way for President Andrew Johnson to appoint the able and ambitious McCormick as Arizona's second governor.

Richard C. McCormick: Building a federal political ring in the tradition and practice of his times, McCormick had a clear perspective on Arizona's early needs—military protection against Indian resistance, wagon roads and postal routes, railroads, encouragement for mining and agriculture, and education. Timing his political ascension carefully, McCormick helped select his successor, A. P. K. Safford, and successfully ran for delegate to Congress three times. Even after his service there concluded, he retained connections in federal agencies that allowed him to influence patronage in Arizona for many more years. Later, New Yorkers elected him to Congress from the First District.

Anson P. K. Safford: Safford came to the governorship with political experience in California and Nevada, and the political support of powerful western railroad personalities. Indian and border troubles had become the major concern of Arizona settlers. Safford—a man no larger than Napoleon—bravely marched at the head of volunteer militia in efforts to suppress hostile Indian bands, and supported Crook's intense campaign to subjugate the Apaches and confine them to reservations. The little governor's next priority, and greatest achievement, was the establishment of a public school system in the territory. As governor he signed an omnibus divorce law, authorizing, among others, his own divorce from his first wife. Safford also had varied private interests, acting as a banker, practicing civil law as a lawyer in territorial courts while serving as governor, and becoming a successful investor in the Tombstone mining bonanza. He retired from the governor's office in declining health, but wealthy enough to become a Florida land promoter.

John J. Hoyt: The following and fourth governor was John J. Hoyt, a capable man who was in office only a short time, during which he codified territorial laws. He was asked to resign to make way for the aging John C. Frémont, who came to Arizona hoping to restore his family's well-being after squandering two fortunes.

John C. Frémont: The salary of $2,600 a year was a welcome though meager reward for Frémont's past service to the Republican party. He came to the office an old man of sixty-five after forty years in the public eye, part of it involved in failed promotions. Governor Frémont was frequently absent from Arizona, promoting his own and Arizona's mining interests in eastern financial centers, a vital need in the territory's development. His absences were bitterly criticized by the partisan Democratic editors as well as by two Republican newspapers. Cantankerous John P. Clum, angry that Frémont had not appointed him sheriff of Cochise County but had handed that political plum to a Democrat, lashed out at Frémont unmercifully in

the Tombstone *Epitaph.* The other perennial Republican critic was
the *Salt River Herald* in Phoenix, partly owned by the territorial
secretary, John J. Gosper, who had obvious gubernatorial aspirations
and sharply resented duties that devolved upon him during Frémont's stock-selling forays in the East.

Frederick A. Tritle: Frémont was finally pressured to resign in
1881, and President Chester A. Arthur replaced him with Frederick
A. Tritle, like Safford a former Nevada officeholder but, by virtue of
several years of involvement in Arizona mining promotions, considered the first Arizonan appointed to the governorship. Tritle's support of railroad construction to facilitate mining properties was
beneficial to the territory, helping copper surge into leadership over
the base metals of gold and silver. During Tritle's term the Thirteenth
Legislative Assembly made a strong move to develop needed internal
institutions such as colleges at Tempe and Tucson, the asylum at
Phoenix, and the prison at Yuma. Excesses in legislative housekeep-
ing expenses, however, unfortunately caused it to be dubbed the
Thieving Thirteenth, an undeserved misnomer. Upon the election of
President Grover Cleveland, Tritle graciously resigned to expedite
the appointment of Arizona's first Democratic governor, C. Meyer
Zulick, who had been a Civil War hero before entering mining in
Arizona.

C. Meyer Zulick: With Zulick of New Jersey as governor and
former Kentuckian Marcus Aurelius Smith of Tombstone newly
elected as delegate to Congress, the Democrats were on the verge of
acquiring political control of Arizona. Removal of the territorial
capital from Prescott to Phoenix was the source of early trouble for
Zulick, but he suffered more from consistent political clumsiness and
bad judgment, resulting in a succession of unpopular acts and indis-
cretions that nullified his well-intentioned efforts to capitalize on his
party's opportunity. The appointed governor was less effective than
the elected delegate in achieving leadership of Arizona Democrats.
One grave mistake by Zulick was his attempt to win bloc support of
the growing Mormon population through repeal of a former legislative enactment aimed at denying the voting franchise to members of

that church who either practiced or believed in polygamy. Although the law was patently unfair, public opinion against the Mormons had grown with concurrent strong enforcement of the federal Edmunds Act, which prohibited polygamy. Religious issues invariably backfired against political opportunists, including Zulick. His chief critic became the *Arizona Star* of Tucson, a Democratic newspaper owned by a zealous reformer and liberal, Louis C. Hughes, later himself to be appointed governor, a role in which he likewise proved a disastrous failure despite the best of intentions. When the election of Republican President Harrison ended his gubernatorial term, Zulick foolishly attempted to delay the orderly succession, leading a feckless band of Democrats hoping to retain their jobs in defiance of the accepted system of political turnover.

Lewis Wolfley: These tactics stalled until July of 1890 the seating of Lewis Wolfley, Zulick's successor and Arizona's only bachelor governor, a man remembered as a meddler rather than a manager. Wolfley had been a civil engineer and land surveyor in Arizona for six years, but his past was clouded by an 1869 dismissal from the federal revenue service in Louisiana. His term as governor initially was impaired by the presence of Democratic holdovers from the prior administration, but was little helped by his own actions. Hoping for a better public image, Wolfley and friends established the weekly (and later daily) *Arizona Republican* at Phoenix, but soon was accused by rivals of pressuring territorial employees to support the newspaper with subscriptions and with a portion of their salaries. Many of the charges against him were politically motivated and marginal in importance, which was par for Arizona politics and journalism in the century.

John N. Irwin: Wolfley's successor was John N. Irwin of Iowa, the last nonresident to be appointed governor. Family illness delayed his arrival in Arizona, during which the territorial secretary, N. Oakes Murphy, was acting governor, a role he served with intelligence and good judgment. Once in office, Irwin was an effective advocate of Arizona development. At a time when home rule was a strong issue, Irwin faced a legislature in which both houses were

Democrats anxious to embarrass the Republican party. Irwin conducted himself well against such odds. He supported creation of the Arizona Rangers as a territorial police force directed primarily at eliminating rustling in the southeastern part of Arizona, and he called a constitutional convention in 1891 to activate Arizona's dreams of advancement toward statehood. Elected delegates to this first constitutional convention were mostly Democrats with strong Populist influences. The result was a provisional constitution too radical for congressional acceptance, especially with features such as Arizona's yen for free-silver policies while the national administration supported a gold-based currency. Irwin, a fair-minded gentleman, erred politically by making several Democratic appointments, which lost him Republican support and gained no appreciable Democratic backing. He courteously resigned upon learning of President Harrison's wish to replace him. Several years later President McKinley appointed him United States minister to Portugal.

N. Oakes Murphy: In May 1892, N. Oakes Murphy became governor in his own right, after serving often as acting governor (as well as territorial secretary) under three previous governors. By measures of intelligence, education, business experience, speaking ability, appearance, and a grasp of the paths to Arizona development (especially in railroading and irrigation), Murphy was among the best qualified of all chief executives in Arizona's history. He was courageous enough to cross party lines to join Democrat Mark Smith in a tireless quest for home rule as a first step toward statehood. Murphy's first term as governor was very short, owing to a change in national administration. Grover Cleveland's defeat of President Harrison in the 1892 campaign opened the way for the appointment in April of 1893 of Louis C. Hughes as Arizona's second Democratic governor.

Louis C. Hughes: As a delegate to the Democratic nominating convention Hughes had vigorously supported Cleveland, and this served to overcome severe opposition to him within the organized Democratic party in Arizona. As an inveterate reformer and zealot, as well as a critic who used his newspaper as a political club, Hughes had made enemies more readily than he won friends. They plagued him all during his term. Hughes unwisely objected to several of the president's appointments in Arizona. As an ardent prohibitionist he attracted the united opposition of the saloon, hotel, and sporting element at a time when Arizona's splendors and climate were being exploited for tourist and resort business. Before coming to Arizona from Pennsylvania, Hughes had built a fine reputation for his sponsorship and support of farsighted welfare and reform programs. As governor he attempted to consolidate control of territorial agencies under one board, thus threatening the patronage that was the lifeblood of his own party. He even opposed the national administration's generous land policies in Arizona. One of the most ridiculous affronts to political reality was the *Star*'s support of Oakes Murphy for delegate to Congress over the Democratic candidate. However statesmanlike Hughes's positions may have been on such issues, they practically guaranteed his own removal from the governor's office.

Benjamin J. Franklin: Lawyer Benjamin J. Franklin—a descendant of, but otherwise unlike, the wise old Revolutionary printer and statesman—was the second Democrat in a row, but less courageous and even more inept than Hughes. Attempting to follow President Cleveland's gold-standard policy, Franklin was pilloried by silver advocates in Arizona. He vetoed several tax exemption bills, which heightened opposition to him and perhaps left him the most inconspicuous of Arizona's governors.

Myron McCord: President William McKinley next appointed Myron McCord of Phoenix as governor, restoring the parade of Republican chief executives. When McKinley had been a congressman from Ohio, his desk in the House of Representatives had been beside that of McCord, who was then representing a district in Wisconsin. Despite strong opposition to his confirmation—based upon a brother's fraud trial in Wisconsin many years earlier, and on McCord's service during the Hughes administration as purchasing agent for the Territorial Board of Control, which had made an unpopular contract with an irrigation development firm for the exploitation of convicts from the prison at Yuma—McCord turned out to be surprisingly popular as governor. He showed outstanding oratorical skill and enthusiasm in promoting Arizona. The outbreak of the Spanish-American War in April 1898 brought McCord into a favorable light as he set aside past political partisanship in which he had been the victim of gross attacks from Buckey O'Neill, editor of a cattle industry journal and twice the Populist candidate for delegate. O'Neill, an officer of the Prescott Grays, a volunteer militia company, had joined James H. McClintock, a Phoenix publicist, and Alexander O. Brodie, West Point graduate and mining developer, in recruiting volunteers for a cowboy regiment that Arizona offered the War Department as its first contribution to the war effort. Governor McCord appointed O'Neill and McClintock captains of the Prescott and Phoenix volunteer companies respectively, and Brodie commander of the Arizona battalion in the First Volunteer Cavalry. Only 210 men of the more than 500 who volunteered from Arizona were accepted for the Rough Riders led by Colonel Leonard A. Wood, a medical doctor who had won the Medal of Honor in the Geronimo campaign of 1886, and Theodore Roosevelt, assistant secretary of the Navy. McCord then resigned as governor to become commander of an Arizona volunteer infantry company that missed out on the hostilities.

N. Oakes Murphy: N. Oakes Murphy returned to the governor's office upon McCord's resignation, the only territorial governor to serve separate terms. In the six years since his first term he had served a term as delegate to Congress and had enthusiastically supported Arizona's mounting demand for statehood. His appointment was well received, but it soon became clear that Murphy had somehow lost the gentle touch and charisma evident in his first term. While he still displayed skill in dealing with the territory's taxation and development and patronage problems, evidently the demanding level of his family's active social life burdened him with scandalous personal difficulties. The governor turned to drinking and gambling, covering his losses by dipping into a contingency fund allocated to his office. Murphy tried to justify the illegal expenditures by asserting that the governor was paid too little, only $2,600 a year. Although federal law authorized a $3,000 salary for territorial governors, Congress appropriated the lesser sum. Despite this laxity in the use of public funds,

Murphy continued in office for a turbulent term, during which he became the first governor to occupy the new capitol, which was dedicated in 1901.

Much of Murphy's last year in office was spent lobbying against federal reclamation proposals. The governor, abhorring restrictive federal controls and ensnarling bureaucracy, believed that private enterprise should take the lead in such activities. President McKinley's visit to Arizona in May 1901, which included a stop at the Congress Mine developed by the governor's brother, Frank, undoubtedly prolonged Murphy's tenure, despite mounting public opposition; but it was McKinley's assassination a few months later that spelled finis for the capable man who had permitted wine, women, and song to impair his political career.

Alexander O. Brodie: Alexander O. Brodie, Teddy Roosevelt's comrade in the Cuban campaign, was a popular choice for governor of Arizona when Teddy reached the White House. A man of strong character and military bearing, Brodie worked harmoniously with the legislature and Delegate Mark Smith. Brodie's friendship with Roosevelt was insufficient, however, to obtain from the president a clear commitment to support of Arizona's statehood aspirations. Even after Teddy visited the Grand Canyon in 1903 as Brodie's guest —a visit that helped crystallize the president's interest in conservation which led directly to creation of the national park system— Roosevelt could not be persuaded to espouse separate statehood for Arizona. A little later, Teddy was to become enamored of the "jointure" movement led by United States Senator Albert J. Beveridge of Indiana, who proposed to link Arizona and New Mexico together as a superstate to be known as Arizona, with its capital at Santa Fe. Arizona vigorously opposed jointure and finally defeated it in 1906, thanks both to Mark Smith's political sagacity and to the broad national support that accrued to Arizona owing to the apparent unfairness of the scheme. Brodie's popularity gained on that fundamental issue and on his positive support of new irrigation projects authorized under the National Reclamation Act of 1902. As construction began on the Laguna Dam near Yuma and the Tonto (later Theodore Roosevelt) Dam on the Salt River, Arizonans recalled that

Brodie had helped organize and build the pioneer but ill-fated Walnut Grove Dam on the Hassayampa that had collapsed during a flood in 1890. His forward-looking interest in development was remembered as sad details of the tragedy receded into the dim past. Brodie's two-year governorship was a creditable though not sensational administration, hence has not been so well remembered as the beginnings of major irrigation projects at around the same time. When Brodie resigned as governor to head the pension office of the War Department in Washington, Roosevelt promoted the territorial attorney general, Joseph H. Kibbey, to the governorship.

Joseph H. Kibbey: By experience, temperament, lack of political liabilities, and past performance, Kibbey was the best prepared of all Arizona governors for the responsibilities of the office. After several years as a schoolteacher he had studied law with his father, a judge in Indiana, then come to Florence, Arizona, as attorney for an irrigation project. Through briefs submitted for litigants in civil actions, and later as a district court trial judge and Arizona Supreme Court justice, Kibbey wrote opinions that shaped and defined Arizona's basic water doctrine. His wisdom and courageous decisions in complex water suits led to "prior appropriation" and "beneficial use" being accepted as the basic principles of water law in the arid Southwest. The Salt River Valley Water Users' Association (organized by Kibbey's articles of incorporation in 1903) became the model for project operations throughout the nation and the basis of contracts between the Bureau of Reclamation and local farmers for the construction of Roosevelt Dam.

During Joseph H. Kibbey's four years as governor of Arizona, his leadership brought the office of chief executive new respect and dignity, even though he confronted an overwhelmingly partisan Democratic legislature. The lawmakers passed several bills over his insistent vetoes; abolished the Arizona Rangers (which had done an excellent job) on the pretext that this agency provided direct patronage opportunities for the governor; and indulged in traditional opposition rhetoric against the Republican governor.

Yet, the legislature could share with pride the accomplishments credited to Kibbey: introducing economy and a new standard of integrity into territorial government. Over intense opposition, an improved tax-assessment procedure brought taxes to more equal levels, and territorial institutions came to operate with greater apparent efficiency. No territorial governor left office with more praise and accolades than Kibbey received from his political associates and even from members of the opposition party.

Richard E. Sloan: William Howard Taft's election as Roosevelt's successor in 1908 catapulted Arizona unswervingly toward the statehood goal it had first asked from Congress in 1871 when McCormick was delegate. Several times a statehood bill had passed the House of Representatives, only to be lost in the Senate because, as Delegate Mark Smith averred in his last floor speech in 1909, entrenched senators of both parties distrusted "fearless and plain-spoken" westerners. One of the leading supporters of Taft's presidential candidacy had been Judge Richard E. Sloan, who as a delegate to the 1908 Republican convention compellingly labored for a positive statehood plank in the party platform. Taft honored Judge Sloan by naming him Arizona's last territorial governor, charged specifically with preparing the territory for its transition to statehood.

In the 1908 election, Arizona voters chose the Republican sheriff of Coconino County, Ralph H. Cameron, as delegate to Congress, replacing the now ailing and aging Smith. Cameron, who owned a copper mine, the Bright Angel Trail, and Indian Springs within the Grand Canyon, hurried off to Washington to confer with President Roosevelt, who still had a short session of Congress to address before the end of his tenure in March. Although no record of his conversation with Roosevelt has been found, subsequent events suggest that Cameron told the president he would sell the trail and the valuable water rights to Indian Springs to the Santa Fe Railroad—the franchise holder at Grand Canyon Village—in the interest of the resort's proper development. Apparently in consideration of that "deal," Teddy reversed his obdurately held position and asked Congress to admit Arizona and New Mexico separately. Taft clinched the effort by insisting that the Republican Congress fulfill the promise of the party platform.

Governor Sloan's appointment was a triumph for Arizona,

quickly endorsed by Governor Kibbey, leaders of both parties, and newspapers of all faiths. In October 1909 President Taft toured Arizona and renewed his statehood pledge. On June 20, 1910, he signed the Enabling Act to begin the statehood process for the admission of Arizona and New Mexico. A week later Governor Sloan called for a special election to follow county party conventions to select fifty-two delegates for a constitutional convention. The election of forty-one Democrats and only eleven Republicans foreordained a liberal document.

Democratic party leaders had yielded to threats of a separate labor slate of delegates by promising to enact a generous package of benefits demanded by union leaders as the price for their support. Inclusion of the progressive initiative and referendum measures and direct primary elections were foregone, but the recall of judges and other elected officials was openly challenged by President Taft, who was averse to making judges subject to political control.

When the constitutional convention delegates convened on October 10, 1910, they chose George W. P. Hunt, a rotund banker, merchant, and union sympathizer from Globe, as president. Labor forces exerted considerable influence through their intimate contacts with Hunt and his pre-election pledges to them, but he conducted the convention with conscientious fairness and dignity. Republican members joined hands with conservative Democrats to vote down only the most extreme proposals. The great progressive reform movement which swept the nation had its effect. The result was a liberal constitution.

Time has shown that it had two major flaws. First, initiative and referendum provided such ease in amending the constitution that errant moods and whims of the electorate permitted significant changes in the basic law which have been difficult to correct. Second, in its enthusiasm for broad, direct citizen participation, the constitution weakened the office of the governor and the executive departments, hampering executive authority by an excess of boards and commissions subject to legislative confirmation. Additionally, taxing functions were divided between state and county officials, a condition that has defied correction for nearly three-quarters of a century. The budgeting process also is divided between legislative and executive branches, another source of anxiety.

Nonetheless, Arizonans hailed the new constitution as the finest created by any state, and the convention delegates adopted it by a vote of 40 to 12. Yet only one Republican voted for and signed the constitution, while one Democrat took a comparably stubborn position, refusing to vote for it and withholding his signature. Voters approved the proposed constitution enthusiastically, although many expressed grave fears that it might be rejected in Washington. The Enabling Act required that the constitution receive the approval of both Congress and the president. President Taft's known objection to the recall provision of the constitution was seen as a major barrier to its acceptance.

By mid-August of 1911, as Arizona prepared for the election that would choose its first set of state officials, both houses of Congress had approved the Flood Resolution to admit Arizona, but, as expected, President Taft invoked his veto. He was forthright in his explanation, encouraging Arizona to remove the disputed provision for recall of judges long enough to attain statehood, after which it could be restored without his involvement. This advice was sound, and Arizona followed it, albeit without full appreciation of Taft's directness.

On December 12, 1911, the territory's voters agreed to exempt judges from recall. On February 14, 1912—fifty years to the day after Jefferson Davis had proclaimed Arizona a territory of the Confederate States of America—President Taft used a gold pen and many wooden replicas to sign the proclamation that made Arizona the forty-eighth state of the Union. The statehood fight was over.

16

Arizona Comes of Age

In later years, when he was serving his seventh term as governor of Arizona, his political foes would call him King George, although he preferred another sobriquet: The Old Roman. Opponents would try to pull him down with jibes at his crudities and his imperfect self-education. But on February 14, 1912, an admiring citizenry saluted him respectfully as Governor Hunt and cheered as he led a small parade of friends and political hangers-on in a march from downtown Phoenix to the state capitol fifteen blocks away.

As a display of the economy and simplicity he promised Arizona as its first elected governor, George Wiley Paul Hunt had announced he would forgo the automobile used by the last territorial governor. Hunt demonstrated the common touch that was the studied and orchestrated hallmark of Arizona's most effective political personality of the early statehood period, a man who, despite his human flaws, was a good choice as the state's first governor.

Two hours before the march began, word had been flashed by telegraph from Washington that President Taft had signed the proclamation that made Arizona the forty-eighth state. Governor Hunt ceremoniously walked to his high noon inauguration at the state capitol, but returned to his hotel a few hours later in an automobile. Thereafter he rode to the capitol in some splendor, forsaking the pledge of rigid economy in order to be at his desk earlier, an example to all public employees.

G. W. P. Hunt: Arizona's first elected governor was a Democrat, heart and soul, a self-made man, and a politician of remarkable acumen. He came from a Missouri slaveholding family impoverished by the Civil War. Having limited opportunities for schooling, Hunt followed the lure of gold into Colorado when he was eighteen. He worked as a waiter in restaurants and boardinghouses in mining camps, prospected without luck, and drifted down into New Mexico and Arizona, following fresh hopes of a mineral bonanza that eluded him. He and a companion entered Arizona in July of 1881. Shortly afterward, Hunt recalled, he rode into Globe astride a burro. Once more he went through the odd-jobs routine, working as a mucker in mines, serving in restaurants, clerking in stores and a bank, cattle-ranching for a while, and gradually edging into politics. Successful in both business and public life, he became president of the merchandising firm and the Old Dominion Bank where he had been a clerk, and served as a Gila County legislator for seven terms before being chosen president of the constitutional convention.

Hunt's political philosophy was a reflection of his origins and the Populist upsurge. He actually was a common man who knew the problems of working people, spoke their language, shared their frustrations and ambitions, and, even after becoming moderately wealthy, aligned himself on the side of labor in what he saw as a class struggle against privilege and power. His political posture was that of an implacable foe of the corporate enemy whose smokestacks belching fumes from copper furnaces signaled the prosperity Arizona enjoyed. Hunt attacked the mining companies incessantly, even while sharing that prosperity as a Globe merchant, as a broker of mining equipment, and—horrid paradox to Populist thinkers such as himself —as a small-town banker.

While he was thus capitalizing on the muckraking attitudes of an era when corporations and big business were the target of political reforms, Hunt's amazing vitality and his confidence in mankind carried him up the political ladder despite the doubtful sincerity of his public hostility toward mining corporations. This stance was a useful political expedient, and nearly always a winning factor at the polls. Meanwhile, Hunt tempered his official acts with an understanding of business problems and needs, based upon his own banking and commercial experiences in an area where mining was the bulwark of the economy.

Hunt had an uncanny feel for vote-producing issues. His popularity was strengthened in following years by the frequency with which he turned up in remote Arizona hamlets, almost always traveling by auto, ceaselessly boosting the Good Roads cause, and thoughtfully (by referring to a card index) remembering the names of leading citizens. While not a total abstainer, Hunt early in his legislative career opposed public gambling and the liquor trade. When prohibition became an issue in 1914, he carefully sidestepped the controversy, diverting public attention toward abolition of capital punishment. The governor became deeply absorbed in penal reform, economically employing convict labor on construction of highways and bridges for the state until the use of prisoners became unpopular with unions and private contractors as federal aid programs made more funds available for contract construction.

Governor Hunt's early control of state government was interrupted by the surprising general election of 1916, in which he trailed Republican Thomas E. Campbell, a handsome native son, by thirty votes. Hunt contested the results in court as Campbell occupied the governor's office. The recount and court decision took a year, with Hunt ruled the eventual winner by forty-three votes. Campbell served a year without pay, but won the office decisively in 1918 over Fred T. Colter, Apache County cattleman and stand-in for Hunt. Afterward Colter was to influence Hunt in Arizona's disastrous policy of nonparticipation in the development of the Colorado River. While out of office during Campbell's full term, 1919–20, Hunt permitted friends to spread the word he would oppose Mark Smith for election to the United States Senate in 1920. Smith and Henry Fountain Ashurst had been elected in 1911 as Arizona's first two senators—Smith for a short term, after which in 1914 he was re-elected to a full six-year term. Smith and his friends met Hunt's challenge in one of the cleverest political maneuvers in Arizona political annals. Secretary of State Robert Lansing, acting for President Woodrow Wilson, offered Hunt a post as United States minister to Siam. Hunt was delighted with the honor and announced his acceptance publicly before he realized he was being removed from the political hustings to protect Smith, who was universally respected. As it turned out, Republican Ralph H. Cameron upset the aged Smith's last grasp, serving as United States senator from 1921 until Carl Hayden defeated him in 1926.

Hunt turned the Siam episode from humiliation into victory. He used his assignment to Siam to mend fences back home in Arizona, sending thousands of postcards to rank-and-file voters as well as generous presents to prominent persons. He returned to Arizona for the most resounding victory of his career over Campbell in the 1922 campaign, winning with nearly fifty-five percent of the total vote. Although a myth of invincibility has come to surround Hunt's memory, in his eight general-election contests he had many narrow victories, as well as a sharp loss to John C. Phillips in the 1928 Hoover landslide. In eight campaigns Hunt received only 273,532 votes to 256,579 for his Republican foes.

Phillips, the 1928 victor, boasted of origins as humble as Hunt's, recalling that he had worked as a stonemason during construction of the capitol building in 1900 before he became a lawyer. Phillips also joked that he was the homeliest man in Arizona. Withal, he was an average leader, limited to a single term before the nation plunged into the Depression. Hunt won back the governorship in 1930, just in time to be caught by hard times.

In the 1932 party primary Governor Hunt faced a crusty Tempe physician, Dr. Benjamin B. Moeur, who had served with him in the constitutional convention and now represented a conservative Democratic coalition against Hunt's waning strength. His political dependents had pushed the Old Roman into the public forum once too often. The white suits and white cap he usually wore were now often rumpled and untidy. His oratorical skills had weakened, his vigor and health were diminished. He lost by a margin of 6,000 votes, and soon was fatally ill. Ever a showman, Hunt had ordered his tomb built in the style of the pyramids on the Nile, which he visited on his return from Siam. Hunt, his wife, Duett, her parents, and Colonel and Mrs. J. W. Ellison, pioneer cattle ranchers from the Tonto Rim area, are entombed in a tiled white pyramid in Papago Park on the north edge of Tempe.

Thomas E. Campbell: Arizona had been fortunate in its selection of a popular and practical politician as its first governor. The second chief executive brought to the state capitol a vision of Arizona's need to broaden its economic foundation and further expand industrial production. Republican Thomas E. Campbell, after a college education, had worked in post offices at Jerome and Prescott, then turned to mining promotions and ownership and also became a stockman. He had been as active in Republican politics as Hunt had been in the opposition party, and was the first native of Arizona elected to the legislature. He had been assessor of Yavapai County and a state tax commissioner. Campbell served one year as governor without salary as a result of the contested election of 1916. His four-year tenure from 1919 through 1922 brought a herculean effort against partisan Democratic opposition to Arizona's acceptance of the Colorado River Compact. That goal was not to be achieved until Arizona ratified the law of the river in 1944 during the administration of Democrat Sidney P. Osborn, second native-born governor of Arizona.

John C. Phillips: John C. Phillips, the second Republican governor, served one term between two of Hunt's separated terms, not long enough to generate and develop leadership. After he had studied law while working as a stonemason and laborer, he had been a probate judge and superior-court judge in Maricopa County. Although Democratic strength was unified against endorsement of the Colorado River Compact, the legislature during Phillips's term created the Colorado River Commission, which sought a way for Arizona to utilize a share of the river's water without fully cooperating with other states. The divided terms of Campbell and Phillips failed to break the monolithic control and momentum Hunt established.

Benjamin B. Moeur: Arizona's second Democratic governor, Dr. B. B. Moeur, was a small-town physician, a native of Tennessee and former Texan, who came into office when the national economy was suffering its greatest illness. Frequently impatient and often profane, Dr. Moeur was a considerate country doctor who traditionally sent poor patients bills marked "Paid" as Christmas greetings. He ran for governor on the ticket headed by Franklin D. Roosevelt, and his tenure was doomed by the national disaster with its high unemployment and widespread financial distress.

Governor Moeur recruited many of his appointees from the business community in an effort to establish confidence and efficiency in state offices. During his first term, property taxes were cut by forty percent but, to keep the state solvent, new direct taxes were imposed on sales and on luxuries such as liquor, wine, beer, and tobacco, and an income tax was instituted. Arizona joined the nation in repealing the prohibition amendment. Overwhelmingly re-elected in 1934, Dr. Moeur was discouraged by the economic crisis that could not be overcome by any authority vested in state government. Consistent with Arizona's efforts to retain its legacy and independent action in Colorado River matters, Governor Moeur sent a unit of the Arizona National Guard to stop construction of the Parker Dam, by which water was to be diverted to Los Angeles. A quick United States Supreme Court response led to embarrassed withdrawal of the Arizona troops. In 1936 Dr. Moeur was eliminated in the primary election in a campaign which callously and erroneously blamed him for the sales tax which had been adopted to save the state from bankruptcy.

Rawghlie C. Stanford: A former county judge, Stanford was the primary victor at a time when Democratic nomination was tantamount to a cakewalk in the general election. Like Phillips, he was a self-educated lawyer who had been a cowboy and a miner and served in the Spanish-American War. Even though economic conditions were a bit better, Stanford's term was hectic and disappointing, unfortunately because of his gentle, patient insistence upon personally talking with everybody who asked for an audience. Carryover officials from the previous regime malevolently urged job seekers to gather in the governor's office, adding to his troubles. He refused a second term, but later was elected to the Arizona Supreme Court for two terms.

Robert T. Jones: Robert T. Jones, who had come to Arizona as a construction engineer and later been a druggist and member of the state senate from Pinal and Maricopa counties, succeeded Stanford and also decided that one term in the embattled governor's office was sufficient. Paradoxically, Jones found his effectiveness and strong political skills impaired by close comradeship with former colleagues in the state senate, a fact which denied him adequate support in the lower house.

Sidney P. Osborn: The next governor, Democrat Sidney P. Osborn, thrived on controversy. At age twenty-four he was the youngest delegate to the constitutional convention, then was elected to three terms as the state's first secretary of state. Osborn frankly and proudly made politics his career, recalling that his father had been a page in the first territorial legislature in 1864. First achieving the governorship in 1940, Osborn was elected to four consecutive terms, a feat beyond the accomplishments even of Hunt. He used his popularity to muster support for programs he advocated and made part of the party's platform, turning to the radio to bring pressure upon the legislature. Upon his firm insistence, the lawmaking body in 1944 ratified the Colorado River Compact at last, abandoning Arizona's obstructionist role. This success was followed in his fourth term by the first effort to conserve underground water as part of the state's irrigation resources and the creation of the Interstate Stream Commission to bring Colorado River water into central Arizona. Arizona had gained economically during the war boom. As industrialization and employment increased with the return of peace, voters in 1946 approved an initiative measure to end compulsory union membership in Arizona, called the right-to-work law. Two attempts by organized labor forces to repeal that measure at subsequent general elections were rejected, each time with an increased vote for its continuation. During the last two years of Osborn's service it became apparent that the governor was critically ill, dying of amyotrophic lateral sclerosis, but he courageously continued to work as well as he could until a few weeks before his death on May 25, 1948.

Dan E. Garvey: Secretary of State Dan Garvey of Tucson became governor upon the death of Osborn, as he also had acceded to the secretary's post with the death of Harry M. Moore two years earlier.

In November of 1948 Garvey was elected to a full two-year term. An amiable and polite gentleman, Garvey was unaggressive, with little taste for the rough-and-tumble controversy in which Osborn delighted. In the 1950 primary campaign he was edged out by the effective and popular state auditor, Ana Frohmiller, who had achieved strong support through well-publicized thrusts against petty waste in state government.

BROADENED POLITICAL HORIZONS

The campaign of 1950 was a turning point in Arizona politics, ending a Democratic regime that had been interrupted only by Campbell and Phillips in thirty-eight years of statehood. Arizona had become emphatically Democratic in registration, overwhelming opposition about five to one. Although much of Arizona's population gain came from states with better political balance, newcomers often registered with the Democratic party because the Republican party seldom presented a full ticket for voters' choice, although closet Republicans emerged in strength at the general election to vote their party's skimpy state ballot. By registering Democratic, citizens could participate in a viable primary and still cast a ballot for a Republican governor and members of Congress. In presidential election years there was generally a brief GOP revival.

Two Democrats of strong personality had dominated the political scene since the first election of state officers in 1911. While Governor Hunt ruled the statehouse for much of that time, in the first election he actually had placed second in popularity to Carl Hayden of Tempe.

Hayden was a pragmatist who practiced partisan political regularity coupled with flexibility on issues of importance, patterned after the success enjoyed by Marcus A. Smith as Arizona's long-time territorial delegate. To assure his popularity and re-election, Smith once told Hayden that he always tested the political wind at home before taking a stand on Capitol Hill. Thus he avoided alienating blocs of voters as public opinion shifted due to fluctuating economic or political factors. Hayden served in the House of Representatives seven terms, 1912 to 1926, when growing discontent with Republican Senator Ralph H. Cameron convinced Hayden he could defeat Cameron and step up to the Senate, where the six-year term eliminated campaigning every other year.

There was little love lost between Hunt and Hayden, the former a willful common man while Hayden was the product of an educated family with overtones of New England and southern formality. Carl Hayden himself was never a confirmed western-type horseman or guntoter, even as sheriff. Their personal coolness never became public knowledge, probably because political acumen led them to override such feelings. As perennial Democratic candidates they frequently campaigned together, often traveling in the same automobile from town to town for political rallies. Simultaneously they developed strong but separate interests in the Good Roads movement, leaving as evidence of their combined devotion to that issue an excellent highway system in Arizona. Hunt promoted the internal system, linking the state capital to outlying county seats, while Hayden early saw that increased automobile travel and the long distances in Arizona would impose upon the state an intolerable financial burden to construct roads to link up with transcontinental systems. Adroitly joining forces with congressmen interested in farm-to-market roads, Hayden early threw his energies into support and enhancement of the federal-aid highway program that enabled Arizona to keep pace with major construction that otherwise it could not have financed.

Hunt was in his tomb in Papago Park and Hayden was secure in the United States Senate as Republicans began the uphill fight that converted the Democratic fiefdom into a genuine two-party system. Rugged determination by elder statesmen of the long-recumbent Republican party in Arizona was coupled to the vigor and enthusiasm of fresh blood to put a new face in the statehouse. These groups stimulated a shift toward more balance in party registration, with the Republican resurgence bringing greater responsibility to state office than was possible in the good-old-boy days of one-party rule.

Howard Pyle: Complacency had settled over the Democratic party. The nomination of the capable and popular Ana Frohmiller found the party organization in shambles, unprepared for a vigorous general-election campaign. In contrast, the Republicans presented a fresh cast with an attractive radio announcer, Howard Pyle of Tempe, as its candidate for governor. For months Pyle hit every town and crossroads in the state in an aggressive flying campaign directed by Barry Goldwater, wartime pilot, head of a pioneer mercantile family, organizer of the integrated Arizona Air National Guard, and member of a new reform city council in Phoenix. Governor Osborn two years earlier had appointed Goldwater to the new Interstate Stream Commission, hoping to develop the Colorado River for Arizona's beneficial use. Goldwater first had been introduced to the basics of Arizona politics by his uncle, Morris Goldwater, venerable Prescott merchant and banker, one of the founders of the Democratic party in Arizona, several times member of territorial and state legislatures, vice-president of the constitutional convention, and for thirty-six years mayor of Prescott.

While the Democrats conducted a desultory campaign, Pyle vigorously exploited the right-to-work issue. Without ever criticizing and hardly ever mentioning his opponent, Pyle kept the campaign on a warm, hopeful, and positive note, and won the election by 3,000 votes. Possessed of patience, a melodious voice, and a strong religious background, Pyle found his gentle efforts to strengthen the executive branch of state government thwarted by the overwhelming Democratic character of the legislature, even though eleven Republicans had been elected to the house in his victory campaign. The ruling Democrats had paranoid fears that efforts to improve governmental efficiency were tampering with the constitution their party claimed as its supreme contribution to Arizona. Governor Hunt himself had found the progressive constitution imperfect, asking for stronger executive authority in the first state legislature in 1912 and for major reorganization in 1927. Campbell in 1921 and Moeur in 1933 had been similarly frustrated. Finding that the legislative branch had an excessive clout over the governor and elected officials, the Republicans began recruiting candidates for house and senate seats throughout the state. That search was a significant state effort spearheaded in 1952 by Dwight Eisenhower's election as president.

Goldwater, after serving as Pyle's campaign manager in 1950, jumped into the 1952 campaign for the United States Senate, challenging Ernest W. McFarland of Florence, who in 1940 had stunningly defeated Henry Fountain Ashurst. Grief-stricken by the death of his wife, Ashurst had conducted a half-hearted campaign. McFarland had been an effective cloakroom senator, and at the time of his defeat was the short-lived Senate majority leader. Teamed with Goldwater and Pyle in the 1952 campaign—all of them cozying close to Ike's coattails—was John J. Rhodes of Mesa, a young lawyer, native of Kansas, who was among a horde of military personnel determined to remain in Arizona after war service. Rhodes upset the veteran Tempe educator John R. Murdock for a House seat, Pyle won an easy second victory, and Goldwater bumped McFarland from the Senate. The election of thirty Republicans in the lower house and four to the state senate finally brought Arizona closer to a two-party system.

Howard Pyle made considerable progress in his two terms, but the governor's popularity suffered a severe setback prior to his 1954 bid for a third term when, because of widespread abuse of welfare programs, he dispatched a large force of highway patrolmen to Short Creek in the far northwest corner of the state on a raid upon a small sect of polygamists. The group was an outlawed offshoot of the Mormon church, which had repudiated plural marriage in 1890. Still, the tone of criticism aimed at the dissidents offended many persons of the Mormon faith who themselves were descended from plural families. Pyle was defeated by former Senator McFarland and left Arizona to become an administrative assistant to President Eisenhower and later president of the National Safety Council.

Ernest W. McFarland: New welfare, development, and recreational programs were approved during McFarland's term with the momentum generated by the infusion of active Republicans into the legislature, although Democrats had regained a few seats lost to the opposition in the Eisenhower landslide. After two terms as governor McFarland attempted in 1958 to regain the Senate seat held by Goldwater. Rejected, he later was elected to the Arizona Supreme Court, thus becoming the only person to serve Arizona in such a variety of offices: county judge, United States senator, governor, and Supreme Court justice. He followed his public service career as owner of a Phoenix television station.

Paul J. Fannin: In the 1958 campaign, during which Goldwater defeated McFarland for the second time, one of the senator's boyhood friends, Paul J. Fannin, best known as a softball player and retired from business at age fifty-one, entered the race for the vacant governor's chair. Openly expressing admiration for Goldwater conservatism, Fannin was arrayed against a former attorney general who had changed his name after leaving California and a youthful miscue with a bad check. Fannin took speaking lessons to overcome his shyness and plunged into his duties with astounding energy and obvious sincerity. He was as surprising as governor as he had been as an unknown candidate. With unusual courage and candor he selected members of both political parties for appointment to state boards and commissions. He dismissed criticism of the strategy within his own party, explaining that as a minority party the Republicans had to depend upon Democrats for victory in elections, so likewise should include them in providing improved government services. Fannin was more successful than any governor before him in obtaining the services and skills of outstanding business and financial leaders to work on programs of statewide interest, especially in promoting industrial development in Arizona and friendly trade with Mexico. His association with the legislature likewise proceeded generally with cooperation and mutual respect. The voting pattern in Arizona had crystallized into a two-party system in the postwar rush of population.

During the 1960 Republican national convention Governor Fannin nominated Goldwater for president as a favorite-son candidate, a maneuver of admiration by the Arizona delegation which the senator immediately rejected. By 1964 the idea that the outspoken Arizona senator might provide the nation with dynamic leadership had grown into a grassroots demand which Goldwater finally accepted, largely out of concern about the growing national debt, internal discord, and the declining military structure of the nation in a hostile world. Goldwater resigned his seat in the United States Senate (to which Fannin was elected). Although he polled twenty-seven million votes, incumbent President Lyndon B. Johnson overwhelmed the Arizonan in a sympathetic Electoral College vote only about a year after the assassination of John F. Kennedy.

As Fannin moved on to Washington, where he served two terms characterized by intense working habits and mounting effectiveness in the field of energy legislation, the governor's office was up for grabs again.

Samuel P. Goddard: Lawyer Sam Goddard of Tucson, who also had come to Arizona in the military service and later studied law at the University of Arizona and Harvard, won the governorship as a liberal with strong support from labor unions and minorities. Although he had been active in community affairs and in social welfare and youth activities, the handsome Goddard suffered from a penchant for creating political discord and was a one-term governor.

Jack Williams: Jack Williams, another Republican radio announcer and former Phoenix mayor who had developed a wide following with a career of friendly boosterism and a readiness to compromise, occupied the governor's office for three terms. During the Williams regime the Republican party achieved a new pinnacle of strength in Arizona, gaining control of both houses of the legislature as well as a majority of statehouse elective offices. Under this impetus a constitutional change was voted, extending what was then the two-year term of office for major state officials to four years, thus reducing the frequency and expense of elections. The consolidation of many state offices, sought for decades, was achieved, strengthening the executive branch of government.

Raul Castro: Governor Williams's decision to retire to private life made the 1974 election a wide-open affair, with victory going to Democrat Raul Castro, born in poverty in Mexico. After his father came to the United States as a smelter worker, Raul obtained a college education, in part through his earnings as a professional boxer. In the Kennedy administration he had served as ambassador to two Latin American nations. Castro was elected Arizona's first four-year governor, but his first two years in office were stormy. His impulsiveness and the heavy pressure for political favors from ethnic supporters led him to resign and return to the diplomatic world.

Wesley A. Bolin: When Castro resigned as governor in October 1977 to accept an ambassadorship to Argentina, Wesley A. Bolin, who had been a popular, smiling, and trouble-free secretary of state since 1949, became governor. The new governor died in his sleep six months later on March 4, 1978.

Bruce Babbitt: Next in succession under revised Arizona law was the dynamic, articulate, and active young attorney general, Bruce Babbitt. Third-generation member of a pioneer mercantile family that had come to Arizona from Ohio in the 1880s and become dominant and powerful as cattle and sheep raisers, Indian traders, owner of wholesale and retail food and department stores, and other business enterprises, Bruce Babbitt was educated first as a geologist at Notre Dame and in England and then studied law at Harvard.

Coming into office at age thirty-five, younger than any other Arizona governor, Babbitt had an avid interest in art, history, and political science, bringing to the governorship great talent and confidence. In the 1978 election, running for a full term, he received 282,605 votes, a margin of more than 40,000 over a veteran Republican campaigner. That total, more than Governor Hunt had received in eight elections, was indicative of the astounding growth in Arizona's population in sixty-six years, but also was a reflection of the popularity of the articulate but somewhat authoritarian Babbitt, marking him as a possible major political figure in Arizona's future.

HALLS OF CONGRESS

During the first three decades of statehood Arizona had only one member in the national House of Representatives. Carl Hayden held the office through 1926, followed by Lewis W. Douglas, son of Rawhide Jimmy Douglas, head of the Phelps Dodge mining corporation. Douglas resigned in 1933 to become director of the budget in Roosevelt's New Deal circles, and Isabella Selmes Greenway, widow of mining engineer John C. Greenway, whose statue was erected in the halls of Congress during her incumbency, replaced him. Mrs. Greenway had been a bridesmaid at the wedding of Eleanor and Franklin

Roosevelt, and later had moved to Arizona, where she raised cattle and owned a pioneer airline.

From 1937 until 1943 John R. Murdock, history professor and dean of Arizona State Teachers College (now Arizona State University), was the lone representative and continued to win elections until defeated in 1952 in the first district (then composed entirely of Maricopa County) by John J. Rhodes, the first Republican to sit in the House from Arizona since statehood. A second Arizona seat was first held by Richard F. Harless, Phoenix attorney, for three years (1943–6) until he retired to seek the governorship. Harold A. Patten (1949–55) and Stewart L. Udall of Tucson (1955–61) consecutively held the post until 1961, when President Kennedy appointed Udall his Secretary of the Interior, a political reward for the support of the Arizona delegation at the 1960 Democratic convention. Udall's resignation from the House brought his brother, Morris K. Udall, into office as his successor, a seat Mo has held continuously since 1961. Seeing the need for reform in internal procedures in the House of Representatives, in 1969, after only eight years of service, Udall daringly challenged four-term Speaker John McCormack for leadership of the House—the first contested election for nomination to the speakership since 1923. Udall's Democratic colleagues slapped down his attempt by a vote of 178 to 58. He also subsequently lost the 1971 contest for majority leader to Hale Boggs. Unabashed, and growing in stature as a bold and articulate liberal, Udall in 1976 ventured into the presidential primaries against Jimmy Carter. Although defeated again, he remained unbowed, exercising growing power through accumulated seniority and witty self-criticism.

Population gains in the decennial censuses of 1960 and 1970 allotted Arizona additional congressional seats and provided opportunities for Democrat George F. Senner, Jr., of Globe (1963–67) and the arrival of two Republicans, Sam Steiger of Prescott (1967–77) and John B. Conlan of Phoenix (1972–77). Steiger, a Brooklyn native who came west to be either a cowboy or a veterinarian but instead became a racetrack announcer and a trouble-ridden congressman, and Conlan, the dapper son of famed baseball umpire Jocko Conlan, vacated their seats in the House to oppose each other in a bitter primary fight for the United States Senate in 1976 as Fannin returned to private life.

Both lost as Democrat Dennis DeConcini of Tucson, son of an Arizona Supreme Court justice during the Osborn regime, won the seat.

This opened two seats, which were won by Democrat Bob Stump, a conservative Tolleson rancher and past president of the state senate, and Republican Eldon Rudd of Camp Verde, a former Marine pilot, lawyer, and FBI agent.

Meanwhile John J. Rhodes and Mo Udall have through hard work and the seniority system risen to prominent positions within their parties and the Congress. Both have aspired to be speaker of the House. Rhodes in December 1973 was elected minority leader by his Republican colleagues, a position of prestige and power second only to speaker. Seniority brought Udall the chairmanship of the House Interior and Insular Affairs Committee, a position of vital importance to a state such as Arizona, where more than seventy-five percent of the area is in federal ownership or control.

Although Arizona's representation in the House and Senate often has been divided between the parties, on issues of paramount concern to the state—such as irrigation, mining, and the development of industry and of natural resources—members of the Arizona delegation almost invariably have overlooked partisan differences to work together for the state's needs.

After losing the race for president in 1964, Barry Goldwater waited until Carl Hayden announced his retirement from the Senate before asking Arizona voters to return him to Washington. Out of respect and personal admiration for Hayden's unparalleled service to Arizona and his seniority, which was of major importance in Arizona's long struggle for the Central Arizona Project, Goldwater was unwilling to oppose Hayden in any way. In 1962, when Hayden ran for the last time and was vulnerable because of failing strength, both Senator Goldwater and Governor Fannin threw their political favor to Hayden, refusing to support a Republican candidate against the prominent Arizona statesman.

Just as Hayden for most of his tenure was Arizona's most revered lawmaker and his office was the focus of the state's concerns and interests in Washington, Goldwater during his career from 1952 until the present has become Mr. Arizona, a fearless, fighting champion of personal and states' rights and enemy of concentration of federal controls. Goldwater's charisma, his personal generosity and many philanthropies, combined with his insistence upon conservation of taxpayers' money, his patriotic support of American military superiority, and his outspoken courage in defiance of bureaucracy, opposition to an increased federal debt, and defiance even of his party's leaders, won him unchallengeable bipartisan support at home. At the end of World War II he took a reduction in rank from major to captain to organize the Arizona Air National Guard, demanding that it be an integrated unit. As a photographer of international recognition, he had as a young man made thousands of pictures of the Navajo Indians and had flown his private plane throughout their vast interior domain on missions of mercy and because of love for the Navajo people, only to find tribal political leadership arrayed against him when in the interest of justice he sided with the equally commendable Hopi Indians in the mid-1970s in the century-old protest against intrusion of Navajo herdsmen upon Hopi lands. Despite such affronts to his devotion to his native state and its cultural riches, Goldwater remained unembittered by such idiosyncrasies of political life.

A few days past his seventy-first birthday on January 1, 1980, Goldwater announced he would seek a fifth term in the United States Senate, hoping thereby to help return the nation to its former position of leadership, to aid in re-establishing prudence and thrift and productivity which have made the nation the envy of the world, and to help make the nation militarily strong again. Unstated was his desire to prevent the kind of harmful partisan struggle for his vacant seat that had followed Senator Fannin's retirement a few years earlier. Goldwater often remarked that he shared with his Uncle Morris, a founder of the Democratic party in Arizona, the conviction that responsible citizens should pay rent through public service for the opportunities and success accorded them, and that as long as he retained personal vigor he would offer his native state a measure of his service in gratitude for the opportunities his family had received in the forty-eighth state.

ARIZONA ATTAINS MATURITY

In the first half of the century after it acquired civil government as a territory Arizona struggled manfully to join the family of states as a full partner. It was annoyed by the indifference of some of the governors imposed upon it by "carpetbag rule" of the federal government in distant Washington. It sought, as the founding fathers had, a greater measure of representation. It opposed but finally submitted to compromises demanded by Congress and a strong-willed president as the price of statehood. Having attained self-rule, it relished a moment of sweet revenge at the expense of President Taft, and then faced the more serious responsibilities ahead.

It learned, all too soon, that independence was more a dream than a reality. In a land of vast federal domain, great distances, and sparse population it found itself unable to survive by its own resources. The cherished self-reliance of pioneers could not cope with all the complex problems in a nation becoming, both within and without its borders, steadily more interdependent in a shrinking world. Arizona entered the Union as a state at a time when the federalism of the founding fathers—the ideal of home rule in partnership with a union of independent states—gradually was being dissolved.

To build the roads it needed, Arizona willingly joined the Good Roads movement with its standardization and funding from Washington; it saw its great grazing lands and scenic wonders placed under federal control for management and administration; its irrigation development and water conservation were dependent upon federal financial resources; its copper industry, to survive, needed protection from cheap imports; its shippers required lower freight rates. Arizona had waited a half-century for greater freedom from federal rule only to pass through a first seventy years of statehood with federal controls increasing.

Forced to compromise to attain statehood, Arizona learned to accommodate to changing times. It shared the great westward sweep of population. It learned that home elections were no universal guarantee of steadfast public officials. It coveted the freedom of self-taxation without realizing any lasting enjoyment in carrying the self-imposed burden. It learned that its constitution, although progressive, was not infallible, and made a few vital changes while recognizing the need for others. It made progress, but not without sacrifices and suffering. It borrowed ideas from other states while attempting to retain individuality even as the pressures of conformity were sweeping over a world with the speed of jet power and the reach of radio and laser beams. It learned that responsibility increases speedily with the emergence from youth into maturity. But it could count its blessings: most of its governors had been honest and dedicated men. Its legislatures had been restrained but compassionate. It placed one native son in the federal cabinet; a second in the most respected position an American can attain in the United States Senate; and favored a third as a candidate for president. Two Arizonans have been appointed to the Supreme Court. Serving on the high court with William Rehnquist is Sandra Day O'Connor, the first woman to achieve this distinction. Another woman, Margaret Hance, is serving her third term as mayor of Phoenix, which by 1980 was the ninth-largest city in the nation. Ahead Arizona could see promising new horizons, and behind it a history so rich in accomplishment that it needs no fabrication or exaggeration to stir pride in every citizen.

17

The Desert Blossoms

In His infinite wisdom God gave Arizona more sunshine but less rainfall than any other state. Mankind, through ingenuity, struggle, and necessity, sought to overcome that disparity and, by and large, has done very well in making this parched land habitable, productive, and attractive. Anthropologists elsewhere may argue avidly that fire, the wheel, iron, the bow and arrow, flight, or taxation was the most significant of man's inventions. In Arizona they could reach an easy consensus that the greatest achievement of man in the Western world was the discovery that the seed of a very simple, wild plant in subtropical America could be put in a hole in the ground, and that with the blessing of rain a new plant with larger seeds would emerge from that effort. Thus Indian maize, the white man's corn, was the first cultivated plant in the Americas. From man's delight in its taste and nutrition, and therefore his need for more maize or corn, he learned to irrigate. Without irrigation there would be no Arizona.

EARLY IRRIGATION

The first Europeans to arrive in Arizona, Coronado's legion, found Indians living along streams in southern Arizona cultivating crops of corn, beans, squash, and melons. As the conquistadors moved into the mountains north of the Gila River, they encountered tiny patches of corn and squash growing on low riverbank terraces, even though no dwellings existed to mark the sites as permanent habitations. Many nomadic Indian bands supplemented their hunting skills and gathering labors with seasonal cultivation of crops at places where subsurface moisture would support growth.

During the mission period and into the early nineteenth century Spanish priests added many cereals, vegetables, and fruits to the native diet. The Spaniards had learned oasis or strip cultivation from their African-Moorish masters during the long Iberian occupation that finally ended in 1492, the year of Columbus's arrival in the Americas. The Spaniards marveled at the similarity of the technique to divert water from streams used in Mother Spain and that found in the New World. Weirs or dams were constructed of brush and rocks to raise the water level, allowing it to flow across fertile soil deposited by the floods of the distant past. The newcomers called these water channels *acequias,* a word of Arabian origin. Men responsible for delivery of water to fields were known as *zanjeros* (literally, ditch diggers), another word reminiscent of pomegranates growing near the Alhambra. When Anglo pioneers began planting crops along Arizona's streams in the interim between the War with Mexico and the Civil War, they simply called the ditches canals and the zanjeros reverted to water tenders or ditch riders. In this early farming phase in Arizona history, settlers frequently cleaned out old canals built by the long-forgotten Indian irrigators identified in Arizona as the Hohokams. These prehistoric Indians had dug hundreds of miles of canals radiating out from the Salt and Gila rivers in central Arizona. These river valleys again became the breadbasket of Arizona with accelerated white settlement prior to 1900.

As Arizona mountains yielded their hidden mineral wealth, Arizona's population grew. To feed the hungry miners and those serving their everyday needs, as well as the soldiers brought to subdue the Indian resistance to this invasion of their homeland, more farmers came, more canals were dug, and more fields were put into cultivation. The engineering problems that had defied Indian peoples who had no domestic sources of energy other than their own muscle applied to stone hoes were soon overcome by steel plows, steam power, and then internal-combustion engines of the white man.

FEDERALIZING RECLAMATION

The National Reclamation Act in 1902 overcame the financial barriers that had inhibited pioneer farmers from full development of available water resources through construction of permanent storage dams. The new federal reclamation program provided a revolving fund by which undertakings in the West (such as the model Salt River Valley project) could borrow the enormous capital needed for major construction and development. The Bureau of Reclamation was created in the Department of the Interior to evaluate and make engineering studies of projects, to build, and then to operate those authorized by Congress until management was shifted to local authorities. The resultant storage reservoirs prevented floods which previously had washed out dams and canals, and at the same time they saved for summer use water that earlier had destroyed downstream fields and delivery systems before being wasted in the sea.

The Salt River Valley Water Users' Association, organized in 1903, allowed owners of eleven private and cooperative canals in the Salt River Valley around Phoenix to pool their water rights and form a corporate body to accept and repay a federal mortgage of $11 million placed upon their land. That price tag was the cost of the Theodore Roosevelt Dam and its ancillary works—three times the original estimate, but a sum totally repaid to the federal treasury by 1955.

By the time the masonry of the dam was completed and dedicated by its namesake on March 18, 1911, on the eve of statehood, most flowing streams within Arizona had been utilized for agricultural use. The Roosevelt Dam stored flood water for about 250,000 acres in the Salt River Valley. Later its resources would be augmented and stabilized by construction of three supplemental dams downstream on the Salt River and by two more on the Verde. Weir-type dams on the upper Gila fed a thriving farming community centered on Safford. Both Indians and whites irrigated from the Gila River west of Florence, and farther downstream near Gila Bend the privately constructed Gillespie Dam provided another desert oasis. Since Spanish times the Santa Cruz River between Nogales on the international border and Picacho Peak had been marked with small fields. At St. David on the San Pedro were similar subsistence farms, and the early

Mormon settlements along the Little Colorado River and Silver Creek managed to hang on despite frequent seasonal washouts of their insecure dams.

TAMING THE COLORADO

There were still millions of unwatered but fertile acres in Arizona, plus almost as many dreams by men who wished to make the untended desert blossom like the rose. Along the western border of Arizona flowed the mighty Colorado, wasting in an average year more than fifteen million acre-feet of water that flowed into the Gulf of California. A fraction of that total was diverted by Laguna Dam near Yuma, completed in 1907, for irrigation partly in Arizona but mostly in the Imperial Valley of southern California, with some left over for crops near the northern border of Baja California in Mexico. As early as 1875 there had been serious talk of bringing Colorado River water to beneficial use in Arizona. Delegate Charles D. Poston ten years earlier had first thrust Uncle Sam into the irrigation business by wheedling a small appropriation for an Indian irrigation project on the Mohave and Chemehuevi reservation north of La Paz. But because of engineering mistakes this effort did not pan out very well.

The startling success of the Salt River Valley project and similar if smaller developments in Utah, Wyoming, and Colorado excited national interest toward full development of the Colorado River. Regional water resource conferences in 1919 and 1920 culminated in 1922 in the Santa Fe Conference, convened under the chairmanship of Secretary of Commerce Herbert Hoover. Representatives of all states in the river's drainage met to draw up an agreement, known as the Santa Fe Compact, for equal division of water between upper basin states (Utah, Colorado, Wyoming, and New Mexico) and the lower basin states (Arizona, Nevada, and California).

Because Arizona alone of the lower basin states contributed substantially to the Colorado River through the drainage of the Little Colorado, Bill Williams Fork, and the Gila-Salt system (while only a few trickles came off the hills of Nevada and California into the Colorado River), Arizona promoters and partisans began developing elaborate plans for farming the vast desert plains extending nearly to the Mexican border. Arizonans expected that their state would draw from the river in proportion to its relative input. The Santa Fe Compact was drafted during the last months of the Thomas E. Campbell administration. When Governor Hunt returned to power in January 1923, he opposed ratification of the compact, and maintained steadfast opposition to cooperative development of the Colorado River throughout his lifetime. Hunt asserted the plan did not guarantee Arizona all the water to which the state was entitled. Two stronger, but then unstated, rationales for his obstructionist position have been identified: one was partisan, the other personal. Governor Hunt opposed the compact initially because it had been conceived during a Republican administration. Moreover, Hunt's close friend and political ally Fred T. Colter of Apache County was promoting an imaginative plan calling for several dams in Arizona between the Utah border and the Nevada line, plus a science-fiction scheme of water delivery to the huge desert plains and valleys, envisaging consumption of the major portion of the water in the river. Colter was to spend a tidy personal fortune and the rest of his life attempting to establish his Highline Canal system as Arizona's official water program. His greatest concession to reality was to modify it frequently as engineering flaws in his concepts were revealed.

For two decades Arizona resisted development of the river by lower basin states. It halted its squabbling with the Bureau of Reclamation and the federal government over the Colorado River long enough to lobby for the San Carlos Project, which Senators Hayden and Ashurst achieved despite the negativism of the Hunt political machine. Waters stored behind Coolidge Dam on the Gila River at the southwest corner of the San Carlos Indian Reservation, dedicated by Silent Cal in 1930, irrigated both Indian and non-Indian lands on the south side of the Gila River in Pinal County.

The spectacular Hoover Dam was built despite Arizona's strenuous objections, providing a new important source of hydroelectric power, guaranteeing freedom from flood damage on the lower river, and creating behind the dam an unexcelled recreational facility as well as a storage basin which retains nearly two years' flow of the river. Generators in its powerhouse intended for Arizona's benefit remained idle as long as the state retained its obdurate attitude. A breakthrough came in 1940, with a proposal from engineer James G. Girand of Phoenix for a Central Arizona Authority, a plan for Colorado River water use which eliminated much of the traditional opposition by incorporating within the concept the useful features of Colter's Highline Canal plan.

CENTRAL ARIZONA PROJECT

The Interstate Stream Commission formed in 1944 seized upon the Central Arizona Project as a practical plan that could unify divergent petty forces and meet the growing need for additional water for agriculture, for cities and towns, and for the mining industry revitalized by the demand for copper in the European war. Colter's unapproved plan was a dream of Camelot. Although homesteading had virtually stopped in 1895, he appealed to persons who hoped to develop new farms on the raw desert with water to be delivered by enormous tunnels as much as ninety miles long reaching from Marble Canyon or the Grand Canyon to the upper Verde River and then into the river basins in the lower desert. His personal fortune exhausted, Colter in his weary, declining years sometimes collected ten cents an acre from owners of desert land in hope they could obtain water from his Highline Canal Project.

Designers of the Central Arizona Project expected it to transport water from the Colorado River into central Arizona via a system of pumps and aqueducts. Its purpose was not to increase irrigated agriculture in Arizona, but to stabilize and protect it from abandonment. The project was to supplement water resources for irrigated lands already producing wealth for the state with winter vegetables, citrus, sugar beet seed, hay, cotton, and other crops for which there was a national need and a ready market. Cities and towns dependent upon pumps for domestic water were finding underground water tables dropping so deep that the cost of pumping was prohibitive, and so they too would benefit from increased water availability.

The Bureau of Reclamation endorsed the feasibility of the project. It justified federal funding because of the huge costs involved and the benefits of the plan to divert water from the Colorado, an interstate stream under federal control. Bills to authorize the Central Arizona Project were introduced in Congress. The Senate voted favorably, responding to the urging of Senators Hayden and McFarland, but the House of Representatives—where California's greater numerical strength was an enormous advantage—turned down Arizona's hopes. Even so, congressional leaders decided in conference with the Arizona congressional delegation that Arizona's right to use water of the Colorado River required legal confirmation. Arizona had to fight in the courts and in the media for a dozen years, during which obstructionists raised tangential new objections to the program, some of which linger on beyond the resolution of the legal question.

Once Arizona in 1944 had decided upon a course of cooperation with the federal government and other states, its citizens and congressional delegation could support supplemental Colorado River development programs while awaiting legal confirmation of Arizona's water entitlement. Between Parker and Hoover dams an earth-and-rock dam was constructed in 1951, called Davis Dam, to provide additional storage to fulfill American treaty obligations to deliver some of the river's flow to Mexico. The dam impounds Lake Mohave, which laps almost against the foundations of the powerhouse below Hoover Dam and adds substantially to rich fishing grounds created along the river channel. The small Imperial Dam later was built a few miles above Laguna Dam to assist in diversion of water for projects in the lower valleys. The Wellton-Mohawk Project on the Gila River east of Yuma was authorized and constructed after World War II, pumping water from the Colorado and carrying it by canals to the valley of the Gila to bring more fertile land into production. Some of the citrus groves there were abandoned in the mid-1970s so that Arizona could deliver less-saline waste water to Mexican farms below Yuma. (It is a little-known fact that much of this Mexican land is controlled by Americans.)

Far upstream on the Colorado River, between Father Escalante's 1776 Crossing of the Fathers and Lee's Ferry, which Mormons used in their migration to the warm valleys of Arizona, the federal government next built the Glen Canyon Dam and close to it the town of Page. The new dam, providing storage and hydroelectric power, is a marvel of engineering skill equal to Hoover Dam. Behind it Lake

Powell stretches nearly 200 miles into Utah, creating a recreational facility even more sensational than Lake Mead behind Hoover Dam.

Arizona filed suit against California to seek a Supreme Court decision on Arizona's share of water from the Colorado River. California, choosing to ignore and exceed its own statutory limitation of 4.4 million acre-feet of water per year, attempted to erase Arizona's allocation of 2.8 million acre-feet from the river's main stream by asserting Arizona had withdrawn that amount by internal use and by reuse of Gila River water. This obstacle to cooperative development was the main point to be clarified in court. Prolonged hearings were held and arguments continued from 1958 until 1963, during which period a Special Master heard the evidence and arguments. Ultimately he endorsed Arizona's position; the Supreme Court confirmed the opinion on March 9, 1964. Four busy years later, after much compromising on details and heroic work by Arizona's water users and its congressional delegates, who worked together and with other states, Congress approved the Central Arizona Project. President Lyndon Johnson signed the enabling legislation on September 30, 1968.

TANGLES TO PROGRESS

Inconceivable new problems arose before actual construction could begin. New federal environmental protection laws created complex problems requiring that endangered species of flora and fauna, archeological remains, and historical sites be protected from adverse impacts of the undertaking. Intensified and overdue national concern for the sensitivities and cultural heritage of Indian bands that had roamed or occupied the path of the aqueducts and the basins of proposed storage reservoirs created a new set of impediments. Increased political power among Native Americans induced the Secretary of the Interior to require that a major portion of Arizona's water allocation be assigned to Indian reservations, where white lessees can be expected to cultivate these public lands with low-cost Indian water, free of certain tax obligations and controls to which competing farmers on non-Indian private lands are subject. Recreational uses, such as skiing and tubing on rivers, often were conceived as having priority over agricultural, domestic, and industrial uses of water.

In addition, abstract and idealistic conservation arguments have frequently swept aside contemporary needs of established communities and productive enterprises.

Despite all these new problems, construction of the Central Arizona Project began in 1973 with work on the inlet basin, high-lift pumping plant, and tunnel through Buckskin Mountain two and a half miles above Parker Dam on the Bill Williams arm of Lake Havasu. In the first five years appropriations for planning and construction reached nearly $500 million. Construction was concentrated on the 190-mile-long Granite Reef Aqueduct to deliver water from Lake Havasu into the Phoenix metropolitan area, with first delivery scheduled for 1985 in Maricopa and Pinal counties and to Tucson in Pima County by 1987. The pumping plant at the Colorado River will lift water more than 800 feet to pour it into the open aqueduct which will carry it toward Phoenix, during which four smaller pumping stations, two tunnels, and several siphons will convey it over mountains and under streambeds for a total pump lift of about 1,200 feet. A somewhat smaller aqueduct will convey water south of the Salt to the Gila River, and then on to a storage basin near Picacho Peak, from which point it will finish its journey to Tucson in an underground conduit system. The project has the capacity to deliver 1.2 million acre-feet of water annually to agricultural, community, and industrial users, who will develop their own delivery systems from the aqueduct. It will provide supplemental water for established farming areas as well as municipal and industrial water for metropolitan areas.

For three decades massive overpumping of underground water resources caused an overdraft as groundwater levels declined an average of eight to ten feet per year with serious land subsidence occurring in several areas, mostly in Pinal County. Pumping will be sharply reduced as Colorado River water is introduced into the central valleys, conserving both energy and water.

President Jimmy Carter in 1977 recommended elimination of three supportive dams within the Central Arizona Project, and, even more significantly, he asked that federal funding for construction be contingent upon further study of groundwater supplies and the adoption of groundwater pumping regulations and management by the State of Arizona. The 1980 state legislature moved quickly to conform to this federal requirement.

Pumping on a large scale was originally a conservation measure. In ancient times the irrigated valleys of the Salt and Gila rivers became nonproductive and were abandoned by the Hohokam Indians as constant irrigation resulted in waterlogging. As the subsurface became saturated with water, alkali and salts invaded the root area of growing plants, killing all growth and poisoning the earth. With modern irrigation of the Salt River Valley, which began in the winter of 1867–68, less than half a century had gone by before similar waterlogging curtailed production on both sides of the Salt River from Mesa westward to Tolleson. The Salt River Valley Project and the independent Tempe Canal Company, with assistance from the Bureau of Reclamation, sank wells which by pumping lowered the water table, allowing the surface soil to be leached of alkali and crop production to be resumed, while pumped water was conveyed to bordering desert lands where new crops previously had been impossible because of a lack of surface water. Thus conservation and reclamation coexisted. During the crop demands of World War II improved technology in pumping and the use of natural gas as fuel saw acreage irrigated from subsurface pumping in Arizona exceeding lands watered by surface systems. Eventually this led to the overdraft condition in which water tables dropped faster than the supply could be replenished by natural rainfall and percolation of the water into the earth. When Colorado River water is supplied to farms irrigated by pumping, the pumps are to be closed down.

Charges to farmers for irrigation water and to municipalities and industries for their withdrawals will repay all operation and maintenance costs and about three-fourths of the construction costs. Patterned after the model Salt River Valley Water Users' Association of 1903, the Central Arizona Water Conservation District was formed in 1971 for the purpose of contracting with the federal government for repayment of $1.2 billion of the total outlay. A small tax is now levied on real property in Maricopa, Pinal, and Pima counties as repayment reserves are being created for this debt even before water is delivered to the non-Indian users, who will repay most of the reimbursable costs of the project.

THE IRRIGATED ECONOMY

Arizona agriculture and thriving urban communities developed within farming areas can face this debt without fear of bankruptcy or failure. They rely on the proven record of desert irrigation, which in Arizona matches and even exceeds the Biblical promise of wilderness converted to a rose garden. From a few thousand acres irrigated along scattered streams a century ago Arizona now has 1.3 million acres under cultivation, most of it supported by pumping, which gradually will be phased out with delivery of Colorado River water. Long before the nation at large recognized that water is its most valuable natural resource, arid Arizona realized that irrigation was its lifeblood and its future. Arizona farms grow a million bales of cotton a year (third in the nation after California and Texas) with per-acre yield of 979 pounds of upland cotton (nearly two bales), virtually double the national average of 524 pounds an acre. Wheat production on Arizona's irrigated farms is 72 bushels to the acre against the national average of 30 bushels; hay produces six tons an acre, nearly three times the national average; barley is 76 bushels as against a national average of 43 bushels. The state's economy, built upon the $1.25 billion produced by crops and livestock each year, plus slightly more than that from minerals, now also yields $3.5 billion in manufacturing. Travel and tourism—2.5 million persons visit national parks and monuments in Arizona each year, fascinated by the natural wonders of canyons and mountains as well as the oases in the desert sunshine belt—attract 10 million motor vehicles coming into Arizona each year and 5 million airline passengers embarking and arriving in Phoenix and 1.5 million more at Tucson.

This economic base is accompanied by a near-perpetual aura of optimism, reinforced year after year by startling statistics of economic and population growth. Doomsayers warn that the desert environment is fragile, that if man tampers with nature he will destroy its balance and productiveness. The few thousand native Americans who used stone hoes to till tiny fields of corn, beans, and squash a few centuries ago held similar fears. They dusted pollen of the early maize upon the streams and prayed to the sun above to bring clouds and rain to replenish the life-cycle. A stubborn Nature did not appreciably change the amount of rainfall that fell on Arizona, but man, highest in order of the creatures that evolved in the process of natural survival, came to Arizona; he did trifle with the environment, and thereupon produced an economy which now supports 2.5 million inhabitants who export the produce of their technology and tillage systems to far corners of the earth.

18

~

Ever Westward

by Geoffrey P. Mawn *

The decade of the 1970s was one of unprecedented growth for Arizona:

- Population increased 943,000 or 53 percent.
- Employment increased 350,000 or 54 percent.
- Manufacturing output increased $4.1 billion or 289 percent.
- Agricultural production increased $1.4 billion or 217 percent.
- Annual retail sales increased $10 billion or 259 percent.
- Savings and loan deposits increased $4.15 billion or 452 percent.
- Bank deposits increased $7.8 billion or 219 percent.
- Sales of electrical power increased 107 percent.

In short, Arizona was among the leaders in virtually every major index of healthy growth. One of the best growth indicators for the past three and one-half decades has been the gain in personal income. In 1946 the total was $669 million; in 1960, $2.634 billion; in 1970, $6.488 billion; and in 1980 the staggering jump to $23.345 billion. At the same time, per-capita income also has advanced sharply: from $1,083 in 1946 to $2,011 in 1960, then to $3,655 in 1970, and up to $8,589 in 1980.

*Curator, Arizona Historical Foundation and Arizona Collection, Hayden Library, Arizona State University.

Why did Arizona have such spectacular success? The answer is simple: People are moving to Arizona. Since World War II Arizona has attracted people to visit and eventually to migrate to the state. Arizona is viewed as a highly desirable place to live, to work, to vacation, to retire, and to locate factories and corporate headquarters. It offers a comfortable, leisurely society with a pleasant climate in the midst of attractive physical surroundings with many recreational opportunities, ease of access by a variety of transportation modes, and all the urban amenities. The resultant migration creates a large labor pool and increased demand for goods and services that attract light industry and service enterprises. This cycle of population growth, production growth, and income growth has repeated itself continuously over the past four decades.

The United States Census of 1980 credits Arizona with a total population of 2,719,225, according to a revised count. Behind this figure is a pattern of population explosion.

Year (Census)	Population	Percentage Change
1910	204,354	
1940	499,261	+144.31
1950	749,587	+50.13
1960	1,302,161	+73.71
1970	1,775,399	+36.34
1980	2,719,225	+53.16

These spectacular decennial population increases have marked Arizona as one of the leading growth states of the twentieth century. Particularly in the post–World War II years Arizona has far outstripped its southwestern rivals of California and Texas in population growth. Migration rather than natural increase is the key to Arizona demography, so that one of the most frequently asked questions in Arizona is, "Where are you from?" More often than not, the answer is the Great Lakes region, other parts of the Midwest, or the Pacific Coast states.

This population growth is not an isolated phenomenon. All the leading growth states (with the exception of Florida) are located in the Far West, either in or west of the Rocky Mountain region. Within this larger area of growth leaders is an overlapping geographical area known as the Sun Belt—the area that extends from Virginia on the east across the southern portion of the United States to California on the west. Thus, Arizona is not an isolated pocket of expansion, but a leader within a region of active growth.

Maricopa and Pima counties, which contain the metropolitan areas of Phoenix and Tucson, respectively, overshadow all others in statistical growth. While many of the nation's cities suffered a decline in population in the postwar period, Arizona's two metropolitan centers scored spectacular gains equaled by few other cities. While American urban population generally declined in the 1970s, Arizona's increased. Of the almost one million new residents that Arizona attracted during the 1970s, approximately 57 percent settled in metropolitan Phoenix and 19 percent in metropolitan Tucson. This growth assured Phoenix of its continued leadership as the financial, commercial, retail, cultural, and employment hub of the state, as well as the largest population center. Except for the new development of retirement communities (such as Sun City and Apache Junction on the fringes of the Phoenix metro area, Lake Havasu City and Riviera/Holiday Shores along the Colorado River, and Green Valley/Continental south of Tucson) and the decline of a few mining centers, in 1980, Arizona's residents were concentrated in urban centers as they had been at the time of statehood. Further, analysts project continued strong growth in the same areas.

Arizona's immediate past was considerably different. During World War I Arizona was a quiet region awaiting decisions and developments that seldom took place. For decades Arizonans had been generating lyric prose extolling the healthy climate and picturesque attractions of both natural and man-made wonders. Boosters during World War I tried to sell federal government officials on the idea of locating multiple infantry training posts near Phoenix and Tucson. The state was known principally, however, as a producer of raw materials such as copper, cotton, and cattle for the war effort.

World War II had a totally different impact. World War II launched the modern era of growth for Arizona. The state was transformed into a predominantly urban-industrial-agribusiness enterprise. Promoters revived plans for military training posts, and federal

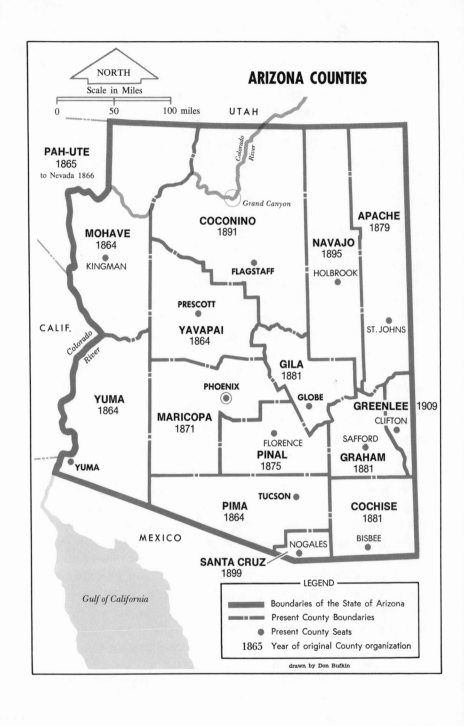

ARIZONA COUNTIES

officials awarded Arizona major air training facilities near Phoenix, Tucson, and Yuma. The bases included what became Luke and Williams Air Force bases in the Salt River Valley, and Davis-Monthan Air Force Base outside Tucson. Tied to these achievements was the establishment of a number of aircraft component-parts plants in the Phoenix and Tucson areas. Chief among these were AiResearch Manufacturing, Consolidated Aircraft, and Goodyear Aircraft. Allison Steel in Phoenix built portable bridges; subcontractors in a dozen Arizona cities turned out components for tanks and planes; and Alcoa operated the world's largest aluminum-extrusion plant in Phoenix. These plants proved the initial spark for the growth of population and manufacturing in Arizona. Wartime industry in Arizona contributed to full employment, and workers flocked to the plants from the Midwest and South.

Although the cessation of hostilities in 1945 resulted in termination of contracts and closure of many war-related plants, people continued to move to Arizona; many former GIs settled in Arizona. The shutdown was only temporary. In 1948 Motorola's Military Electronics Division established temporary engineering facilities in Phoenix. The favorable wartime experiences of the pioneering manufacturers encouraged the relocation of other corporations that built a "light industry" base for the state's postwar economy.

The advent of the Korean Conflict in 1950 added momentum to the industrial shift to Arizona. AiResearch, which closed in 1946, reopened operations in 1951. Reynolds Metals acquired and reopened the Alcoa aluminum-extrusion plant. Hughes Aircraft spearheaded an aircraft-manufacturing boom by opening a Tucson plant in 1951 and eventually expanded to become one of the nation's most important developers and producers of guided missiles and related technology. Motorola added a second plant in Phoenix in 1955 and opened a third the following year. Since then Motorola has emerged as Arizona's largest single industrial employer. Two other important arrivals of 1956 were General Electric, which established its computer manufacturing and research headquarters near Phoenix, and Sperry Phoenix, which added aviation testing and research.

Electronics has become the descriptive byword for the phenomenal growth of manufacturing during the 1950s, 1960s, and 1970s.

Hundreds of electronic research and component-manufacturing industries have located in Arizona. The necessary burden of freight costs is easily offset by high profit margins and pleasant environment. Many of these new electronic industries are related to the defense industry. Supportive research and manufacturing highlighted aerospace control, guidance, and instrumentation systems. The impetus for this modern electronics focus was the U.S. Army's decision in 1954 to move its electronics proving facility from Fort Monmouth, New Jersey, to a reactivated Fort Huachuca in southern Arizona and the federal government's subsequent support for expansion of this Southwest Signal Center. The Army Electronic Proving Ground, located at Fort Huachuca, and the Yuma Proving Ground were helpful magnets in attracting a growing list of electronics and transportation manufacturers to Arizona. The resultant bond between government requirements and private-industry research and development was close. For example, during the 1960s Pan American Airways and Bell Aerosystems even moved their research laboratories onto the grounds of Fort Huachuca to provide greater efficiency in test and evaluation programs.

Following the lead of the trend setters, many other national and regional manufacturers built operations in Arizona. The roster of Arizona's electronics and related aerospace firms includes the blue-chip names in the field: Motorola, General Electric, Goodyear Aerospace, Sperry Rand, Hughes, AiResearch, Unidynamics, Honeywell, Digital, Intel, IBM, ITT, Talley Industries, Western Electric, Gates Learjet, Burr-Brown, and dozens of lesser-known but equally respected firms.

Arizona provided a receptive business climate for new manufacturing operations. Labor was abundant. The state's right-to-work legislation provided a balance favoring the business community; state legislatures enacted laws to encourage new plants and to keep taxation reasonably low.

Manufacturing is Arizona's largest basic industry. Since 1957 it has provided the state with both economic diversification and stability. Three-fourths of the state's manufacturing is in durable goods, electric and electronic equipment, non-electrical machinery, fabricated metals, and transportation equipment. New, modern, efficient plants and rapid technological advancement put these light industries in competitive positions in a rapidly expanding marketplace; a commitment to research and development keeps them competitive. Manufacturing establishments in Arizona number more than 3,000 firms with a value-added output of more than $5 billion. Forty-six of the Fortune 500 firms currently operate in Arizona, and several of them, such as Greyhound, have established their headquarters in the state.

This phenomenal growth of light industry and electronics brought about an amazing transformation in Arizona's economy. Until World War II, agriculture, livestock, mining, and tourism formed the basis of the economy. Commonly referred to as the "four C's"—Cotton, Cattle, Copper, and Climate—these old standbys also provided the foundation for economic development in the postwar period.

Since World War II, agricultural crop income built on the traditional plantings of cotton, vegetables, alfalfa, barley, wheat, and citrus products has risen from $102.9 million in 1946 to a peak in 1953 at $320 million. Crop output rebounded from the 1950s economic fluctuations and survived the devastating effects of the suburban transition of the post–Korean Conflict decades to its 1979 peak of $905 million. This figure supplies a strong argument for scientific farming and increased mechanization: although less than two percent of Arizona's land is devoted to agricultural acreage, it produces tremendous volume and dollar value. Stored water introduced onto fertile, arable land combined with the nearly year-long growing seasons permits three to five high-yield crops per year. The result is that Arizona's crop yield per acre far exceeds the national average. For example, in 1980 short or upland cotton averaged 1,062 pounds to the acre, compared to the U.S. average of 410 pounds per acre, and this figure is lower than an Arizona record yield of 1,162 pounds per acre in 1963.

Although Arizona's agricultural production is highly diversified, cattle and cotton constitute a high proportion of income totals. Cattle represents about three-fourths of livestock marketings, and cotton accounts for more than half of crop income.

The livestock industry is the most important element of the agricultural economy. Since 1940, extensive irrigation has made possible feed production that has resulted in feedlot marketing of cattle and calves becoming the most important segment of Arizona's livestock industry. Cattle for feeding are shipped in from local ranges, Mexico, and states as far away as Florida. Recent diversification in the cattle industry made the cattle business an $827 million operation in 1979.

The second important element of Arizona's agricultural economy is cotton. The beginning of World War II spurred an increased demand for cotton. The years immediately after the war saw a steady expansion of Arizona's cotton industry, so that by 1950 Arizona was one of the top cotton-producing areas in the world. Since the peak years of the early 1950s Arizona's cotton acreage in the 1970s was reduced almost fifty percent.

A large part of this reduction is accountable to other factors in Arizona's postwar economy. The steadily expanding sprawl of residences and industrial sites has had a profound impact on the use of land, water, and energy resources. Urbanization and spiraling water and energy costs have provided a lucrative incentive for farmers to sell their land to developers. What were prime farmlands, for example, northwest and southeast of Phoenix are now suburbanized Glendale and Peoria, and Chandler and Gilbert, respectively. In recent years 10,000 acres of irrigated farmland in Pima County were sold to the city of Tucson and to mining companies which bought the land for the attached water rights.

Water is *the* essential factor in the farmer's future. Almost all of Arizona's farmland is irrigated acreage; about ninety percent of Arizona's water is used for agriculture. Increased residential, commercial, and industrial development means greater demands on the few sources of water. Arizona's consumption of water annually exceeds replenishment by 2.2 million acre-feet. (One acre-foot equals 325,850 gallons.) In some parts of Arizona the water table has dropped significantly through demand usage. The Central Arizona Project, which will bring Colorado River water to central Arizona during the 1980s, promises to cut the state's water overdraft by about fifty percent. Its goal, however, is to support urbanization and to maintain existing farmland, not to support new production. Three to four acre-feet of water (about a million gallons) required to raise a single crop on one acre of land would support twenty-five people for an entire year.

Another industry dependent on water and hydroelectric power is mining. During most of the immediate post–World War II period the Big Five of mining—copper, lead, gold, silver, and zinc—represented virtually all of Arizona's mining industry. Copper has always dominated the statistics, for more than three-fourths of the total value of nonfuel mineral production. The year 1979 marked a modern peak of slightly over one million tons with a value of approximately $1.9 billion, which represents more than fifty percent of the copper produced in the United States. The total economic impact of the industry on the state is estimated at more than $5 billion.

During the postwar decades the mining industry has posted marked gains and faced a variety of problems. Increased mechanization and improved technologies have reduced costs and increased yields. The quality of ore in Arizona's mines has become steadily poorer, but more efficient extraction methods have more than offset this disadvantage. Excess copper inventories caused by market variations, competition from low-priced foreign-produced copper, and labor controversies have caused mines to close, production to lag, and copper prices to fall. Only a portion of these uncertain market conditions are relieved by advances in technology which have provided new uses for copper in solar energy, electrically powered motor vehicles, and other sectors of the economy.

Although the other elements of the Big Five—lead, gold, silver, and zinc—have had mining and marketing problems, their decline has been counterbalanced by increased production of miscellaneous minerals and by-products. As late as the early 1950s the combined value of minerals other than the Big Five totaled just under $9 million. By the early 1960s the output value of miscellaneous minerals and by-products such as sand and gravel, stone, molybdenum, lime, asbestos, gypsum, cement, perlite, pumice, and uranium climbed to $63 million, over three and a half times the combined value of lead, gold, silver, and zinc; in 1979 the value of these miscellaneous minerals and by-products rocketed to more than $400 million.

Arizona's transportation system has changed significantly during recent decades. From the late nineteenth century through the mid-twentieth century, railroads served the territory and provided fast, dependable, and economical transportation that brought visitors, settlers, and supplies into Arizona. Railroads made feasible the shipment of the state's mineral and agricultural products to distant markets; this role continues, but at a drastically reduced tonnage.

During the middle decades of the twentieth century, automobile, bus, and truck transport made steadily greater inroads into the predominance of the rail system. Ground transportation has experienced exceptional growth in Arizona since World War II, thanks in part to matching federal funds for development of the state's highway system. In 1980 Arizona registered 2,465,040 motor vehicles of all types, which utilized a highway system of more than 57,500 miles. As a result, more than half the communities in the state are totally dependent on highway transport for freight service. Interstate truck freight service carried electrical and electronic equipment, cement, apparel, paper and pulp, furniture, and other manufactured items which contribute to the importance of Arizona as a wholesale and warehousing center for the Southwest. Passenger transportation has been pre-empted by the two transcontinental bus lines which offer passenger and package express service to many Arizona communities.

As elsewhere, there has been a revolution in air transportation. Taking advantage of the finest flying conditions in the nation, Arizonans are very air-minded. Arizona was in the forefront of the twentieth century transition to air transport. Tucson boasted the first municipal airport in the country in 1917; in 1927 the state's first successful air service offered travel three times a week between Phoenix, Tucson, and Los Angeles. By the 1960s almost every city and town and many ranches and mining areas had airfields. For decades Sky Harbor International Airport in Phoenix has been one of the busiest municipal fields in the United States, ranking among the nation's top five in total traffic volume. Increases in passenger volume strain the efforts of authorities to construct adequate terminal facilities. In 1951 there was a total of 240,786 arrivals and departures; this figure grew to 859,744 in 1960 and 2.9 million in 1970. In 1979 the seventeen international, transcontinental, and regional carriers that service Sky Harbor accounted for 7.02 million arrivals and departures; Tucson arrivals and departures for 1979 totaled 1.94 million.

The automobile still remains the basic mode of transportation.

Arizonans own approximately one car for every two residents of the state. As distances continue to increase the commute radius to work, trips to shopping centers, and access to recreational activities, Arizonans' dependence on the automobile is likewise increasing. Despite the restraints of possible gas shortages and rising costs, the luxury of air-conditioned automobile transportation seems a basic necessity for everyone.

Airline travelers, highway tourists, and in-state travelers all have developed an enormous portion of the Arizona economy: tourism. Fortunately for Arizona, travel and tourism have built a major bulwark against the threats of recession for the Arizona economy. In 1979 tourists in Arizona spent an estimated $4.04 billion—a figure that propelled tourism into the second-largest industry in the state.

Arizona tourism once simply involved stopping between "Colossal California" on the west and "Titanic Texas" to the east. Once the needs of tourists were simple: food, gas, and lodging. Times have changed. During the 1950s visitors increased significantly, traveling both *to* and *in* Arizona. During the 1970s a further adjustment of the travel picture resulted from the real or feared gasoline shortages which shifted travel modes so that airline traffic increased and motor vehicle traffic decreased.

Arizona's success in travel and tourism is the result of the state's harmonious diversity which answers the dreams of millions of people. During recent decades Arizona's historic liabilities of desert climate and inland location have become assets. In addition to the effect of a warm, dry climate on health and morale, Arizonans boast about the eighty-percent-plus days of sunshine. Winter and spring weather in southern and central Arizona is near perfect. Daytime hours are characterized by sunny skies and mild temperatures, and nighttime air is crisp and clear. The high mountain areas offer skiing. Summer brings low humidity which moderates temperature extremes of the heat in the southern deserts, and there are mountain escapes for picnicking, camping, and vacationing.

Arizona currently meets the needs of both tourist and vacationer. Enterprising businessmen meet the basic needs of traveling tourists who come to Arizona to see the broad assortment of unparalleled natural scenery, ranging from the awe-inspiring Grand Canyon of the

Colorado to the photogenic wonders of the national forests, national parks, Indian lands, and cacti-covered, flower-colored desertscape. Larger enterprises answer the needs of vacationers seeking continuing variety and entertainment.

As was pointed out earlier, one of the greatest contributors to tourism has been the development of air conditioning. Originally twentieth century tourism was a seasonal concentration during the winter, but the age of refrigeration, beginning with the evaporative cooler, has attracted a second, summer season of tourism as well as bringing a dramatic change to the life-style of Arizonans.

Another major element of the postwar economy has been the federal relationship. Not only did the federal government construct the multipurpose water storage dams with hydroelectric capabilities on the Salt, Gila, and Colorado rivers which supply inexpensive electrical power, but for years the U.S. government has been the largest landowner in Arizona. It controls about 54 million acres, approximately 32.5 million acres of which are owned outright and 21.5 million are Indian reservations held in trust. The biggest share of these federal lands comprises seven national forests administered under multiple-use and sustained-yield management policies so that they provide outdoor recreation, hunting and fishing, forage for livestock, and commercial timber. Although the federal forests, monuments, and parks are not subject to local taxation, one-fourth of all their revenues is returned to counties in which they are located to be used for schools and roads. More important, the federal government spends almost twice as much in Arizona as it collects in taxes. In fiscal year 1980 the U.S. government expended $6.2 billion in Arizona, or about 1.2 percent of the total government budget of $529 billion. The bulk of these funds in Arizona was expended by the Department of Health and Human Services and the Department of Defense. In other years the federal government has spent large sums of money in public construction, such as the Glen Canyon Dam, the interstate highway system, missile sites around Tucson, and the Central Arizona Project. It is these massive federal contributions that are ignored when Arizonans discuss their own "Sagebrush Rebellion" to remove or to lessen the federal government's influence in the state.

The newest developing element of the postwar economy is the

initiation of a strong border-economy relationship with the Republic of Mexico. The proximity of Mexico has had a strong impact on Arizona. Both Arizona and the Mexican border state of Sonora benefit from the expenditures of visitors. Mexico lacks adequate production and an integrated manufacturing and distribution system to handle its vast, untouched natural resources of oil, coal, copper, iron, timber, and fish. Its exports through Arizona consist largely of edible products such as cattle, seafood, fresh vegetables, beverages, and a variety of raw materials. Its imports, which generally have outweighed exports, consist primarily of capital goods and manufactured consumer goods. The unfavorable balance in Mexico's international trade is financed through foreign indebtedness from investments, many of them from Arizona financial institutions. Resolving the traditional tensions between the United States and Mexico—involving such issues as illegal aliens, produce and textile exports, border crime and smuggling, and oil and gas prices—will probably benefit the economies of both nations and, in particular, of the border states of Arizona and Sonora.

In addition to its international trade, Arizona is a lucrative investment locale for foreign investors. Foreign nationals own billions of dollars' worth of Arizona land and property. For example, foreign investors own more than 22,000 acres of agricultural land in Maricopa County valued at more than $65.9 million. Further, more than thirty-seven major foreign business enterprises have invested in Arizona properties on speculation. A preliminary and incomplete report in 1974 by the Department of Commerce indicated that foreign investment in Arizona property, plants, and equipment amounted to $295 million. The foreign owners and investors include individuals and corporations from Canada, Germany, France, Belgium, Japan, the Netherlands, Sweden, England, Italy, Saudi Arabia, Egypt, Bermuda, the Bahamas, and the British Virgin Islands.

Native and adopted Arizonans continue to live in a desert society on their own terms. Both groups seek modern creature comforts that were beyond the imagination of pioneer Arizonans. The modern view combines man's ingenuity and technology to mold a comfortable life-style within a hostile environment. Desert living means air conditioning, water fountains, swimming pools, and irrigation. The fragile ecology of the semi-arid desert threatens periodic drought or seasonal floods, seasonal restrictions of hydroelectric power or limitation of fossil fuel sources of energy, and uncertainty from the proposed alternatives of solar energy and nuclear power. Getting back to nature means running the Colorado River rapids, hiking the mountain wilderness, horseback riding, and motorized houseboats or speedboats on man-made lakes or, believe it or not, surfing on man-made ocean waves. For many, adjusting to the desert is a matter of the affluent society of equestrian manors, tennis ranches, golf resorts, and colonial homes—many landscaped with displaced desert vegetation outlined with artificially colored rock. All these aspects of Arizona desert living reflect man's dominance over an adverse environment. The fullness and ease of the desert life-style should make us more grateful for what we have, more appreciative of our technology, and more protective of the balance of our environment. Arizona's historic land is a promise for the future!

Bibliographical Essay

Newcomers to Arizona sometimes are surprised when natives and old residents say the forty-eighth state has a history. Their mental backpacks are crammed with the misconceptions of myths, movies, and the magnetic media. They expect to find Arizona occupied by stereotypes: cowboys and Indians and floozies in a menage of strife, sin, and bloodshed. They are shocked when told that Arizona is no longer—if ever it was—a part of the Wild West. Arizona often is described with either pride or a sneer as Goldwater Country, in recognition of the straight-talking senator. But Arizona also has been the home of astronaut Frank Borman, president of Eastern Airlines. It is the fastest-growing of the contiguous forty-eight states as well as the last of them in chronological time. On the other hand, in population and in many other indices of growth and prosperity it outstrips all the rest.

No state in the American West has a more exciting history than Arizona, unless it would be California, which must acknowledge that some of its historical roots spring from earlier settlements in Arizona. Californians can and do embellish their historical pageant with the one ingredient lacking in Arizona—a seashore and seaports on a vast ocean. Arizona is landlocked, but it has not been isolated. Against spectacular geography its record of human habitation surpasses that of all other known communities in North America. The village of Oraibi, looking down upon a land where the ebbs and flows of history have been enacted with every emotion of mankind, has been inhabited by the Hopi Indians for at least eight centuries.

War and peace, disaster and tranquility, success and failure, charity and avarice, inspiration and animalism—all have been demonstrated here, and all have left some record in this land. If the full record is not found in books, that is the fault of writers and researchers, not of history. Arizona's anomalous character seems, indeed, to have permeated its historians, most of them from outside the state. "Hay is cut with a hoe and wood with a spade," as J. Ross Browne observed a century ago, and, as he then observed, there are still politicians without policy, though Indians, "the most barbarous on earth," were long since quelled. Arizona would seem to be a state with a history and yet with very few historians.

Arizona's character has not been contrast alone, for other states can boast of near-equal or greater differences in terrain and altitude, and hence in temperatures as well as in flora and fauna. Few, however, can enumerate greater or more varied accomplishments by man. Arizona has been a pathway to the riches of California's goldfields and has produced bonanzas of its own. It provided a battleground— remote and, by the standards of Gettysburg, actually insignificant— in the tragic Civil War. It yielded right-of-way for two transcontinental railroads. It has provided a home for more Indians and Indian tribes than any other state—Indians such as the Hopis, of incomparable gentleness, and the Apaches, in the past unmatched for ferocity. Its horde of copper has been among the richest in the world. It pioneered in the irrigation of arid lands. But, above all, its percentage of sunshine—that transparent golden energy prized above other elements with the exception of water—is the highest, most constant, and most dependable in the United States.

In such an environment, high accomplishment was natural. Here men performed deeds of valor, of desperation, of determination, and sometimes of disgrace, nearly all worth recording on the pages of regional and local history. And not a few Arizonans have left their marks on the world panorama.

While this broad Arizona story is familiar in a general way to historical buffs throughout the state and some elsewhere, most Arizonans know it imperfectly and some not at all. In marked contrast to the widespread dissemination and appreciation of regional and local history in Colorado, Utah, Texas, and California, the level of public awareness of the past has not been high in Arizona. This disparity cannot be explained alone by the fact that Arizona has been a state only seven decades.

Because the native populations were so numerous, and because Nature provided an environment suited for preservation of evidence of civilizations that reached their zeniths and disappeared long ago, Arizona has an unsurpassed aboriginal history. The archeological and ethnological literature of Arizona's past is exhaustive and, in many aspects, quite technical. This distant past can best be understood through broad interpretive efforts of the kind achieved by Edward H. Spicer with great effectiveness in *Cycles of Conquest* (Tucson: University of Arizona Press, 1962). Nowhere else is the history of the effect of the white man's occupation upon Native Americans presented so completely and lucidly by one author.

The first 300 years of Arizona occupation and exploration belonged to Spain and Mexico, and most records of the period have never been published. The Archive of the Indies in Seville, Spain, and the national archives of Mexico contain extensive original reports of Spanish efforts to entrench Church and State on the northern frontier of New Spain, including present Arizona. Little of this period had been known until the last half-century, when Herbert Eugene Bolton and his students began penetrating the mysteries of the Spanish Borderlands. Fascination with this phase of Arizona history is neverending. For instance, the Spanish effort to contain the Apache and Comanche enemy on the northern frontier has best been examined fairly recently in a book called *Lancers for the King* by Sidney B. Brinckerhoff and Odie B. Faulk (Phoenix: Arizona Historical Foundation, 1965). Here the story of the presidial cordon stretching from the Colorado River of the West almost to the Gulf of Mexico is told for the first time.

Remarks in the present essay, however, treat mainly of general works that concern the century since the creation of the territory of Arizona. Supplemental and more specific notes are provided for each chapter of this book, together with reading lists recommended for those who wish to dig deeper than is possible in one easily held volume.

Anglo-Americans first learned of Arizona through oral accounts from meandering trappers; next they heard from travelers who wrote of their horizon-reaching adventures in the Great West; and finally they had access to reports from well-planned scientific exploring and surveying parties. The public waited, however, until long after the Anglo military occupation of Arizona to learn the barest details of the first Spanish settlement. American history, in fact, was woefully lacking in realization of the southwestern Spanish heritage until the beginning of the twentieth century. The merest fragments of knowledge had entered print before the War with Mexico of 1846–48. Foremost among these had been the highly fictionalized account of the travels of Sylvester and James Ohio Pattie on beaver-trapping expeditions along the Gila, Salt, and Colorado rivers. *The Personal Narrative of James O. Pattie of Kentucky* (as edited by the Rev. Timothy Flint; Cincinnati, 1831) projected the young Kentuckian and his father, who died in California, as heroes in the grand image of Daniel Boone and Davy Crockett. The book told avid readers there was a land of "rugged and pathless mountains, subject to every species of danger, want, and misery" between Santa Fe and San Diego, yet its presentation was forbidding rather than inviting. Fortunately for the history buff, it has been reprinted at least twice.

The land cessions by Mexico—the spoils of war—and the resultant military and boundary surveys threw more light upon the contents and topography of the land. It had been partly mapped by Lieutenant William H. Emory during the course of the War with Mexico as he marched with General Stephen Watts Kearny and the Army of the West toward the conquest of California. Emory's fine work *Notes of a Military Reconnaissance from Fort Leavenworth . . . to San Diego* (Washington, D.C., 1848) also has been republished. It was followed by a closer look at the acquired territory taken by the boundary survey party led by John R. Bartlett and reported in his *Personal Narrative* (New York, 1854), also available in a reprint edition. Accounts of other travelers, similar to those of Emory and Bartlett, contained fragments of history, items incidental to the scientific data which it was the author's responsibility to collect. Emory's contemporary Lieutenant Colonel Philip St. George Cooke reported in great detail the march of the Mormon Battalion from Santa Fe to San Diego. In the same period Lieutenant John G. Parke completed the *Report of Explorations for Railroad Routes . . . from . . . the Gila to the Rio Grande near the 32nd Parallel, 1854–55,* published as volume 7 of *The Pacific Railway Explorations.* Joseph C. Ives's *Report Upon the Colorado River of the West . . .* (Washington, D.C., 1861) added further to the growing literature in print on Arizona. These works likewise did not provide much in the way of history, but all such reports have become exceedingly valuable tools for the research historian and serious reader.

It remained for another army officer, Lieutenant Sylvester Mowry, who was himself later an important mine owner and entrepreneur, to begin the compilation of Arizona history. In his promotional pamphlet *Memoir of the Proposed Territory of Arizona,* published privately at Washington in 1857, Mowry summarized the economic potential of Arizona. He borrowed from comments of explorers for railroads, including Parke, and he boldly presented as fact the speculations of mining promoters such as Herman Ehrenberg and Charles D. Poston. He also reviewed briefly Arizona under the Spanish domain. Here, for the first time, was a general history, albeit a short one.

Emory, Bartlett, Parke, Pattie, Ives, and others had told Americans how to reach Arizona and what they might expect to see once there; but they did not provide any real reasons why Americans might want to visit or settle there, nor did they hold out the golden promise implicit in Mowry's plea for territorial status. The latter was achieved on February 24, 1863. The movement for creation of civil government, paradoxically, was to wait more than a century. The publication of Dr. Benjamin Sacks's work *Be It Enacted: The Creation of the Territory of Arizona* (Phoenix: Arizona Historical Foundation, 1964) told the story from a better perspective than had principals in the events. The important roles of Mowry and General Samuel P. Heintzelman and their deserved recognition as co-authors of civil government had been usurped long before by Poston's self-designation as Father of Arizona.

Many nineteenth century impressions of Arizona and a goodly share of its history were journalistic in origin and nature. Newspaper and magazine writers began visiting Arizona with considerable frequency after J. Ross Browne came in 1864 with Poston, who had been appointed the first superintendent of Indian affairs for Arizona. Browne produced a series of bright articles printed first in the San Francisco *Bulletin,* next in *Harper's Magazine,* and as a book in 1869, *Adventures in the Apache Country: A Tour Through Arizona and Sonora.* Not only was it the first major contribution to Arizona history, but also it remains one of the best. Fortunately, it has been reissued at least four times.

Late in the 1870s, as the Southern Pacific Railroad approached the borders of Arizona from the west, heralding a new day for the terri-tory, efforts to stimulate immigration produced a number of booster handbooks. Privately published in most instances, they had indirect subsidies through advertising, transportation, and accommodations provided gratuitously to authors, and through cooperation from mer-chants and communities who could see Arizona's future prosperity linked to the inflow of residents and capital. Two of these, Hiram C. Hodge's *Arizona as It Is* (the least reliable of the group) and Richard J. Hinton's ponderous *The Hand-Book to Arizona, 1877,* have been reprinted. A third, *The Resources of Arizona,* by Patrick Hamilton, was published in four editions between 1881 and 1884, each larger than the last. It had a direct subsidy from the territory of Arizona, as the author was the official immigration commissioner.

After Browne published *Adventures in the Apache Country,* little of worth appeared for fifteen years except four chapters in Raphael Pumpelly's popular travel narrative *Across America and Asia* (New York, 1870). In 1884 Wallace W. Elliott of San Francisco published his *History of Arizona* in a large format. Only five years later Hubert Howe Bancroft brought out his *History of Arizona and New Mexico* as Volume XVII of his monumental *Works* in thirty-nine volumes. Both of these works have been reprinted. Bancroft's book marked the end of the period characterized by booster literature, and highlighted the beginning of objective historical study in and about Arizona. Bancroft chose to link Arizona with New Mexico in one volume, because of their common Hispanic culture. He could not see, as present perspective permits, that most of Arizona's significant devel-opment came as a backwash of the great gold rush and land booms in California. Arizona and New Mexico took different paths immedi-ately upon their political separation in 1863.

A great outpouring of magazine and newspaper reports of travel, of scientific studies, of military activities, and of mining came with completion of two transcontinental railways across Arizona in 1882 and 1883. It was easier to reach Arizona than before, but many of the vivid impressions formed by the travelers in the riskier stagecoach era were repeated, if not exaggerated, by writers with romantic notions of what the Wild West should be—or should have been. The romantic view has persisted to the present and has grown more distorted with motion pictures and television.

Little of the writing on Arizona could be considered truly artistic until 1892, when Arizona and the Southwest became the focus of the talented and eccentric author Charles Fletcher Lummis. He described the beauty and charm of the Indian country of northern Arizona and supported railroad promotion effectively, if not intentionally, with *Some Strange Corners of Our Country*. The efforts of Lummis were followed by the adventure novels of Alfred Henry Lewis and Charles King. Of the early popular illustrators, only Frederic Remington was inspired by the Arizona scene.

In the early twentieth century Arizona suffered from an insufficiency of serious historical study. Competent writers such as Ross Santee, Edwin Corle, and Stewart Edward White carried on the deft tradition of Lummis, but rarely undertook scholarly or historical themes. Attempts at serious objective history were somewhat defective. The eight-volume *History of Arizona* (Phoenix, 1915–18) by an early state historian, Thomas E. Farish, was little more than a series of loosely connected chronicles, largely collected from newspapers. About the same time Farish was pasting together his volumes, there appeared an effort that stands as the best multivolume history of the state. However assiduously Colonel James Harvey McClintock applied himself to the three-volume *Arizona: Prehistoric—Aboriginal— Pioneer—Modern* (Chicago: S. J. Clarke Publishing Co., 1916), errors and incomplete explanations characterized many of its pages.

Among single-volume works that have attempted a comprehensive view of Arizona's history, Rufus Kay Wyllys's book was outstanding. He was for a decade Arizona's finest professional historian, a student of Bolton, thoroughly inspired by his adopted state. Wyllys wrote *Arizona: The History of a Frontier State* (Phoenix: Hobson &

Herr, 1950) as a primary work he hoped could be followed by more detailed studies. An early death denied Arizona the full advantage of this brilliant and productive scholar.

This book is another effort to present in one volume an informal overview of Arizona history. It is not a definitive or a complete account of the state, whose phenomenal growth has been spectacular and would require several volumes for full delineation. Minimal attention is given herein to the violence and misdeeds of gunfighters, outlaws, and other maldoers of the past, because that superficial aspect has been overdone already by the popular media in the transparent cloth of entertainment—and it *is* entertainment more than serious or significant history.

A short, annotated reading list is provided for each chapter of this book, frequently containing works used as secondary sources. These supplemental readings are offered for readers who may deplore or applaud the absence of footnotes and documentation in this book.

1. Creation

For vivid visual impressions of Arizona and supplemental reading, no resource can surpass the files of *Arizona Highways* magazine. The curious spell of the desert is inspirationally articulated by the great naturalist Joseph Wood Krutch in *The Desert Year* (New York: Sloan, 1951). Equally appealing, light-hearted, with broad sweeps of historical and social comment, is Douglas Rigby, *Desert Happy* (Philadelphia: Lippincott, 1957). An excellent scientific and historical treatment is Roger Dunbier, *The Sonoran Desert* (Tucson: University of Arizona Press, 1968). Elements of an area larger than Arizona forcefully appear in Elna Bakker and Richard G. Lillard, *The Great Southwest: The Story of a Land and Its People* (Palo Alto: American West, 1972). A classic is John C. Van Dyke, *The Desert* (New York: Scribner's, 1930; Tucson: Arizona Historical Society, 1978).

2. Peoples of the Past

An encompassing overview of Peoples of the Past is provided by Gordon R. Willey, *An Introduction to American Archeology,* Volume One, *North and Middle America* (Englewood Cliffs, N.J.: Prentice-Hall, 1966). Clear perspective on variations within Arizona is provided by Paul Martin and Fred Plog, *The Archeology of Arizona* (Garden City, N.Y.: Doubleday—American Museum of Natural History, 1973). Handsome pictorial presentations with lucid text are in Elna Bakker and Richard G. Lillard, *The Great Southwest: The Story of a Land and Its People* (Palo Alto: American West, 1972) and Donald G. Pike with photographs by David Muench, *Anasazi: Ancient People of the Rock* (Palo Alto: American West, 1974). The brilliant scholarship of Emil W. Haury has brought him premier ranking as the leading expert on the Hohokam Culture. Particularly significant are three books among his extensive publications: *The Excavation of Los Muertos and Neighboring Sites in the Salt River Valley, Southern Arizona,* Papers, Vol. 24, No. 1 (Cambridge, Mass.: Peabody Museum, Harvard University, 1945); *The Stratigraphy and Archeology of Ventana Cave, Arizona* (Tucson: University of Arizona Press, 1950); and *The Hohokam* (Tucson: University of Arizona Press, 1976).

3. Enter the King's Captains

The pioneer work on the first Spanish penetration into the American Southwest is Herbert E. Bolton, *The Spanish Borderlands* (New Haven: Yale University Press, 1921) and it was enlarged upon by Bolton's *Coronado: Knight of Pueblos and Plains* (Albuquerque: University of New Mexico Press, 1949). The area and the era are brought into modern perspective with the informal and very readable W. Eugene Hollon, *The Southwest: Old and New* (New York: Alfred A. Knopf, 1961). Priestly attitudes are delineated in a fine overview by the Jesuit scholar John Francis Bannon, *The Spanish Borderlands Frontier, 1513–1821* (New York: Holt, Rinehart & Winston, 1970). The role and reputation of Coronado's guide are elucidated yet decimated by Cleve Hallenbeck, *The Journey of Fray Marcos de Niza* (Dallas: Southern Methodist University Press, 1949). Solid documentation is provided by George P. Hammond and Agapito Rey, translators of *Narratives of the Coronado Expedition, 1540–1542* (Albuquerque: University of New Mexico Press, 1940). Indian reactions to this invasion are lucidly revealed in Edward H. Spicer, *Cycles of Conquest: The Impact of Spain, Mexico, and the United States on the Indians of the Southwest, 1533–1960* (Tucson: University of Arizona Press, 1962). The continuing frustrations of life on this frontier are superbly supplemented by John L. Kessell in *Kiva, Cross and Crown* (Washington, D.C.: National Park Service, 1979).

4. For the Glory of God and King

The exhaustive translation and editing of basic records in the Archive of the Indies in Seville and the Archivo General de la Nación in Mexico by Professor Herbert Eugene Bolton and his students established the Spanish Borderlands as a vital segment in the history of the Americas. His own pioneering works are the foundation for understanding the actions of soldiers and priests, and include:

Rim of Christendom: A Biography of Eusebio Francisco Kino, Pacific Coast Pioneer (New York: Macmillan, 1936)

Kino's Historical Memoir of Pimería Alta: A Contemporary Account of the Beginnings of California, Sonora, and Arizona, 1683–1711 (Berkeley: University of California Press, 1948)

Anza's California Expeditions, 5 vols. (Berkeley: University of California Press, 1930)

Outpost of Empire: The Story of the Founding of San Francisco (New York: Alfred A. Knopf, 1939)

Unfortunately, a definitive biography of Father Garcés has yet to be published. Father John Francis Bannon, Jesuit scholar and student of Bolton, who summarized the period carefully in *The Spanish Borderlands Frontier, 1513–1821* (New York: Holt, Rinehart & Winston, 1970), provides new light on the period in *Herbert Eugene Bolton: The Historian and the Man, 1870–1953* (Tucson: University of Arizona Press, 1978).

5. Time of the Apaches

The definitive work of monumental proportions explaining the dislocations, turmoil, and changes created in Indian life by the Spanish invasion is Edward H. Spicer, *Cycles of Conquest: The Impact of Spain, Mexico, and the United States on the Indians of the Southwest, 1533–1960* (Tucson: University of Arizona Press, 1962). Purposes and weaknesses of the presidio system are told in two excellent works: Max L. Moorhead, *The Presidio: Bastion of the Spanish Borderlands* (Norman: University of Oklahoma Press, 1975) and Sidney B. Brinckerhoff and Odie B. Faulk, *Lancers for the King* (Phoenix: Arizona Historical Foundation, 1965). Pressures extending to the most distant enclaves of Spanish settlement are revealed in Oakah L. Jones, Jr., *Los Paisanos: Spanish Settlers on the Northern Frontier of New Spain* (Norman: University of Oklahoma Press, 1978) and Max L. Moorhead, *The Apache Frontier: Jacobo Ugarte and Spanish-Indian Relations in Northern New Spain, 1769–1791* (Norman: University of Oklahoma Press, 1968). David J. Weber, *The Taos Trappers: The Fur Trade in the Far Southwest, 1540–1846* (Norman: University of Oklahoma Press, 1971) updates earlier works on the American fur trade, specifically concentrating on the southern Rockies and the Gila River basin. John L. Kessell's forcefully written *Friars, Soldiers, and Reformers* (Tucson: University of Arizona Press, 1976) tells of internal efforts to soothe and satisfy the natives in Arizona.

6. Distant Trumpets

The War with Mexico generated a volcanic outpouring of analytical and guilt-ridden literature which sputters and regurgitates cyclically. General comments on the causes and campaigns of the war are clearly presented in: Frederick Merk, *History of the Westward Movement* (New York: Alfred A. Knopf, 1978) and Samuel Eliot Morison, *The Oxford History of the American People* (New York: Oxford University Press, 1965). The two expeditions that crossed Arizona for the conquest of California are amply described in: Dwight L. Clarke, *Stephen Watts Kearny: Soldier of the West* (Norman: University of Oklahoma Press, 1961) and Philip St. George Cooke, *The Conquest of New Mexico and California: A History and Personal Narrative* (New York: G. P. Putnam's Sons, 1878; reprint, Albuquerque: Horn and Wallace, 1964). William H. Emory, *Notes of a Military Reconnaissance from Fort Leavenworth . . . to San Diego,* originally published as a government document in 1848, has been abridged and annotated as Ross Calvin, *Lieutenant Emory Reports* (Albuquerque: University of New Mexico Press, 1951). An insight into personal daily life of the Mormon volunteers is found in Daniel Tyler, *A Concise History of the Mormon Battalion in the Mexican War* (reprint, Chicago: Rio Grande Press, 1964).

7. Ho for California!—and Back Again

Written as a doctoral dissertation and therefore suffering from pedantic academic style, an accurate and precise account of the difficult negotiations for the Gadsden Purchase is found in Paul Neff Garber, *The Gadsden Treaty* (Gloucester, Mass.: Peter Smith, 1959). A highly individualized and grossly self-aggrandizing account of the Poston-Ehrenberg venture into the Gadsden Purchase appears in a work credited to Poston since the material originally was published serially in the *Overland Monthly*. Annotation by John Myers Myers overlooked substantive errors. The small book chronicles main incidents of the expedition, but Poston's role and explanations should not be accepted literally as stated in Charles D. Poston, *Building a State in Apache Land* (Tempe: Aztec Press, 1963). The definitive account of Arizona's long struggle for separate identity and territorial status apart from New Mexico is presented brilliantly by B. Sacks, M.D., *Be It Enacted: The Creation of the Territory of Arizona* (Phoenix: Arizona Historical Foundation, 1964). This work deflates Poston's claim as "Father of Arizona," demonstrating that he was among a half-dozen pioneers and politicians with equal claim to that parenthood. Diane M. T. North's recent work, *Samuel Peter Heintzelman and the Sonora Exploring & Mining Company* (Tucson:

University of Arizona Press, 1980), provides a valuable introduction and portions of Heintzelman's journals in a handsome and scholarly format. The detailed history of the early stage lines is presented in Roscoe and Margaret B. Conkling, *The Butterfield Overland Mail, 1857–1869* (Glendale, Calif.: Arthur H. Clark, 1947).

8. Stopped at Stanwix Station

Frontier attitudes toward Indians in the Gadsden Purchase are illuminated in Frank C. Lockwood, *Pioneer Days in Arizona* (New York: Macmillan, 1932) and his *The Apache Indians* (New York: Macmillan, 1938). For a contrasting and highly romanticized, sympathetic view with an Indian focus, see Elliott Arnold, *Blood Brother* (New York: Duell, Sloan & Pearce, 1947); from this latter book came the movie *Broken Arrow,* in which Jeff Chandler appeared as Cochise, cast as a matinee idol. John C. Cremony, *Life Among the Apaches* (San Francisco: A. Roman, 1868) related his experiences on the same frontier as a member of the American boundary commission, which he served as a translator. Later he commanded a company of California cavalry in Civil War operations in Arizona. Campaigns of the Civil War are well presented in two books, one with a Southern viewpoint, the other by a Union follower: Robert Lee Kerby, *The Confederate Invasion of New Mexico and Arizona, 1861–62* (Los Angeles: Westernlore Press, 1958) and Aurora Hunt, *Army of the Pacific* (Glendale, Calif.: Arthur H. Clark, 1958). The death of Mangas Coloradas and the search for gold in Arizona during the Civil War were recorded autobiographically by Daniel E. Conner, edited by Donald Berthrong and Odessa Davenport, *Joseph Reddeford Walker and the Arizona Adventure* (Norman: University of Oklahoma Press, 1956). Inexplicably, the editors failed to credit Swilling with leadership of the Walker Party, although that significant fact was noted in the Conner manuscript at the Arizona State Library and Archives and is corroborated by other sources and circumstances.

9. New Home in the West

Achievement of Arizona territorial status is best told in B. Sacks, M.D., *Be It Enacted: The Creation of the Territory of Arizona* (Phoenix: Arizona Historical Foundation, 1964), and the day-to-day realization of that dream is vividly described in Pauline Henson, *Founding a Wilderness Capital, Prescott, A.T., 1864* (Flagstaff: Northland Press, 1965). Composite descriptions of Arizona at the period are provided in the reprint of J. Ross Browne, published as *Adventures in Apache Land, or a Tour Through Arizona—1864* (Tucson: Arizona Silhouettes, 1950) and John Nicolson, *Arizona of Joseph*

Pratt Allyn: Letters from a Pioneer Judge (Tucson: University of Arizona Press, 1974). The colorful and significant career of Charles D. Poston awaits a suitable biography. Two attempts failed to clarify the enigmatic activities of this articulate, garrulous, and unlucky pioneer. A. W. Gressinger, ed., *Charles D. Poston, Sunland Seer* (Globe: Dale Stuart King, 1961), is based on Poston's countless self-laudatory articles. Poston himself was more directly the author of *Building a State in Apache Land* (Tempe: Aztec Press, 1963), which is a reprint of Poston articles that appeared in 1894 in the *Overland Monthly*. Both contain factual chronological threads of events in which Poston participated, but the accounts are colored and distorted by his vanity and self-aggrandizement. Jack Swilling's importance as a key figure in major historical events was not adequately explained in the one attempt at a biography of this remarkable pioneer, which was greatly flawed by fictional padding: John Myers Myers, *I, Jack Swilling* (New York: Hastings House, 1961).

10. Settling the Indian Question

A vast and unending literature describes in detail, analysis, and sometimes boredom all aspects of the Indian wars in Arizona, but the main elements will be found in four outstanding compilations:

Edward H. Spicer, *Cycles of Conquest: The Impact of Spain, Mexico, and the United States on the Indians of the Southwest, 1533–1960* (Tucson: University of Arizona Press, 1962);

John G. Bourke, *On the Border with Crook* (New York: Scribner's, 1891; Chicago: Rio Grande Press, 1962);

Ralph H. Ogle, *Federal Control of the Western Apaches, 1848–1886* (Albuquerque: University of New Mexico Press, 1940);

Dan L. Thrapp, *The Conquest of Apacheria* (Norman: University of Oklahoma Press, 1967).

The remarkable achievements of John P. Clum are recounted in a book written by his son, largely as a compilation of many self-laudatory articles which Clum wrote in his advanced years and should therefore be taken with a liberal amount of salt. Woodworth Clum, *Apache Agent: The Story of John P. Clum* (Boston: Houghton Mifflin, 1936).

11. The Wheel in the West

The scope of Colorado River steamer traffic is graphically and textually revealed in Richard E. Lingenfelter, *Steamboats on the Colorado River, 1852–1916* (Tucson: University of Arizona Press, 1978). The meeting of the camels and steamboat may be seen from two perspectives by consulting

Arthur Woodward, *Feud on the Colorado* (Los Angeles: Westernlore Press, 1955) and Stephen Bonsal, *Edward Fitzgerald Beale: A Pioneer in the Path of Empire, 1822–1903* (New York: Putnam, 1912). David F. Myrick, with access to official Southern Pacific corporate records and the papers of the Big Four, has carefully detailed the history of that railroad's venture into Arizona in his monumental *Railroads of Arizona*, Vol. I: *The Southern Roads* (Berkeley: Howell-North, 1975).

12. Hidden Wealth Revealed

Perspective on the proliferation and promotion of mining in pioneer Arizona and its endorsement by public officials, boards of trade, and almost all elements of the business world will be found in the massive Richard J. Hinton, *The Hand-Book to Arizona: Its Resources, History, Towns, Mines, Ruins and Scenery* (San Francisco: Payot, Upham & Co., 1878; Tucson: Arizona Silhouettes, 1954; Glorieta, N.M.: Rio Grande Press, 1954). A careful historical treatment of the mining industry in Arizona is Charles H. Dunning and Edward H. Peplow, Jr., *Rock to Riches* (Phoenix: Southwest Publishing Co., 1959). A pioneer in development of new extraction techniques, Ira B. Joraleman, has also written an excellent book about the metal, *Romantic Copper: Its Lure and Lore* (New York: Appleton-Century, 1935). The work recently has been enlarged and made more current under a new title, *Copper: The Encompassing Story of Mankind's First Metal* (Berkeley: Howell-North, 1973). The stature of Dr. James Douglas and of the firm he brought to prominence is told in two companion works: Hugh H. Langton, *James Douglas: A Memoir* (Toronto: University of Toronto Press, 1940) and Robert Glass Cleland, *A History of Phelps Dodge* (New York: Alfred A. Knopf, 1952).

13. Cowboys, Cattle, and the Law

A lifetime could be spent (in the sense of expelled or wasted) reading books about cowboys, the cattle industry, and outlaws, and years could be devoted to poring through compartmentalized pulps dealing with each aspect of the complex culture they created, such as branding, saddles and other horse gear, boots and pants, and cowboy wenching. A more productive but selective list of supplemental readings supportive of this chapter could include but not be restricted to:

Philip A. Rollins's classic work *The Cowboy* (New York: Scribner's, 1922) has been republished with a jaw-breaking subtitle, *An Unconventional History of Civilization on the Old-Time Cattle Range* (Albuquerque: University of New Mexico Press, 1979);

Will C. Barnes and William McLeod Raine, *Cattle, Cowboys and Rangers* (New York: Grosset, 1936).

There is fine humor mixed with a mass of detail and lively anecdotes in C. L. Sonnichsen, *Cowboys and Cattle Kings: Life on the Range Today* (Norman: University of Oklahoma Press, 1951).

Three works give a reasonable overview of the achievements of the Arizona Rangers, but take the first ghost-written work with plenty of salt:

Thomas N. Rynning, *Gun Notches: The Life Story of a Cowboy-Soldier* (New York: Stokes, 1931);

Joseph Miller, *The Arizona Rangers* (New York: Hastings House, 1952);

Frazier Hunt, *Cap Mossman: Last of the Great Cowmen* (New York: Hastings House, 1951). This is equally good for the first part of the book devoted to the Hashknife Outfit, the most colorful of Arizona cattle empires. The Graham-Tewksbury feud, also called the Pleasant Valley War, is best but incompletely recounted in the elaborate footnotes in the 1952 revised edition of Earl R. Forrest, *Arizona's Dark and Bloody Ground* (Caldwell, Ida.: Caxton Printers, 1952).

14. South from Zion

Although written in 1921, three decades before time allowed the passions of prosecutions for polygamy to cool and permit their open discussion, James H. McClintock, *Mormon Settlement in Arizona* (Phoenix: Privately published, 1921) presents a detailed, commendable effort to describe the "peaceful conquest" of the desert by Latter-day Saints. A candid family history, one of the first to admit the presence and problems of plural marriage, is David King Udall and Pearl Udall Nelson, *Arizona Pioneer Mormon: David King Udall, His Story and His Family* (Tucson: Arizona Silhouettes, 1959). The candor and clear analysis with which settlement along the Little Colorado River was described in 1973, a century after the first colony there failed, reflects new objectivity and scholarship being applied to the history of Mormon colonization. Charles S. Peterson, *Take Up Your Mission* (Tucson: University of Arizona Press, 1973) presents that history as the work of a talented, unfettered scholar reared in the hardscrabble land he describes very well. An enlightened overview of the LDS role in development of the Intermountain West is presented by authors who are believing Mormons in good standing: Leonard J. Arrington and Davis Bitton, *The Mormon Experience: A History of the Latter-day Saints* (New York: Alfred A. Knopf, 1979) blends honest glimpses of history with modern church perspectives. The horror of the Mountain Meadows Massacre and the strange banishment and fate of John Doyle Lee are recited by Mormon author Juanita Brooks in

John Doyle Lee: Zealot, Pioneer, Builder, Scapegoat (Glendale, Calif.: Arthur H. Clark Co., 1962).

15. Perils of Partisan Politics

Clearly, the best perspective on territorial politics of Arizona could be gained by a few years spent in reading the half-dozen leading newspapers of the period, followed by some months given over to poring through several record groups in the National Archives containing correspondence between federal officials and agencies and the chief executives sent to Arizona Territory during its half-century of prolonged quest for full membership in the family of states. Only a few scholars have been privileged to give such ardent attention to that period; others of us must depend upon the best compiled records of the period, which include:

James H. McClintock, *Arizona: Prehistoric—Aboriginal—Pioneer—Modern* (Chicago: S. J. Clarke Publishing Co., 1916);

George H. Kelly, *Legislative History of Arizona, 1864–1912* (Phoenix: State Historian, 1926);

Rufus Kay Wyllys, *Arizona: The History of a Frontier State* (Phoenix: Hobson & Herr, 1950);

Howard R. Lamar, *The Far Southwest, 1846–1912: A Territorial History* (New Haven: Yale University Press, 1966). By comparing the territorial experiences of the four-corner states of Utah, Colorado, New Mexico, and Arizona, Professor Lamar provides a yardstick for assessing carpetbag or colonial rule, in which Arizona comes off quite well.

Jay J. Wagoner, *Arizona Territory, 1863–1912: A Political History* (Tucson: University of Arizona Press, 1970).

16. Arizona Comes of Age

Not enough time has elapsed to give the first seven decades of statehood the mellowing patina that adds to historical perspective and understanding. Yet a number of published works give interesting glimpses of Arizona in the process of maturing:

J. Morris Richards, *The Birth of Arizona: The Baby State* (Phoenix: Privately published, 1940);

George F. Sparks, ed., *A Many Colored Toga: Diary of Henry Fountain Ashurst* (Tucson: University of Arizona Press, 1962);

Lawrence Clark Powell, *Arizona: A Bicentennial History* (New York: W. W. Norton, 1976);

Marshall Trimble, *Arizona: A Panoramic History of a Frontier State* (Garden City, N.Y.: Doubleday, 1977);

Robert L. Peabody, ed., *Education of a Congressman: The Newsletters of Morris K. Udall* (Indianapolis: Bobbs-Merrill, 1976);

John S. Goff, *George W. P. Hunt and His Arizona* (Pasadena, Calif.: Socio Technical Publications, 1973);

Marjorie H. Wilson, "The Gubernatorial Career of George W. P. Hunt," Tempe, Arizona State University, Doctoral Dissertation, 1973;

Barry M. Goldwater, *With No Apologies: The Personal and Political Memoirs of United States Senator Barry M. Goldwater* (New York: Morrow, 1979).

17. The Desert Blossoms

The story of man in the Southwest is also the story of irrigation; the rainfall is so light human existence is virtually impossible without irrigation to support the cultivation of food crops. A great deal of the history of irrigation in Arizona is to be found in a vast array of government publications and reports: proposals, feasibility, and engineering studies of the Bureau of Reclamation, hearings and investigations of committees of Congress, hundreds of thousands of pages of testimony presented to a Special Master of the United States Supreme Court in *Arizona* v. *California,* and as well in newspapers of Arizona, which on a daily basis for nearly a century have recorded this triumph of man over the desert environment. Books to add to such information may include the following:

Dean E. Mann, *The Politics of Water in Arizona* (Tucson: University of Arizona Press, 1963);

Jack L. Cross, ed., *Arizona: Its People and Resources* (Tucson: University of Arizona Press, 1960 and 1972);

Edward Peplow, Jr., ed., *The Taming of the Salt* (Phoenix: Salt River Project, 1970);

Central Arizona Project (Phoenix: U.S. Department of the Interior, Bureau of Reclamation, 1978);

Madeline F. Paré and Bert M. Fireman, *Arizona Pageant* (Tempe: Arizona Historical Foundation, 1978);

Arizona Statistical Review, 34th Edition (Phoenix: Valley National Bank, 1978);

Rich Johnson, *The Central Arizona Project, 1918–1968* (Tucson: University of Arizona Press, 1977).

18. Ever Westward

Very little has been published on the impact of World War II and the Korean Conflict on Arizona, or on the decades that followed. Most of the factual information for this chapter came from the following sources:

Valley National Bank, *Arizona Progress;* First National Bank, *Profile of Arizona;* and Western Savings and Loan, *Forecast 80* and *Forecast 81;*

Paul Bracken with Herman Kahn, *A Summary of Arizona Tomorrow, 1912–2012* (Croton-on-Hudson, N.Y.: Hudson Institute for Arizona Tomorrow, Inc., 1980);

Phoenix Magazine; Tucson Magazine; Mesa Magazine; Arizona Highways; and *Arizona,* Sunday supplement to *Arizona Republic;*

Arizona Yearbook, various years through 1981–1982.

Index

abolitionists, 173
aerospace industry, 234
agriculture, 118, 227, 235–6; early
    Native American, 35–6, 41–
    45, 217–18; Mormon, 178–80; *see
    also* irrigation
air conditioning, 240; *see also*
    refrigeration units
aircraft manufacturing, 233
Air Force bases, 233
air transportation and travel, 145–6,
    233, 238
Alamos, 149
Alarón, Hernando de, 51, 55
Allyn, Joseph P., 110, 115
Alvarado, Pedro de, 51
American Colonization Company,
    174
American Indians, *see* Indians;
    Native Americans
Anasazi culture, 36, 38–41
animals, 25–6, 29–33
Anza, Capt. Juan Baptiste de,
    65
Apache County, 182
Apache Indian wars, 104–5, 122,
    132–3
Apaches, 7, 8, 11, 43, 45, 64, 80–
    81, 102–7, 129; Aravaipa, 127–
    128; Chiricahua, 122, 129–

33; Lipán, 71; raids by, 68, 71–
    3, 93–5, 105, 117, 131–2, 163;
    Tonto, 112, 117, 126, 127;
    Warm Springs, 133; White
    Mountain, 131–2
Aravaipa Apaches, 127–8
architecture: Mogollòn, 37, Pueblo,
    39
Arizona County, 97
Arizona Guards, 101
Arizona Miner (newspaper), 110,
    115
Arizona Rangers, 166, 190, 194
Arizona Republican (weekly), 189
Arizona Star (newspaper), 189, 191
Arizona Territory, 117, 151; estab-
    lishment of, 108–13; governors of,
    184–96
arms, ordinances against, 170
Arthur, Chester A., 188
Ashley, James M., 109
Ashley bill, 109
Ashurst, Henry Fountain, 200, 208,
    221
Asia, migration from, 28–30
Atchison, Topeka & Santa Fe Rail-
    road, 144
Athapascans, 40, 43–5; *see also*
    Apaches; Navajos
automobiles, 238–9

aviation, *see* air transportation and travel
Awatovi, 59, 60

Babbitt, Bruce, 211
Bagdad Mine, 159
Baja California, 86–8
barbed wire, 165
Bartlett, John Russell, 85
Bascom, Lt. George, 104–5
Bascom Affair, 104–5
Bashford, Coles, 115–16
Bashford, Levi, 110
Basket Makers, 38, 39, 41
Baylor, Lt. Col. John R., 100, 102–3
Beale, Lt. Edward Fitzgerald, 4, 81, 135–7
Beltán, Bernaldino, 57
Benton, Thomas Hart, 77–8
Bering Sea land bridge, 28, 30
Beveridge, Albert J., 193
Big Dry Wash, Battle of, 132
Big Sandy River, 22
Bill Williams Fork, 22
Birch, James, 94–5
birds, 25, 26
Bisbee, 154, 156, 158, 159
blue-sky mining promotions, 157–8
Board of Indian Commissioners, 125
Bolin, Wesley A., 211
Bolton, Herbert Eugene, 9
Brodie, Alexander C., 192–4
Browne, J. Ross, 6–8, 113–15
Brunckow, Frederick, 153
Bucareli y Ursúa, Viceroy Fray Antonio María de, 64
Buchanan, James, 78
Bureau of Indian Affairs, 123
Bureau of Reclamation, 219, 221–3
Butterfield, John, 95, 140
Butterfield Overland Mail, 8, 12, 95, 99, 140–1

Cabeza de Vaca, Alvar Núñez, 9, 48–9, 51
cacti, 24, 25
California, 63–7, 77–84, 86, 88, 92, 96; Colorado River development and, 223, 224; War with Mexico and, 79–83
California Republic, 78
camels, 137–8
Cameron, Ralph H., 195, 201, 206
Campbell, Thomas E., 200, 202, 207, 221
Camp Grant Massacre, 127–8
Carleton, Col. James H., 101–5, 111
Carson, Kit, 80, 81, 84
Carter, Jimmy, 225
Casa Grande, 42
Castro, Raul, 210
Catholicism, 49, 52, 53
cattle industry, 162–7, 170–1; barbed wire fencing and, 165; finishing cattle in pens, 165; Indians and, 164–5; *see also* livestock industry
cattle rustling, 166
census of 1864, 113
Central Arizona Project, 15, 222–226, 235
Central Arizona Water Conservation District, 226
Charbonneau, Baptiste, 82
Chemehuevis, 43
Chinese railroad workers, 143
Chiricahua Apaches, 122, 129–33
Christianity, conversion to, 57–61, 69
Christie, Van, 115
Church of Jesus Christ of Latter-day Saints, *see* Mormons
Cíbola, 51, 54–5
Civil War, 100–4, 116; mining during, 150–2
Clark County (Nevada), 176
Cleveland, Grover, 190, 191

Clifton, Henry, 153
climate, 12, 239
Clovis-type points, 31, 32
Clum, John P., 131, 187–8
Cochise (chieftain), 104, 105, 129–130
Cochise Man, 32–6
Cocopahs, 43
colonists: French, in Sonora, 87;
  Spanish, 11, 47, 60, 63–72, 120–121, 138, 163, 218; Texas, 75–7
Colorado, 82
Colorado Plateau, 18, 19, 22
Colorado River, 18, 21, 22, 44, 176,
  177; Central Arizona Project
  and, 222–6, 236; development of,
  220–7; steamboats on, 135–6
Colorado River Commission, 202
Colorado River Compact, 200, 202,
  204
Colter, Fred T., 200, 221, 222
Columbus, Christopher, 46
Colyer, Vincent, 128–30
Comanches, 40, 64, 71
Conlan, John B., 212
constitutional convention: of 1891,
  190; of 1910, 196, 197
constitution (of Arizona), 196–7,
  207, 215–16
Cook, Nathan P., 92, 98
Cooke, Col. Philip St. George, 81–82
Cooke's Wagon Road, 139
coolers (cooling systems), 12–13
Coolidge Dam, 221
copper, 147, 148, 152–4, 156–61,
  237
Copper Queen Consolidated Mining
  Company, 156
Coronado, Francisco Vásquez, 10–11, 51, 52, 54–6
Cortés, Hernando, 47
cotton, 227, 235, 236
courts, 113

cowboys, 162, 166–72; rodeo,
  169–71
Cozzens, Samuel W., 174
Crocker, Charles, 143
Crockett, Davy, 76
Crook, Gen. George, 122, 128–30,
  132–3

dams, 219–22; *see also individual
  dams*
Davis Dam, 223
DeConcini, Dennis, 213
defense industry, 234
Democratic party, 188–90, 196,
  205
Department of Arizona, military,
  127, 128
desert, 19; animal life of, 25–6; *see
  also* Lower Desert
desert coolers, 12–13
Desert Culture, 32, 34
Desert Hohokams, 34, 41, 43
Díaz, Fray Juan, 65
Díaz, Capt. Melchio, 55
Doña Ana County, 97
Douglas, James, 154, 156
Douglas, Lewis W., 156, 211
Douglas, Rawhide Jimmy, 156, 158,
  159
Duffield, Milton, 110, 113, 173
Dutch Reformed Church, 123

economic growth and development,
  231, 233–6
education, Mormon, 181
Ehrenberg, Herman, 76, 88, 90–2
El Camino Real, 65
election: of 1864, 113, 114; of
  1916, 200; of 1950, 205
electronics, 233–4
Elías, Jesús M., 116
El Paso & Southwestern Railroad,
  156

Emory, Lt. William H., 82
Enabling Act (1910), 196, 197
Escalante, Fray Silvestre Vélez de, 66
Espejo, Antonio de, 57
Esteban, 9–10, 48, 52–4
executive branch of state government, 196, 207, 210

Fannin, Paul J., 209–10, 213
Fargo, William, 95, 140
farming, *see* agriculture
federal government, relation to, 240
Fitzpatrick, Thomas "Broken Hand," 80
Florida, 48
Font, Fray Pedro, 65
foreign investment in Arizona, 241
Fort McDowell, 117
Fort Union, 100, 101
Fort Whipple, 111, 112
Fort Yuma, 139
France, 87
Franciscan priests, 56–9, 63–8
Frankfurter, Felix, 159
Franklin, Benjamin J., 191
Frantz, Joe B., 163
Frémont, Jessie Benton, 4
Frémont, John Charles, 4, 76, 78, 80, 122, 187–8
French colony in Sonora, 87
Frohmiller, Ana, 205, 206
fur trade, 72–4

Gadsden, James, 86, 142
Gadsden Purchase, 12, 86, 87, 91, 92, 96, 97
Garcés, Fray Francisco Tomás, 63–68
García Conde, Gen. Pedro, 85
Garvey, Dan E., 204–5

Gatewood, Lt. Charles G., 133
Geronimo, 122, 131–4
ghost-dance cult, 131
Gila Bend, 15
Gila City, 150
Gila County, 160
Gila Indians, 99
Gila monster, 26
Gila Range, 147–8
Gila River, 21–2, 83; dams on, 219; Wellton-Mohawk Project on, 223
Gila River Valley, 43; Mormon settlements in, 179
Gillespie Dam, 219
Girand, James G., 222
glaciers, 28–30
Glen Canyon Dam, 223–4
Goddard, Samuel P., 210
gold, 107, 157
Goldwater, Barry, 207–9, 213–14
Goldwater, Michel, 151
Goldwater, Morris, 207, 214
Good Roads movement, 200, 206, 215
Goodwin, John N., 110, 112, 113, 115, 126–7, 186
Gosper, John J., 174, 188
governors: elected, 198–211; territorial, 184–96; *see also* executive branch of state government
Grand Canyon, 18, 55, 152
Granite Reef Aqueduct, 225
Grant Peace Policy, 123–4, 128
Greenway, Isabella Selmes, 211–12
Greenway, John C., 156
Grey, Zane, 167
Groom, Robert, 112
Guadalupe Hidalgo, Treaty of, 82, 83, 85, 86
guns, ordinances against, 170
Gurley, John A., 109, 110
Guzmán, Nuño de, 49

Hamblin, Jacob, 176
Hance, Margaret, 216
Harless, Richard F., 212
Harrison, Benjamin, 190
Hassayampa River, 107
Hawikuh, 54, 55
Hayden, Carl, 169, 205–6, 211, 213, 221, 223
Hayden, Charles Trumbull, 179
Hayes, Rutherford B., 2, 4
Heintzelman, Maj. Samuel P., 90, 108, 110
Heintzelman Mine, 91
Hemenway-Cushing Archeological Expedition, 42
Highline Canal system, 221, 222
highway system, 206, 238
Hohokam people, 34–6; *see also* Desert Hohokams; River Hohokams
home rule, *see* statehood
Honeymoon Trail, 182
Honorato, Fray, 52
Hoover, Herbert, 220
Hoover Dam, 221–2
Hopis, 55, 58–60, 66, 176, 214
horned toad, 27
horses, 70–1
Houston, Sam, 76–7
Howard, Gen. O. O., 129–30
Howell, William T., 110, 116
Howell Code, 116
Hoyt, John J., 187
Hualpais, 44, 66, 126
Hughes, Louis C., 189–91
Hughes Aircraft, 233
Hunt, George W. P., 196, 198–201, 205–7, 221
Hunter, Capt. Sherod, 100, 102

Imperial Dam, 223
income, per capita, 229

Indian Affairs, Bureau of, 123
Indian reservations, 122–4, 129–30, 164–5, 224
Indian Rights Association, 125
Indians, 43–5, 49, 53–5, 67–8, 93, 99–100, 116, 119–34, 138–140, 185; attitudes of settlers toward, 121–5; cattle industry and, 164–5; Central Arizona Project and, 224; conversion to Christianity, 57–61, 69; Crook's campaign against, 129–30, 132–3; genocide of, 124–6; Grant Peace Policy toward, 123–4, 128; horses and, 70–1; irrigation system of, 218; mission, 64, 69–72; Mormons and, 175, 176; raids by, 70–3; *see also* Native Americans; *and individual tribes*
Industrial Workers of the World (IWW), 158, 159
industry, 233–6; *see also* mining
Interstate Stream Commission, 222
irrigation, 114–15, 118, 193, 217–220, 227, 235–6; early forms of, 217–18; pumping water for, 226
Irwin, John N., 189–90
Ives, Lt. Joseph C., 136

Jackass Mail, 12
Jackson, Andrew, 76
Jerome, 153, 158
Jesuits (Society of Jesus), 58, 60–63, 148
Johnson, Andrew, 186
Johnson, Capt. George Alonzo, 135, 136
Johnson, Lyndon B., 209, 224
Johnston, Gen. Albert Sidney, 101
jointure movement, 193
Jones, Robert T., 203–4

Jones, Thomas ap Catesby, 78
Jones, W. Claude, 116

Kearny, Brig. Gen. Stephen Watts,
  80–2, 139
Kennedy, John F., 212
Kibbey, Joseph H., 194–6
Kickapoos, 71
Kino, Father Eusebio Francisco, 11,
  61–2, 69, 162, 163
Kiowa Apaches, 71
kivas, 39

labor unions, 158, 204
Laguna Dam, 220
Lake Havasu, 22
Lake Powell, 223–4
Lamanites, 175, 176, 179
Lansing, Robert, 200
La Paz, 112, 151
Las Vegas, 176–7
law and law enforcement, 168–9
Lee, John Doyle, 177
Lehi, 178, 179
León, Francisco S., 116
Lesinsky brothers, 153
Lincoln, Abraham, 110
Lipán Apaches, 71
Little Colorado River, 22; Mormon
  settlements along, 174, 177–
  178, 220
livestock industry, 235–6; *see also*
  cattle industry
Llano Man, 31
Los Muertos, 42
Lower Basin, 26
Lower Desert (Sonoran Desert), 19,
  22–7, 35; animal life, 25–6;
  trees and plants, 23–5
Magma Mine, 158, 160
mammoths, 31

Mangas Coloradas, 80–1, 106
manufacturing, 233–5
Marchessault, Damien, 151
Marcos, Fray, 9–10, 52–5
Maricopa County, 231
Maricopa Indians, 121, 127
McCleave, Capt. William, 106
McClintock, James H., 192
McCord, Myron, 191–2
McCormack, John, 212
McCormick, Richard C., 110, 112,
  113, 115–17, 186–7
McDougall, James A., 109
McFarland, Ernest W., 207–8, 223
McKinley, William, 190, 191, 193
Mendoza, Viceroy Antonio de,
  49, 51–3
Merill, P. C., 179
mesquite, 24
Mexico, 75–9, 121; boundary with
  U.S., 77, 83, 85–6; French
  colony at border, 87; Mormons
  and, 175–7, 182; trade between
  Arizona and, 241; War with,
  79–83, 175; water projects and,
  223; Zimmermann Affair and,
  159
migration to Arizona, 230
Miles, Gen. Nelson A., 133
Mineral Creek, 21
mining, 88, 90, 91, 108–9, 118–
  119, 143–4, 147–61, 179–80,
  199, 237; blue-sky promotions,
  157–8; efficiency of methods of,
  160–1; in 1870s, 152–3; labor
  difficulties, 158–9; placer, 150–2;
  World War II boom in, 159;
  see also copper; gold; silver
missionaries, 59–64, 67–9, 148; *see
  also* Franciscan priests; Jesuits
Moeur, Benjamin B., 201–3, 207
Mogollon Culture, 36–8, 40, 41
Mohaves, 43, 126, 136

molybdenum, 157
Morenci-Clifton district, 148, 153, 158
Mormon Battalion, 81–2, 163–4, 175
Mormons (Church of Jesus Christ of Latter-day Saints), 144, 175–183, 188–9, 208; Arizona settlements, 176–80; churches, 180, 181; communalism among, 180–181; education, 181; gentiles (non-Mormons) and, 182; Indians and, 175, 176, 179; marriage customs of, 182–3; Mexico and, 175–7
Motorola, 233
Mowry, Sylvester, 98–9, 103–4
Mowry Mine, 103, 104
Mule Mountain, 147
Murdock, John R., 208, 212
Murphy, N. Oakes, 189, 190, 192–193

Naco archeological site, 30–1
Narváez, Pánfilo de, 48
National Reclamation Act (1902), 219
Native Americans: agriculture, 35–36, 41–5, 217–18; earliest, 28–33; first habitations built by, 34–46; at Ventana Cave, 32–5; *see also* Indians; *and individual cultures and tribes*
Navajos, 43, 71, 105, 176, 214
Nevada, 82
New Cornelia Mine, 156
New Mexico, 57, 59–60, 80, 82, 86, 91–2, 96, 97, 100, 101; jointure of Arizona and, 193
New Mexico & Arizona Railroad, 144
Niza, Fray Marcos de, 9–10, 52–5

O'Connor, Sandra Day, 216
O.K. Corral, gunfight at, 170
Oñate, Juan de, 57–8
O'Neill, Buckey, 192
Oraibi, 66
Osborn, Sidney P., 204, 207
Oury, Granville H., 100
Oury, William S., 76, 95, 128
Overland Stage Company, 95
Owings, Lewis S., 98

Pah-Ute County, 176
Paiutes, 43
Papago Indians, 24, 33, 43, 128
Parker Dam, 203
Park of the Four Waters, 42
Patten, Harold A., 212
Phelps Dodge Corporation, 156
Phillips, John C., 201, 202
Phoenix, 42, 117, 118, 145, 231
Picacho Pass, Battle of (1862), 102
Pico, Gen. Andrés, 81
Pierce, Franklin, 86
Pima County, 160, 231
Pima Indians, 43, 62, 82, 121, 127
Pimería Alta, 62, 64
Pinal Mountains, 147
Pizarro brothers, 47
placer mining, 150–2
plant life, 23–5
Polk, James, 79
population growth, 229–31
Poston, Charles D., 88, 90–2, 100, 109–11, 113, 115, 149–50, 220
Poston, James Lee, 100
Prescott, 174; as capital, 113, 115, 117
Prescott & Arizona Central, 145
prohibition, 200, 203
Provincias Internas, 64, 72
Pueblo Grande, 42
Pueblo Revolt (1680), 59–60

Pueblo tradition (or culture), 39–41
Pumpelly, Raphael, 100
pumping of underground water, 225, 226
Pyle, Howard, 207, 208

Quechans, 43
Quivira, 56

railroads, 85–6, 92, 96, 141–5, 164, 237–8
rainfall, 22–3
Raousset-Boulbon, Count Gaston de, 87
rattlesnakes, 26
Read, Rev. Hiram W., 112
Real de Arizonac mining district, 149
recall of judges, 197
Reclamation, Bureau of, 219, 221–223
Redondo, José María, 116
refrigeration units, 14–15
Rehnquist, William, 216
Republican party, 109, 185, 205–7, 209, 210
Rhodes, John J., 208, 212, 213
right-to-work law, 204, 207, 234
Rio Grande, 77, 83
Rio Grande Valley, 55
Rivera y Moncada, Capt. Fernando de, 67–8
River Hohokams, 39, 41–3
river systems, 19, 21–2; *see also individual rivers*
rodeo cowboys, 169–71
Ronstadt, Frederick A., 92
Roosevelt, Theodore, 192–5
Roosevelt Dam, 194, 219
Rough Riders, 192
Rudd, Eldon, 213

Safford, Anson P. K., 128, 179, 186, 187
Salado culture, 39–42
Salt River, 21
Salt River Herald, 188
Salt River Valley, 21, 41, 117, 118, 145, 219; Mormon settlements in, 178–9
Salt River Valley project, 219, 220, 226
Salt River Valley Water Users' Association, 194, 219
San Antonio & San Diego Mail Line, 93, 140
San Carlos Indian Reservation, 129–32, 221
San Carlos project, 221
San Carlos River, 21
San Francisco, 141
San Francisco River, 21
San Juan River, 38
San Pascual, Battle of (1847), 81
San Pedro River, 21
San Simon River, 21
Santa Anna, Antonio López de, 76, 77, 86, 87
Santa Cruz River, 21, 219
Santa Cruz River valley, 159–60
Santa Fe, 73, 100, 101
Santa Fe Compact, 220, 221
Santa Fe Conference (1922), 220
Santa Fe, Prescott & Phoenix Railroad, 145
Santa Fe Railroad, 144–5, 195
Santa Fe Trail, 73, 74
Santa Maria River, 22
Santa Rita Mining Company, 108
San Xavier del Bac, 63, 68
Schiefflin, Ed, 147, 153
scorpions, 26–7
Scott, Gen. Winfield, 79
seminaries, Mormon, 181
Senner, George F., Jr., 212
separation movement, 91–2, 96–8

Serra, Friar Junípero, 63
Sherman, Gen. William Tecumseh,
3–6
Short Creek, 183, 208
Sibley, Gen. H. H., 100–1
Sierra Madre, 60
Sierrita Mine, 160
silver, 90, 91, 143–4, 147–9, 152–
154, 157
Sinagua culture, 39, 40
Sky Harbor International Airport,
238
Slaughter, John, 169
slavery, 52, 75, 76, 96
slaves, freed, 173–4
Sloan, Richard E., 195–6
Smith, Lot, 177
Smith, Marcus Aurelius (Mark),
188, 190, 193, 195, 200, 201,
205–6
Snaketown, 42
Society of Jesus (Jesuits), 58, 60–
63, 148
Sonora, 86–8, 241
Sonora Exploring and Mining Com-
pany, 90, 91, 108
Sonoran Desert, 19, 22–7, 35;
animal life, 25–6; trees and plants,
23–5
Sonora Railroad, 144
Southern Pacific Railroad, 136,
141–5, 156
Spanish-American War, 192
Spanish explorers, 9–11, 46–58,
147, 148
Spanish settlers, 11, 47, 60, 63–
72, 120–1, 138, 163, 218
stage lines, 140–1
stage stations, 93–5
Stanford, Rawghlie C., 203
Stanwix Station, 102
statehood, 185, 189–90, 193, 195–
197
steamboats, 135–9, 141

Steiger, Sam, 212
Stockton, Commodore Robert F.,
80
Stoneman, George, 127–8
Stump, Bob, 213
summer, 12
Sun Belt, 231
Swilling, Lt. Jack, 106–7, 117–18,
151
Swilling Irrigation and Canal Com-
pany, 117, 118

Taft, William Howard, 195–7
Taos, 73
tarantulas, 27
taxes, 196, 203
Taylor, Gen. Zachary, 79
Tempe Canal Company, 226
Territory of Arizona (Confederate),
100
Texas, 75–7, 99–101
Texas & Pacific Railroad, 142
Theodore Roosevelt Dam, 194, 219
Tombstone, 143–4, 153
Tonto Apaches, 112, 117, 126, 127
Tovar, Don Pedro de, 55
transportation system, 237–9; *see
also* air transportation and travel;
highway system; railroads
travel and tourism, 227, 239–40
trees, 23–4
Tritle, Frederick A., 188
truck transport, 238
Tubac City 63, 64, 91, 97
Tucson, 83, 92, 111, 231, 238; as
capital, 116–17; during Civil
War, 101–4
Turner, William F., 100
Twin Buttes Mine, 160

Udall, Morris, 48, 212, 213
Udall, Stewart L., 212

unionization of mine workers, 158
unions, 204
United Verde Copper Company, 153
Upland Desert, 19
Utah, 82, 175, 176
Utes, 71, 176

vegetation, 23–5
Ventana Cave, 32–5
Victoria, Queen, 103

Wade, Benjamin F., 109
wagon travel and transportation,
    139, 141
Walker, Joseph Reddeford, 151
Walker party, 106–7
Warm Springs Apaches, 133
Warren, George, 154
water law, 194; *see also* Colorado
    River Compact
water resources, *see* dams; irrigation;
    river systems
water tables, subsurface pumping
    and, 225, 226
weather, 12, 239
Weaver, Paulino, 151

Weekly Arizonian, 91
Wellton-Mohawk Project, 223
Wheeler, Jim, 159
White Mountain Apaches, 131–2
Williams, Jack, 48, 210
Wister, Owen, 171
Wolfley, Lewis, 189
Women's National Indian Associa-
    tion, 125
Wood, Col. Leonard A., 192
Woodford, Wilford, 178
Woolsey, King S., 126
World War II, 231, 233
Wrightson, William, 109
Wyoming, 82

Yavapais, 44, 107, 117, 125–7,
    130
Young, Brigham, 81, 175, 177, 180
Yuma, 65, 142–3
Yuma Crossing, 67–8
Yumans, 43

Zimmermann Affair, 159
Zion, Mormon concept of, 175
Zulick, C. Meyer, 188–9